TED BUNDY

CONVERSATIONS WITH A KILLER

TED BUNDY

CONVERSATIONS WITH A KILLER

THE DEATH ROW INTERVIEWS

STEPHEN G. MICHAUD & HUGH AYNESWORTH

with foreword by Robert D. Keppel,
former Chief Investigator

STERLING
New York

STERLING
New York

An Imprint of Sterling Publishing Co., Inc.
1166 Avenue of the Americas
New York, NY 10036

Originally published in 1989 by New American Library, Penguin Putnam USA, Inc.
and in 2000 by Authorlink Press, an imprint of Authorlink.

This Sterling edition published in 2019

ISBN 978-1-4549-3768-5

Distributed in Canada by Sterling Publishing Co., Inc.
$^c/o$ Canadian Manda Group, 664 Annette Street
Toronto, Ontario M6S 2C8, Canada

For information about custom editions, special sales, and premium and
corporate purchases, please contact Sterling Special Sales at
800-805-5489 or specialsales@sterlingpublishing.com.

Manufactured in Canada

2 4 6 8 10 9 7 5 3 1

sterlingpublishing.com

Cover design by David Ter-Avanesyan

Front cover and title page photograph © Jerry Gay
Back cover images: Digital N/Shutterstock.com (tape);
Yes - Royalty Free/Shutterstock.com (slash)

Authors' Note

Some of the names have been changed to protect privacy.

Foreword

The first fact of serial murder is that these crimes exist most clearly in the mind of the serial killer himself. That was the most important lesson I learned in the course of investigating Ted Bundy's initial killings in the northwest.

And this is why *Ted Bundy: Conversations with a Killer* is such a valuable resource.

Few, if any, serial killers have ever talked at such length, and with such clear self-knowledge, as Ted Bundy did with Stephen Michaud and Hugh Aynesworth.

Ted was resourceful, intelligent, and relentless; he was forever hunting, always perfecting his approach to his victims. He chose ways to dispose of their bodies with infinite care, and he assiduously studied how police investigations are conducted in order to further reduce his chances of being caught.

Bundy, above all, did not want to be caught, ever.

What is more, for police investigative purposes, his case is prototypical. There is no question that it remains the exemplar of what works, and *what does not work*, when local law-enforcement agencies are faced with the fact that some unknown subject, almost certainly a male, has begun to periodically murder people, usually women or children.

In Seattle and surrounding King County, we didn't *know* we had a serial killer until Ted had killed at least eight young women in the region, probably more. The "Ted" investigation's starting point was a summer day in 1974 when a white male subject, seen driving a Volkswagen and calling himself "Ted," had apparently lured two women, separately and at different times, from a popular local lake park in broad daylight. All that we knew for certain was that Janice Ott and Denise Naslund had vanished.

It would be two months before parts of their skeletons were discovered on a hillside east of Seattle, and another six months before the severely fractured skulls of four other Bundy victims (all of these women were killed prior to the summer of 1974) were found in a similar wooded location.

The situation for local law enforcement was unprecedented – as it is every time a serial killer begins operating – and the case immediately presented us with a wide range of unique problems. One was coordination. At least five different and separate police agencies were involved in the early "Ted" investigation. We were separated from one another by distance – it is *265* miles from Corvallis, where Bundy abducted one of his victims, to Seattle – and by other features of geography: another coed victim had disappeared from a campus east of the Cascade Mountains, a physical barrier that seemed to preclude, at first, the possibility of a common suspect.

Communications were a related difficulty. Each individual police agency had separate priorities. What was important to one agency was not necessarily important to another. We all used different methods of paperwork. Nor was it practically possible to keep everyone informed at the same time about developments in the case.

These troubles were further aggravated by external factors. Seattle was a frightened, panicked city. Not every politician who spoke out at the time had the sense not to inflame those fears.

Some segments of the news media clamored for information we could not divulge. And we all felt the stress of public pressure to apprehend "Ted" before he killed again.

Little could we know that Bundy had driven on in his Volkswagen to Utah and was murdering there (and in Colorado and Idaho), even before we had any good idea of how many women he might have murdered in our area.

Then there were problems we had no way of anticipating. Among these was the sheer volume of information (some potentially vital, the rest mostly useless, all of it difficult to evaluate) that quickly overwhelms a serial murder investigation. Officers and detectives are individuals with individual ways of pursuing leads. Until we had developed standardized tip sheets – *who*, *what*, *when*, and *where* forms that could be compared, collated, and studied systematically – the information we collected was really just a blizzard of jotted notes, most of them unintelligible except to the person who wrote them.

Another unwelcome surprise was how serial murders tend to invalidate certain basic assumptions of traditional homicide investigation. Specifically, there is usually a connection of some sort between victim and killer. They are often related or acquainted. Because of this, and because at first we could not assume that all, or even any, of "Ted's" victims were complete strangers to him, we were obliged to go by the book, investigating each victim's circle of contacts and who among them might have a reason for killing her. Although this work generated much information, it turned out to be only marginally useful.

Similarly – and this problem was peculiar to Ted Bundy as a suspect – we discovered the uselessness of showing his photo to possible witnesses. Even without the disguises and masks Ted used, he looked different in just about every photo taken of him.

The two we had seemed to be of two different people, neither of whom resembled the "Ted" at the lake.

We learned lessons of a different type when it came to organizing ourselves into a multi-agency investigative task force. First of all, the formation of a task force represents a police consensus that there is indeed a serial killer on the loose. That can be an important psychological hurdle. Once everyone agrees on the nature of the problem, far less time will be wasted on extraneous investigation not germane to the "task" implicit in the term "task force." A task-force approach promotes better organization of case materials, too. And it absolutely forces a detective to think of what is important to the overall, long-range mission, rather than what seems important that day.

Finally, the Bundy case demonstrated some intriguing apparent truths, borne out in later serial murder investigations. We know, for example, that the actual killer is often *apt* to be among the first suspects known to the police. One important practical application of this knowledge is that when a detective reviews a difficult, long-term case it is worthwhile to go back and look at what was done in the first few months. More than likely, the killer's name or a key clue to his identity will appear in those early files.

Bundy's name was reported to us three times, once by one of his girlfriends. But we had 3500 other suspects, too. Although by standard investigative procedures we eventually would have taken a long look at Ted Bundy, this process was speeded by the use of a computer.

Today, computers are taken for granted across such a wide range of uses, including police work, that it is necessary to recall what a relative rarity they were in the mid-1970s. We in the King County police force didn't have one. But given the nature of our extraordinary problem with "Ted," we saw that we needed to attempt extraordinary new measures if we were going to find him. It was in this context that we thought of the King County payroll computer (a huge and primitive machine by present standards) as a tool for digesting and sorting the mass of data we had collected. We discovered that the computer's power is essential to serial murder investigation. These machines won't solve a case – or at least they haven't yet – but the computer allows an investigation to be focused. In hunting for "Ted," we had numerous lists of potential suspects that we fed into the county payroll computer. We entered the names of the victims' classmates, names from their address books, names of all our suspects, a list of registered Volkswagen owners, and so forth. Then we began asking the machine for coincidences. Whose name appeared on one, two, three, or four of the lists? Ted Bundy and twenty-five others appeared four times.

We also personally sorted through the suspect files, looking for a top one hundred, so to speak, of the most promising individuals for further investigation. Bundy's name was in that group, too.

Thirteen months after we had begun searching for "Ted," we had Theodore Robert Bundy, age twenty-nine, a former Republican campaign worker and at that time a law student in Utah, literally at the top of our pile. Then came the telephone call from the Salt Lake County sheriff's office informing us that Theodore Robert Bundy had been arrested for a traffic violation and had been found with a lot of suspicious paraphernalia in his Volkswagen bug: namely, a pair of handcuffs, a crowbar, a pantyhose mask, and several lengths of rope.

Ted's chance arrest undeniably abbreviated his killing career, but it also ratified the use of computers to focus serial murder investigations. Because of the computer, we were poised to take a concentrated look at Mr. Bundy and, I believe, would have been able to help single him out as a suspect for police in four western states who did not know at that time that they were looking for the same serial killer.

All these years later, the computer has become an instrument of serial murder detection in the form of VICAP, the FBI's new national serial murder tracking program. In the state of Washington, we have established HITS (Homicide Information and Tracking System), which contains information on *all* murders in the state, not just serial killings. HITS now instantly provides homicide detectives in Washington with information that ordinarily would take them months or years to compile.

The Bundy saga did not end in August of 1975 in Utah. He escaped custody twice and made his way to Florida in early 1978, where he killed three more victims; he was sentenced to death twice in 1979 and once again in 1980, the second time for the murder of a twelve-year-old girl, the crime for which he was ultimately executed, in January of 1989.

Just after his apprehension in north Florida, Bundy provided police interrogators with broad hints of who he really was and what he had really done over a period of many years. Yet Ted was not then going to confess. And once he was sent to Death Row, few of us in law enforcement expected that he would ever talk, until, as did happen, Bundy perceived a possible personal advantage in doing so. Certainly, no appeal to his conscience was going to elicit the information we needed.

Then, in the autumn of 1980, while I still was a detective with the King County police, Michaud and Aynesworth came to see me. They explained that they had been talking to Bundy for their book, *The Only Living Witness*, and that they believed I should hear some of the content of their taped sessions with Ted.

They did not claim that what they had was a confession or anything that a prosecutor could take to court; Bundy had secrets that he was not then going to divulge. But what I listened to was shocking: Ted Bundy talking about himself in the third person, telling Michaud and Aynesworth, in considerable detail, what it was like to be a serial killer.

This interview technique, allowing subjects to speak in the third person, gives them the chance to talk directly about themselves without the stigma of confession. Michaud and Aynesworth, given the luxury of extended time with Ted, put him at his ease. They avoided the error of impatience and were usually careful not to seem as if they were judging Bundy for the aberrant homicides he described. It was Bundy himself who first described his crimes as despicable.

What their tapes and transcriptions demonstrated to me and to every other law-enforcement officer who has reviewed them is how effective the third-person approach can be. It was a pioneering effort. And I believe that it helped open the way for my own subsequent and substantive interviews with Bundy. At the very least, Michaud and Aynesworth's exhaustive review of his hidden life helped to break down Ted's dread of confession. As I later learned directly from Bundy, a long-term serial killer erects powerful barriers to his guilt, walls of denial that can sometimes never be reached.

In 1984, my own extended confrontation with Bundy began with a letter from him offering to aid the northwest police in the search for "Ted's" successor in the region, the so-called Green River Killer, whose murders of prostitutes had come to light two years before. Bundy invited me, as a representative of the

Green River task force, to the Florida state prison, where we met twice to discuss "River Man," as he called him. It was a singular experience to talk with one serial killer about another. And although Ted didn't confess to me, either, in these sessions, they were a second step.

The interviews established a personal level of communication between us. Perhaps as important, I seemed to emerge in Bundy's mind as the one investigator he could trust, the detective to whom it eventually would be easiest to confess, in the first person, his crimes.

At last, just before his execution, Bundy did talk directly about himself to me and then to other western law-enforcement officers who also had "Ted" cases. He finally confessed to thirty killings but admitted in detail to only a handful in an orchestrated effort to trade information for two or three more months of life. It didn't work.

Ted did not tell us everything he did – or even *most* of what he did – in detail, and I wonder whether some of the behavior he described to us should ever be publicly known. That leaves, for the general reader and law-enforcement professional alike, Ted's broader testament to his life as a killer contained in this volume. Because of the interviewers' efforts, Ted's crimes can now exist more clearly in everyone's mind, including those of the police officers who some day may have to hunt another Theodore Robert Bundy.

– Robert D. Keppel, Ph.D.
President, Institute for Forensics
Formerly Chief Investigator,
Washington State Attorney General's Office

Part One

Ted Bundy's most apt – and accurate – single-sentence self description was offered not to us but to the group of north Florida cops who interrogated him soon after his final arrest in Pensacola in February of 1978. Said Bundy to the police, "I'm the most cold-blooded son of a bitch you'll ever meet."

Not until he had explicitly confessed to his crimes (at least thirty murders) in the last days of his life did the full meaning of what Ted meant by "cold-blooded" become apparent. Bundy wasn't just a savage killer; he was a degenerate, too. All along there had been evidence that he sometimes mutilated his victims. But the perversity he acknowledged to Bob Keppel and the other investigators went beyond what any of them had ever guessed, or imagined, to be true.

Yet the Ted that we came to know – at his invitation, initially, to act as his investigators and biographers – was also complex, often fascinating to interview, and a consummate gamesman. Besides the sickness of "the entity" he revealed to us, there was also the intelligence, arrogance, and even the charm that made Bundy such a compelling – while at the same time repellent – figure.

In either incarnation, whether Ted was talking about his school days or detailing the essence of victim "possession" – he never seemed to stop striving for a fuller, more comprehensible explanation for who he was and why he had become a killer. The other factor always at play was his innate need to manipulate.

We discovered this at the outset in Bundy's first letter to us, written November 4, 1979, from Florida State Prison. He had been on Death Row there for just over three months after his sentencing in Miami on August 1 for the murder of two sleeping coeds in the Chi Omega sorority house at Florida State University in Tallahassee on January 15, 1978.

"It's too cold to sleep," he wrote. "It may even be too cold to write. An arctic breeze blows through the broken windows across the hall from my cell, dropping the temperature to the point where my breath turns to fog. Who called Florida the sunshine state? He should be in here with me."

Nowhere in the letter did Bundy mention his pleas of innocence except to note that there are "those who wish to accept them unconditionally and to the exclusion of all guilt evidence." These people, Ted wrote, were his solace. "As long as I have strong supporters," he explained, "I have all I can ask for."

Bundy urged us to emphasize the mystery surrounding him; he specifically urged us not to search for evidence that he was guiltless as he claimed. "The facts to prove unequivocally that I'm innocent are not there," he informed us. Bundy didn't get to the point of his letter until two pages later:

"I don't care what you write just so you get it right and just so it sells."

The letter was signed: "Best regards, Ted Bundy." Of the several self-delusions in Ted's letter, the one that irritated us most was his assumption that we, as journalists, were ready to act as his tools.

We had a basic agreement with Ted – already worked out in close consultation with his ardent partisan and soon-to-be wife, Carole Boone, that we would reinvestigate the murder allegations against him, plus interview Bundy at length for any information he might have to help us disengage him as a suspect in any of the two dozen killings he was then accused, or suspected, of having committed.

Because the cases were interrelated, to clear him of one would necessarily clear him of several, maybe *all* of them. Doubtful as that possibility seemed, the chance that Bundy really was telling the truth – that he was innocent – was sufficient reason to undertake the project. Conversely, we told him and Carole that the evidence of his guilt would be fully investigated, too, and that we would be constrained to share such information with the proper police agencies. His letter to us in November, about five months after we'd gone to work, outlined an entirely different understanding and signaled the impasse we reached with Ted a few months later.

We split the work. Hugh went to the state of Washington, then Oregon, Utah, and Colorado to retrace Bundy's trail and to seek, as we'd agreed, the overlooked – or possibly suppressed – evidence that Carole's dear "Bunny" was an innocent man. Consistent with his letter, but contrary to what we'd been promised, Bundy had absolutely nothing to offer – not a thread of exculpatory detail.

Nor did any of the many alternate suspects (Carole's favorite subject) in any of the Bundy murder cases prove viable upon review. The "facts and circumstances which point toward innocence" Bundy mentioned in his letter to us dissolved into nothing, upon close scrutiny.

Meanwhile, I digested what Hugh learned, read over the enormous legal record, and then journeyed to Orlando, Florida, to attend Bundy's January 1980 trial for the murder of twelve-year-old Lake City, Florida, schoolgirl Kimberly Diane Leach. Each day I attended court. Each night in my motel room, I conducted taped interviews with Ted, who spoke from a telephone in the Orange County jail.

He said he could not, at that time, talk about any of the cases against him. That would have to await his return to the

Florida State Prison at the end of the trial. Therefore, beginning with our first taped conversation on January 8, 1980, Bundy confined our discussions to general biographical material. We began at the beginning, with Ted's first four years of life in Philadelphia. He remembered those days fondly, recalling his grandfather Samuel Cowell as a mythic figure he adored as a little boy.

Apparently, he was repressing the truth. Seven years later, as part of an attempt to save his life by demonstrating Bundy's insanity, a psychiatrist would characterize Ted's grandfather as an abusive brute and worse.

We knew nothing about this in 1980, but we did know that Ted was illegitimate. In the first of many discussions we had on this topic, I wondered at what age *he* had first pondered the mystery of his parentage.

"Did I ever wonder about my father during that period of time?" he asked rhetorically. "No, I didn't. Not that I can ever say for sure. Perhaps somewhere down in my little childhood mind, at the time, I probably did. But if at all, it was fleeting," he said.

Logically, we moved on to Louise, Ted's mother, who brought him from Philadelphia at age four to Tacoma, Washington, where she soon met and married Johnnie Bundy, a cook at a local military base, who became the father of her next four children.

"My mother taught me the English language," Ted said from his cell. "How many times did she type my papers as I dictated them to her? (She) gave me great verbal skills.

"I would have written them out in shorthand but would dictate things I had left out. Or I'd insert different language. I became very good at thinking on my feet. All the way through high school and college, I never got below an 'A' on a major project. And I attribute that to my mother.

"But as far as Mom's ability to communicate through writing, she has beautiful handwriting, very good vocabulary, but she never says anything! She says, 'I love you,' or 'I'm sorry we haven't written. Everything's fine,' or 'We miss you… Everything will turn out'… Blah, blah, blah.

"My mother and I, and this well may go for all the kids, didn't talk a lot about real personal matters. Certainly never about sex or anything like that.

"I don't resent it, but I don't know why this is. There's something in her background that prevents her from opening up. 'What's happening? What's going on? What's happening with life?' There's this log-jam of feeling in her that she doesn't open up and explain.

"I don't think it's necessarily a conscious avoidance of putting into letters newsy, gossipy kinds of things. She doesn't even *think* about doing it. She's not a gossipy person. She's not a socializing-type person. She's not a joiner in the sense she belongs to women's clubs and card games and talks over the back fence.

"We never spoke about her childhood. Aside from the fact she grew up in my grandfather's house, with my aunts and my grandma. On Roxbury Avenue, in Philadelphia. And that she was extremely successful in high school. The head of everything. Jesus! I read her yearbook. She was president of this and president of that. She headed up this committee and that committee. And had a straight 'A' average. Her big disappointment was that she had one 'B' in three years of high school!

"A terribly popular person. And then – I don't know – something intervened.

"She's an extremely intelligent person. But she masks it. She has a great deal of potential. But then at a point, it seems, she shied away. I can remember her having some resentment that there was only one scholarship offered in her school, and the richest girl got it. Of course, my mom didn't have enough money to go to school.

"She never thought that was very equitable – that the other girl, who had straight 'A's, got the scholarship. Even years and years later, I detected a strong sorrow in her voice when she told me about it. She certainly has a lot of character, but she doesn't project it. And she certainly did not try to transform her children into some image of what she wanted to be or what she thought she was.

"There's no question that I was more influenced by my mom than by my dad. Because, in many ways, my dad injected himself even less into the psychological intellectual development of his children. Mom sort of ran the roost in many respects, although he was the acknowledged head of the family.

"Our life, as I was growing up, outside the home (was) centered around the First Methodist Church. Whether it was church camps in the summertime or pot-luck dinners or plays. Certainly on Sundays and holidays! Yet I wouldn't call my mother a religious fanatic in any sense of the word. She wasn't constantly reciting Bible verses to us or anything like that. As a child, I didn't read the Bible unless I was absolutely forced to.

"I often babysat while Mom and Dad attended church events. They seemed to get so much out of it. I didn't learn until much later that they had met that way – at a church social.

"I believe I attended Sunday school from the time I was in kindergarten all the way until I graduated from high school. We studied the Bible all through those years, but it amazed me in college that I had retained next to nothing about Christ or the Old Testament or my religion, in the dogmatic sense.

"The essential lessons were certainly clear. Especially the ones I adopted with glee during the Vietnam war. My poor mother had to listen to me talk about the hypocrisy of Christianity under the circumstances.

"On balance, my parents were apolitical. Except when it came to school-bond issues. My mother would always try to get out the vote for the school levies. That was her commitment to electoral politics.

"I guess you'd call my mother a Republican. I don't know where Johnnie stands. He, even less than my mother, would venture opinions on political matters. I think that's significant when you think how politically oriented I was.

"When I was a youngster, I don't think we even subscribed to the local newspaper. Both of my parents were very frugal. Neither smoked nor drank. Lord knows, they couldn't have afforded to if they wanted to."

Ted was uneasy about Johnnie Bundy, and about himself. As far back as he could remember of his days as a boy in Tacoma, he chose to be alone.

"One of the reasons," Ted recalled, "I believe I'm such a verbal person – that I feel I can get much more from listening than from reading – is that in my younger years I depended a lot on the radio. I'm a radio freak!

"As a kid, I would listen for hours and hours to the Lone Ranger, Big John and Sparky, and all that stuff. I remember once I sent away for a little radio. It had no battery or plug.

It was tuned by adjusting the length of the antenna. It had a ground wire with a clip and I would attach the clip to the rail of my bed. I'd go to sleep with that earplug in my ear and wake up in one corner of the bed wrapped up in the tiny little wires. I'd get under the covers and listen as long as I could every night. Never did understand how it worked!

"Later on when I was about in the sixth grade, I had a regular radio, and one of my favorites was a program on KGO in San Francisco, a talk show from about ten into the early morning hours. I'd really get into it. It was a call-in show.

"And as people would be calling in to speak their minds, I would formulate questions as if they were talking to me. I was very, very into news and news broadcasts, but I didn't read very much.

"I would lie in bed for hours and hours, listening to news broadcasts exclusively. *Meet the Press*, or whatever. My favorite thing on Sunday nights was to hunt the radio bands for talk shows, call-in programs, documentary-like things. They're still my favorites. I'd listen to talk shows all day rather than listen to music.

"People might think I was terribly serious-minded. But I genuinely derived pleasure from listening to people talk at that age. It gave me comfort. Often it didn't matter much what they were talking about. And I realized, even then, that a lot of the affection I had for programs of that type came not because of their content, but because it was people talking! And I was eavesdropping on their conversations.

"I never discussed any of this with my parents."

Ted's early habit of isolation no doubt contributed to his later inability to integrate himself socially. Of course, as he revealed in a television interview broadcast nationally the day of his execution, as a boy he was already roaming his neighborhood and picking through trash barrels in search of pictures of naked women.

1980

January 9

"I never really got into organized sports, because it seemed so *serious*. Even as far back as Pee Wee football, the coaches drove the kids unmercifully. Long, sweaty, dirty practices! And very costly to buy the uniforms. My family didn't always have the money – not comfortably so, anyway.

"I always felt I was too small. This feeling began to emerge in junior high school. That I didn't have the weight or physique for sports. It wasn't true, but I never pushed myself.

"My dad never had any feeling for it, none at all. He never came to my football games. My mom didn't like it because it cost money. I didn't have that parental stamp of approval. My dad never played baseball or basketball or football with me. We never threw the ball around. I was never trained in the basic sports skills.

"So I was all on my own. I attempted to get on the school basketball team and a couple of baseball teams, but I failed. It was terribly traumatic for me. I just didn't know what to do. I thought it was something personal. I always thought I should do better. It was a source of some agony.

"I have to tell you. These kinds of innocuous admissions about always being concerned that I was underweight... not liking team sports and being traumatized by not making the hardball team. Whatever it is. Observations about my mother and not communicating in a way that was satisfactory for me. I've really never discussed this with *anyone* before.

"Not anyone! Not with my mom, my brothers and sisters, Liz (his one-time fiancée) or anybody. Maybe there's never been an occasion for it. But you'd think there *would* have been an occasion for it, wouldn't you?"

January 10

"It was not so much that there were significant events (in my boyhood), but the *lack* of things that took place was significant. The *omission* of important developments. I felt that I had developed intellectually but not socially.

"In junior high, everything was fine. Even went to some parties. Nothing that I can recall happened that summer before my sophomore year to stunt me or otherwise hinder my progress. But I got to high school and I didn't make *any* progress. How can I say it? I'm at a loss to describe it even now.

"I didn't understand it as much as I do now – and I don't *really* understand it completely now. Maybe I didn't have the role models at home that could've aided me in school. I don't know.

"But I felt alienated from my old friends. Not that they didn't like me, but they moved into broader spheres, and I didn't. Whether the guys had cars or jobs or big bank accounts or fancy clothes – whatever it was – I didn't seem to be able to grasp a lot of that.

"In high school, I would be characterized as shy to introverted. With exceptions. I loved skiing. I mean, I was basically responsive. I didn't walk down the ball like a dummy. I spoke up in class. Believe me, if anything characterizes my classroom performance, it's being precocious. I've always been that way. In those kinds of settings. It's a formalized setting. And the ground rules are fairly strict. And your performance is measured by different rules than what happens when everybody is peeling off into little cliques down the hallway.

"I don't know why. And I don't know if there's an explanation. Maybe it was something that was programmed by some kind of genetic thing. In my earlier schooling, it seemed like there was no problem in learning what the appropriate social behaviors were. It just seemed that I reached a wall, as it were, in high school.

"It never crossed my mind to see a counselor. I didn't think anything was wrong, necessarily. I wasn't sure what was wrong and what was right. All I knew was that I felt a bit different.

"My way to compensate for that was to say, 'Well, I don't go in for those things. I don't like the drinking. I don't care for this carrying on, the frivolity. I'm a serious student. I'm above all this.' To some degree, that was my way of defending myself against something I didn't want to admit I desired to be a part of.

"A lot of my pretensions about being a scholarly type, a person interested in serious studies, was really a defense mechanism. I was accused on a couple occasions of being aloof, arrogant, and snobby. But it was just this defense mechanism to protect my somewhat introverted nature. I used that to compensate for my outright fear of socializing. Maybe, also, it was a way to protect myself, because I couldn't achieve those kinds of social goals that I wanted.

"Emotionally and socially, something stunted my progress in high school. Not that I ever got in trouble. Or wanted to do anything wrong.

"While I wanted to be a part of the secret societies and clubs, or whatever, I lacked either the social skills or motivation to do it. I seemed to be intimidated by the more gregarious people in my class – although I didn't dislike them, either.

"Oddly enough, it was through my deep interest in skiing that I became involved with the most socially minded and socially active people in my class. But I *still* never really came out of my shell.

"There were all kinds of things happening to me mentally. I felt inferior, in part because of the money thing. My family didn't have money problems per se, but I was always envious of the kids who lived in all those brick houses where the executives and doctors lived. I felt kind of deprived, at a disadvantage to those people who had the money, the successful parents, all the goodies."

January 11

In his senior year at Woodrow Wilson High School in Tacoma, Bundy went to work as a volunteer in a local political race. The experience delighted him. Three years later he served as official driver for a Republican candidate for lieutenant governor. And in 1972, he worked for the GOP gubernatorial candidate, Dan Evans.

"Politics gave me the opportunity to be close to people," he said. "To be socially involved with them… as a consequence of working with them. You get very close. You drink each night – and people sleep with each other. It's a sort of built-in social life. Which I never had.

"In my younger years, I was, as I've said before, socially unskilled. That's one characterization, and it rings true. But politics gave me a lot. It gave me a direction and an education in a lot of things tangential to politics – things I needed to know. In politics you can move between the various strata of society. You can talk and mingle with people to whom otherwise you would have absolutely no access."

January 12

Yet politics didn't solve another developing problem, later diagnosed by a defense psychiatrist as a bipolar mood disorder: manic depression.

"You asked about my mood swings," Bundy mused. "I'm very aware of them myself. Maybe it's not quite accurate to use the term 'mood swings,' but it *is* hard for me to understand what happens. That is, to anticipate them or look back and try to determine some pattern. I've been able to make neither rhyme nor reason out of what happens.

"It's not dictated by the cycles of the moon or anything else that I'm aware of. And again, perhaps the phraseology 'mood swings' isn't accurate. It's just *changes*. It's harder than hell to describe, but all I want to do is lay (sic) around. I'm not motivated to do *anything!* I just consume huge volumes of time, really, without doing a thing.

"I'm not particularly depressed. There's just no momentum. There's no desire to do anything. It's just blaaaah! It cannot be characterized by depression or deep sadness.

"I don't dwell on sad things – but I sure as hell could! I don't dwell on the heartache. I do dwell on the nicer things. Even in those lackadaisical periods, I'm capable of being genuinely cheerful and gregarious. At least for a limited period of time.

:ver the situation calls for. Then, (just) as quickly, I'll slip back into the pattern of just vegetating.

"It became a part of my character, of my facade, that I would conceal these periods of inactivity, as it were. It's really a combination of being inactive, with no motivation or direction.

"I became expert at projecting something very different. That I was very busy. It is clear now, I think, that a huge part of my life was hidden from everyone – secret, as it were. It didn't take much effort at all.

"While I may have been left to myself a lot in high school, it was not as singular and pronounced as the pattern I later developed, in the early '70s. I may have been a bit inward, but I was not entirely an introvert in high school. I certainly didn't have a secret life that nobody knew about then. That's the truth! I didn't have a life that I was *shielding* from anyone."

January 14

The opposite of the depression was the manic high, as Ted described it in his recounting of his successful escape from the Glenwood Springs (Colorado) jail on New Year's Eve of 1977. He had already been convicted of kidnapping in Utah the preceding year and was awaiting trial for the murder of a nurse, Caryn Campbell.

"I felt that way when I popped out of jail in Glenwood Springs. I had the feeling that things were just *happening!* Everything was just going my way. The stars were right! How can I explain it? My karma was good! I mean, *nothing* went wrong. If something did go wrong, the next thing that happened was *so* good it compensated. It was even better.

"People say it was such a sly escape. Well, it wasn't. Yet my karma was so right that it compensated for all my errors. I mean, I just walked out the front door of the jailer's quarters. I didn't hide behind a trash can, like they said. I just walked right down the street. I didn't walk toward Main Street. I walked (in) the other direction and up the dark streets toward this large apartment complex by the railroad tracks. There were several cars parked there.

"I checked out several of them, crunching along in the frozen snow. Couldn't find any cars with keys in them. I don't know how to hot-wire a car, right? So I kept looking in all these cars, opening the doors and checking around for keys under the mats and so on. I got out of the damn jail at seven-thirty and at eleven I was *still* looking for a car!

"I must have tramped up and down every side street, honest to God now… I walked every side street and neighborhood in Glenwood Springs. No lie. In fact, I walked up and down some of them twice.

"I walked from the jail to the high school and past. Up by where the used-car lots are. Over across to the east side of town and down to the river again. And back up and around and down. And I couldn't find a car. And it started to snow, very, very hard.

"Dig this! I found a car with keys in it. It was an old jalopy. This was maybe about nine o'clock. I was looking for a car with snow tires. I was no dummy. I said, 'Let me look some more.' I looked some more and said, 'Well, I'd better take that car.' As I was walking back to get it, somebody came hurrying out of a building, hopped in the car, and drove away.

"It was one of those nights. You see, if I *had* taken that car, it would've been reported almost immediately.

"Finally, around eleven p.m., I found this little MG. It had a front-wheel drive with studded snow tires on the front. I hopped in and revved it up. It went like 'bud-d-d-d-d-d... buh-buh-buh-buh-buh.' There was no second gear. The gear shift was chattering away. I got it in first; there's no reverse. The heater didn't work and windows immediately steamed up. But I was goin' for it.

"It was parked on a residential street by the river. I cleaned off the windows as best I could. Got everything set – and drove right down the wide street by the police station! Stopped at the stoplight. Made a right turn. Drove over the bridge spanning the Colorado River. It was low on gas, so I stopped and filled up just over the bridge. Self-serve. Paid my money and got moving.

"The snow was falling heavily. But I got this thing up to first and then on into third. Vroom! Vroom! Vroom! The thing wouldn't get out of third. It took me about twenty minutes to get it into fourth. And then there's an incline, you know. There were cars all over the place – semis, cars, buses – sideways and slipping. People puttin' chains on.

"I just put this damn thing into third and floored it. I'm zooming around, weaving here and there, like a slalom course. I closed my eyes because there were state patrolmen all over the place, helpin' people. Flares and everything! I didn't even slow down. Vroom!

"I knew that if I stopped in this little fucker on the hill, I wouldn't get anywhere because I couldn't get it in second. It's a four-lane highway most of the way to Vail. Couldn't see the road. After a while, I couldn't drive it in fourth. I could only go in first. The snow was deeper than the hood of the car, right? Finally, it just goes 'phhheeeew.' It wouldn't move.

"I had tennis shoes on, from the jail. I couldn't push the car off the side of wherever I was. Couldn't tell where the highway was! I was scared to death a highway patrolman would come along. A couple cars passed me in the middle of nowhere. I was, for a while at least, more scared of dying of exposure than anything else.

"I was about twenty-five miles from Vail and at least that far from Glenwood Springs. In a blizzard – a bona fide blizzard!

"This guy comes along in a Mazda. I waved at him and he slowed down. Helped me shove my car – get that, *my* car! – off the highway. 'Best to leave the car because my wife's having a baby in Denver. I gotta get to Denver,' I told him. "He said he was from Ogden – in the army, returning from some base in Kentucky. He said, 'Hop in. I'd enjoy the company.' We had trouble getting moving because his tires were almost slick. Just about then a huge snowplow came along, hooked a chain to us, and got us moving. We followed him, pretty close, the rest of the way to Vail.

"When we got to Vail, we found out the pass was closed. Since he didn't have chains, they wouldn't let us try, so we came back down.

"There was a Vail cop right off the freeway as we came back down the mountain. As he pulled over, I rolled down the window and asked him where we could hang out for a while. It was probably about two a.m. He directed us to the Holiday Inn, where they had a nice big fire going. But it was clear the pass was going to be closed for quite a while. Nothing was getting any better.

"I got back out and tried to hustle a couple of rides, to no avail. Finally a Trailways bus was scheduled to leave. I said,

'Sorry, Buddy, I gotta get moving.'

"When I got to Denver, I was *still* feeling those good vibrations. I shared a cab with three other guys to the airport. I was feeling so good, I paid for it!

"I walked in the airport and directly to the row of counters, looking for the first flight to Chicago. I had planned to go to a big city. Lots and lots and lots of traffic. No way to trace me. It was New Year's Eve. I knew they didn't have much of a chance to trace me.

"TWA had an 8:55 flight. I plopped down my money and didn't even slow down because there was less than five minutes to make it. I had a Bell Telephone plastic carrying bag with an extra shirt, some underwear, and miscellaneous items in it.

"I just kept on movin'. Settled in on the plane. Slowly buckled up and said, 'I need a scotch and soda, fast!' It felt just right – the whole time, just perfect. You see, there was nothing clever about the escape. Nothing clever about the engineering. In fact, it was sloppily done."

The high lasted only a few more days.

"In Ann Arbor," he went on, "it was just *boom, boom, boom!* I was just cool. I was talking to people in bars. Oh, I felt good! I felt the drive, the power. I had what it took.

"I lost that. I felt it slip away like in the old movies where you see the ghost lift out of the body lying on the ground. It slipped away from me a few days later in the bus station in Atlanta. It just evaporated. I could just feel it go.

"I was waiting for the bus in the Omni (Auditorium), watching a convention on the main floor there. There were all these people going to a Hawks game. And I was watching these people – these people who had *real* lives, backgrounds, histories, girlfriends, husbands and families. Who were smiling and laughing and talking with each other. Who seemed to have so much of what I wanted!

"All of a sudden I felt smaller and smaller and smaller. More insecure. And more *alone!* Watching groups of couples talking with one another, strolling toward the gate. Bit by bit by bit, I felt something drain out of me. And by the time I got off the bus in Tallahassee, things just did not feel right. From the time I first set foot on Tennessee Street, I kept saying to myself, 'I gotta leave here.'"

The depression came just days before Bundy, in a drunken rampage, committed bludgeon attacks on five coeds, two of whom were Chi Omega sorority sisters who died.

January 15

Bundy compared his disintegration to that of the protagonist in James Clavell's early novel *King Rat*.

"A marvelous, marvelous book," Bundy remarked, "about a Japanese prisoner-of-war camp. King Rat himself masters the environment. But when they're liberated, he's worse than nothing. He's back to his old self again. He's nowhere. I might be there. I don't know.

"My first test of that confirms that I'm a master of this (prison) environment, much more than the other. I sort of reverted to type. I felt overwhelmed by things. I felt out of control. I felt I couldn't manipulate, if that's the word, the environment around me. I couldn't get hold of the things I needed to get hold of. I couldn't get a job. I didn't do the things that I should have done.

"I knew what I had to do and I didn't do it. It just boggles my mind. I failed miserably. I did everything I shouldn't have done. You have to remember, I was on the run, so I couldn't truly be myself. If I was truly shrewd and in control of myself, I would not have done the things that I did, which were terribly stupid."

I told Ted that it sounded as if he actually enjoyed being locked up.

"Anybody matures," he answered, and then he went into another speech. "I'm sure, no matter *where* they are. So many times in these past couple years I felt like I was looking down from atop a mountain and seeing so many things I had never seen before. And appreciating so many things I never appreciated.

"I feel so much more confident about myself. It's really marvelous. But here I am – in here.

"I think that at last I have perspective. And a sort of self-confidence. It may be borne, in part, out of this immense publicity. I don't know. I'm recognized in a terribly bizarre kind of way. I feel immune. I feel nobody can hurt me.

"I'm not sure why I feel that way. Maybe I would have reached this new perspective without being in prison. Anyway, everything from changing my diet – which is a real trip – I take very seriously. I feel comfortable, so much more confident when I talk to people. I *know* who I am.

"I know I don't have to apologize to people for anything. Nobody can spring anything on me. Not that people do this. But nothing's going to come out of left field. I feel like I'm a cat. I feel aware of things. Diet is one thing. Yoga. Some of the more esoteric things I overlooked before.

"Being in prison has helped me understand a lot about human behavior, because in prison behavior is very elemental, and it's very blatant. Very brutal. But it's an analog to the more subtle, more sophisticated behavior on the streets. Nobody surprises me anymore. I believe I know *why* people act the way they do. I understand incentive. I understand the profit motive for the very first time, having been around drug dealers. I understand economics in a way I never understood it before.

"I understand violence – and I am not afraid. I am not afraid of a thing. And it's a terribly secure thing. I am not afraid of death. Maybe that's a function of it, also. I'm not intimidated by anything or anybody. And I used to be very intimidated by situations. And people. Not understanding motivations. I can now speak my mind and be not at all self-conscious about it.

"I don't think people perceived me this way, but I saw myself as meek. I perceived myself to be easily intimidated. And somewhat unsophisticated. Uninteresting – even unattractive. Not in a *gross*, accentuated way that would keep me shuddering in my apartment all day, but in a mild way that sort of took the edge off things.

"When people were genuinely interested in me, I seldom picked up on it. Simply, I just didn't appreciate my worth. It's strange, isn't it, that under these circumstances, today I probably have a stronger self-image that I ever did before?

"It's a revelation. It's marvelous. Now I'm not certain that if you took me out of this environment and put me back on the streets that I might not revert back to my former, Walter Mitty-like kind of thing. I'm not a Walter Mitty. That's not a proper comparison.

"I was scared to death in the Salt Lake City jail (where Bundy was taken after his first criminal charge for the kidnap of an intended murder victim, nineteen-year-old Carol DaRonch, the only woman known to have escaped Bundy once he had her in his car.) I thought I was going to die every night the first few days I was in jail back in October of 1975. I was *scared to death!* Daily. I thought they were going to kill me.

"Animals sense it. Just like the old adage that a dog can tell when somebody is afraid of it. They sensed it – and some guys jacked me up on it. I mean, nothing *happened*. But they

said, 'Hey, Bundy, did you really do that?' This or that. Nobody
fucks with me anymore about that.

"I've come up against the toughest, meanest dudes on Death
Row. They'd slit your throat in a second. I count them as my
friends. They give me no trouble. I don't expect I'll ever have
any trouble with 'em unless I try to fuck 'em somehow. It's not
really men they're in awe of. It's the reputation or something
that goes along with it.

"After I was sentenced in Salt Lake City, I was put on "A"
Block at Utah State Prison, where Truman Capote filmed *The
Glass House*. I was scared to death for a while. A couple of guys
kept chanting, 'We don't like rape-os.' Gave me the bad eye.
Called me a baby raper and all that shit.

"Nobody would ever do that to me now. They might talk
a lot. But they won't say anything to my face. The reputation
stops 'em. They're afraid I'll do something to them. And I
probably would, if it came down to it. It may be the way I carry
myself. They may have respect for me the way I handle the
authorities. The way I fucked with them. The way I made them
pay to get me. No one has said a cross word to me. Not even has
there been a mean word.

"They – all of 'em – will try to get over on you when you first
come in. They'll jam on you. They'll try to get you to get them
drugs and promise to pay you back. They're always trying to hit
on the new guy for candy and cigarettes. I tell 'em to fuck off.

"Sydney Jones is a stand-up convict. About 260 pounds of
mean, black sonuvabitch who they built a special pair of handcuffs
for because he tears the ordinary ones apart. Sydney asks me for
stuff and I say – in a humorous way – 'Fuck you, Sydney.' My
Christmas package came and Sydney said, 'Bundy, I want some
cookies.' I told Sydney, 'Listen, I gotta take care of myself.'

"He was after my law books. He's after everybody's law books. It's nothing personal. I said, Sydney, if you want those law books, tear your cell door off, come rip mine off, tear the window out – and we'll take the law books with us!'

"He once took over "Q" Wing. In September of 1978. He and his buddy, John Jefferson. The doors in "Q" Wing are not remotely operated. Each cell door has its individual key. So they found a way of screwing with the lock mechanism so all they had to do was jiggle the door and it would open.

"They did this for a year or two. All they'd do at night was open the door or go smoke dope or screw each other or whatever they were into. But none of them, surprisingly enough – it just burned me up – tried to escape or anything. They just fooled around.

"So then these two guys one day decided to take over the wing. They didn't know *what for*! Neither of 'em had a murder beef. They were just doin' these things because they were hell-raisers. They just lost their heads. They didn't know what to do, so eventually they gave up."

January 23

As the Leach trial ground into its third week, Ted began to lose his poise. In a conversation with Carole Boone (whom he'd marry at the end of the trial), he complained of the strains of being a defendant in a case where the verdict is a foregone conclusion.

"Vic (Africano, his lead lawyer) gives me a speech at lunch-time. He says, 'What's going on? Why are you so upset?' I told him why. He said, 'It puts us on edge when you're so upset. People might notice.'

"I said, 'Who do you want to be on edge? Me or you?' He said, 'Your demeanor… it's important. It can hurt you.'

"Fuck that bullshit! We lost this thing two years ago. What kind of shit is this? He's trying to talk to me like we have a fighting chance.

"I told Vic I'm coming unglued. I just can't keep it together anymore. I'm sorry. I'm just starting to lose it. I was strong as long as I can be strong. He said, 'Do you think the nurse might be able to get you something to calm you down?'

"I don't know what these guys expect of me. Not only to go through jury selection and listen to all that rot, but then to listen to witness after witness *lie, lie, lie*. I'm fed up with it. I need some goddamn special attention. I *demand* it!

"What makes me mad is I'm allowing myself to be played into a corner on this. Like there's really something at stake here. I'm letting myself be forced to play a role. And I sit there *eating* every second of it! I'm starting to hate myself for doing it. It's the goddamn phoniest set-up. And yet I allow myself to play that role. I feel awful. There doesn't seem to be a point to anything.

"It might be the best thing for me to try to go to sleep. Because all I want to do right now is be unconscious or loaded or fucked up. Or something. I just can't deal with it."

Then his mood shifted.

"One of my fondest dreams," he told Carole, "is to have all the underwear and socks I ever could conceivably use. It's one of my fantasies. To be able to wear new socks every day! And I must admit, I have had three or four dozen socks, all purchased on (stolen) credit cards.

"I have always felt deprived of underwear. I always felt that I would have *really* made it if I had all the socks and underwear

I could ever use. Even in Pensacola (where Ted was arrested for the last time), I went to a shopping mall and bought some socks. I was buying socks everywhere.

"This is for real. I mean, I've got a sock fetish. No question about it. I must have six or seven pairs right here with me in my cell.

"I am really *sick* when it comes to socks. These are some of the things for people who really want to know what makes Ted Bundy tick. They're parts of the combination to the deepest, most secret recesses of my mind.

"I'm very close to my feet. Right now. I'm lying on my back with my foot propped up on the bars. And I'm studying my toes. For a good portion of the night. They're probably the most attractive feet you've ever seen.

"I'm sure all these law-enforcement officers around the country are looking through their unsolved crimes for anything to do with the presence or absence of socks.

"Socks are such a serious part of my life. They're so very important to me. They kept reading the list of socks and all [in court] and I felt proud. Honestly, it didn't even begin to occur to me that people might wonder why I had all those socks. I just felt proud that *I* owned all those socks. Like a man who stands at the back of his ranchhouse and looks out over the range and sees all them cattle.

"The only time I began to have a little bout of sheepishness was when I read about a white sock with a blue band and green stripe on the toe. Those are odor eaters – and that was getting too personal."

January 25

This night Bundy recounted the highlights of his career as a thief.

"Let me give you an idea," he said, "of the way I operated. For instance this little Sony television I had. I can't remember when this happened, but one day I decided I had to have a TV set. I had been out at Northgate Mall in Seattle and I saw the Sony in the display window.

"Later I was sitting at home – this was some time after I started going to the university of Washington – and I was drinking Mickey's Big Mouth, which is my favorite beer. That stuff makes me nasty. All of a sudden I said, 'I'm going to go *get* that Sony!'

"I parked the car close to the mall and walked in the store. The display window had a door that opened from the china-cutlery area.

"It was about four o'clock. It wouldn't have made any difference, daytime or nighttime. Anyway, I just walked right in the display window. Who's going to question you if you just walk right in, like you belong there?

"I was really pumped up. Intoxicated. I ambled on through the chinaware department and opened the door – and there were people looking right in the window at me, right? I reached in and gave a little wave to the people and picked up the TV and walked out of the window, closing the door behind me. Then walked straight through the sales area and out the door, and straight to my car.

"The TV worked terrific and survived many years until the apartment was burglarized. I got my stereo in much the same fashion.

"The thought of burglary or anything really criminal," he went on, "never crossed my mind. I felt no remorse whatsoever about taking something like that out of a store. I'd only take what I needed. Not that that makes any difference.

"I got my stereo by simply walking in and out of this hardware store in Seattle. Every time I wanted to get something just to pump myself up a little, I'd drink a few beers, 'cause I felt I wouldn't have any inhibitions. I'd move quickly and not look over my shoulder. I wasn't nervous – and that's important!

"So I just walked into this place and went over to the display area and unhooked the stereo – the turntable and the amplifier – and put them in a cart. Nobody was around. I pushed the cart back through the paint department and outside to where you can get potted plants, and then right on out the back by where they stack the fertilizer.

"I pushed it to my car and unloaded it and then planned to go back for the speakers! As I headed back toward the store, I saw at least half a dozen hardware people running around with their little vests on, running this way and that! One of them ran up to me and said. 'Did you see a man pushing a cart with a stereo in it?' I swear to God this happened.

"I said, 'Let me think. Yes, I just saw a fellow carrying some stuff and headed toward the bowling alley over there.' All of a sudden, the fear of God was in me! I said to myself. 'Goddamn, Ted, you've gone too far now!' So I moseyed over to the Volkswagen, slipped in, and drove away.

"I got the speakers late… another time. I wanted to find a pair that matched. You need to get speakers that are to be driven by your system, right?

"But I did *stupid* things. If I had spent as much energy trying to make a million dollars, I would have been able to buy all this stuff. Later I walked into this place with a big box under my arm. This is the truth. It was like a big toilet-roll box. And, 'What? Me worry?' I walked in – and I had all sorts of things to lose if I got busted – I walked to the back of the store and unplugged the two speakers, semi-large, and plopped them in my box, sealed the box back up, and walked right out the front door.

"That gives you an idea what kind of nut I was. There was my kitchenware, several lovely prints and pictures I had on my wall, and a Navajo rug that retailed for $1,200.

"That was *something!* It was a bona fide Navajo rug. I saw it in this gift shop in the new Hilton Hotel in Salt Lake – and I was feeling no pain that night. I had spotted this rug some time before, and I just wanted it. It was *really* me! The damn thing had a $1,200 price tag on it. It couldn't be all bad.

"So, without hesitation, I walked into the shop and walked up to it. There was only one person working in the shop. I didn't look over my shoulder or anything. It had this big rock setting on it, along with a lot of dishware. A couple dozen items anyway, including the ninety-pound rock.

"Well, I lifted the rock and put it over to one side and lifted all the other shit up and rolled the fucker up and put it under my arm and walked. I thought, 'If they get me going out the door, I'll just say, "Hold this for me.' I just kept walking, with it under my arm, like I'd just bought the evening paper. That was that.

"One of my fondest memories was the night… I've always had this passion for plants, right? But plants are so damned expensive. Liz was justifiably freaked out by all this because she knew that I couldn't afford these things and she knew I was risking a lot and was stupid for doing it.

"But you know, these were just, uh, you know, little luxuries. And I had this deep desire for this Benjamina tree.

"I've got to tell you this story! There's a big nursery close to the university in Seattle. Lots of greenhouses and beautiful, beautiful plants. I used to go there and drool at all the plants. Well, on this occasion – just before I left for Utah – I got this urge. 'I *want* a tree,' I said to myself.

"And this thing was eight-feet tall! All I had was a Volkswagen (bug) with a sunroof. I walked in the side entrance of this place where this beautiful Benjamina was and picked it up. It was heavy and bulky. Anyway, I got it and started walking. I got to my car. I lifted it up and down through the sunroof. There's a good five feet sticking out the top!

"And I calmly walked around, got in the car, and took *off*. I don't know what would have happened if somebody would've stopped me and asked me, 'Sir, just what did you have in mind here?'

"In those days, I wouldn't go into stores and shoplift. This is the honest-to-God's truth!" he said. (When Bundy got to Tallahassee in 1978, low on cash and the object of a nationwide manhunt, he virtually subsisted on shoplifting.) "What I went for," he added, "were things that I couldn't afford – expensive things.

"I know that doesn't negate the fact that these actions were stupid and senseless... and the risks I was taking – considering, you know, my professional possibilities – it was ridiculous.

"The big payoff for me was actually *possessing* whatever it was I had stolen. It wasn't the act, necessarily. Ofttimes I would have to get intoxicated to get loose enough to be able to do it right. Apart from that, I really enjoyed having something on my wall or sitting in my apartment that I had wanted and gone out and taken."

Bundy's description of his motives for thievery – possession – would echo eerily when he later talked about why he
killed. The fact that he was a murderer of young women also
gave another of his anecdotes, meant to amuse us, a chilling
resonance.

"After I was in there a while," he said, "things loosened
up at the Glenwood Springs jail. They were allowing me
to go down with shackles on to the trustees' cell to watch
TV. And smoke *massive* amounts of marijuana. *Goddamn*,
I got ripped! These were really nice young guys, nineteen
or twenty, and they'd go out on work-release and bring this
stuff back at night. We'd get just rip-snortin' *fucked up*. Time
after time.

"On one occasion – I think it was a Saturday – they had
these two juvenile runaways, females, who they put in the
women's cell. These girls were saying things like, 'Hey guys,
let's get together.' They were really precocious. One was
semi-attractive, the other somewhat obese. I imagine they
were somewhere between fifteen and eighteen.

"There was an old jailer on duty that night, so we decided to
see what could be done. If we'd have had a set of keys, there's
no question that we would've gotten it on.

"I took the initiative. I said, 'Hey baby, what's happenin'?
We think you're terrific. How about gettin' together?' This was
through the wall. The other guys were just listening in.

"The door to the girls' cell had a window with a grating you
could look through. So we sneaked around and I said, 'Well,
you girls are good-looking. Let see what you've got!'

"This went on for some time. The excitement was mounting
and they were getting into it too, right? We told them that later
on the guard would fall asleep and we'd be able to get his keys

and get in there with 'em. They said, 'Really? Really?' This could not have happened, of course. Just part of the little game we were playing.

"So bit by bit, I first convinced them to shed their tops – and then their bottoms. They were parading around and dancing and being coy, okay?

"There were three of us at the little window, the grate we were peeping through, but only one person could look in at a time. Now, the final revelation here was going to be when we got em to shed their panties."

Voice rising in excitement, Bundy went on: "I hadn't seen a real woman in the altogether since February 28, 1976, when Liz and I last slept together. So I can't be held accountable for my motivations being purely perverse and voyeuristic at this point. I mean, I wanted to see a real live woman in the flesh!

"Well, they were edging their panties down slowly, slowly... when we heard the rattle of doors and we all scampered back to the trustees' cell. And immediately, I hear the call: 'Bundy! The Pitkin County deputies are here to pick you up and take you to Aspen.'

"And I cursed, 'The sonuvabitches! The sonuvabitches!' I was so pissed off!

"It was two or three days later when I returned that I learned that the other guys had consummated this stripping act. And, you know, it is not wholly inconceivable – given the fact that the jailer was a nice, kindly old man – that I might have slipped the keys away from him. I was thinking of it; I really was.

"The sight of this one particularly attractive, fresh, firm young nymphet was just fantastic! And I'm sure that if we would have gotten in there, they would have gotten into it. Of course, they were minors and all I needed was a charge of statutory rape – or rape of any kind. Whatever. What we got was a little peep show."

February 6

Two hours after the jury had convicted him, Bundy recorded a tape for us in his cell. Obviously shaken, he ran the gamut of emotions – from sighs and lengthy pauses to an occasional sob – as he fought to keep his composure.

"It's February 6, 1980, about four o'clock in the afternoon," he began. "I'm back in my cell in the Orange County jail. Two hours or so ago the jury rendered its verdict – or rather, I should say, it rendered its verdict to the effect they found me guilty of murder in the first degree, uh (clears throat).

"I really have trouble right now finding a place to begin. I don't really feel like I have (sigh) any really cute insights or observations or analyses to add to what happened this afternoon. I'm tired, sad (voice breaks). And while I wouldn't really say that I was despondent, clearly I'm, uh, extraordinarily disappointed.

"Anyone who has ever been through a criminal trial as a defendant – whether it be a burglary of an automobile or a robbery or a case such as the one I've been involved in, a case of first-degree murder – cannot help but be (voice breaks) drawn in to the defense of the case. And, not withstanding, perhaps, the *reality* of the situation, begins to develop a whole (sigh), develop glimmers of optimism… that the jury will see things the way my attorneys and myself have seen them.

"Between my conviction in Miami toward the end of July of '79 and the beginning of this trial, I had what I thought... had fairly convinced myself I would be convicted. Not on the merits of the case. Not on the facts introduced by the State. And not on the effectiveness or lack of effectiveness of my counsel. But my conviction was assured principally as a result of the extensive knowledge that pervaded communities throughout Florida concerning my prior convictions and allegations about my background.

"Of course, the most significant of these extrajudicial influences was the publicized trial, the *televised* trial in Miami... for the Chi Omega murders. I doubt that any intelligent observer, whether he be a law person or someone involved in the legal profession, doubted for a second that it would be, uh (voice breaks)... extremely difficult (sighs) to find a community *in* Florida where I could find a jury that had not been tainted by the massive and pervasive amount of publicity concerning *me* and the cases with which I was charged – the cases for which I had been convicted.

"Still, within me at least, there always remained an undercurrent of optimism, *hope*, that things would turn out the way they should turn out. But the jury (coughs) didn't see it my way. The jury selected to deliberate the case in the Kimberley Leach murder (swore that they) were truly able to put aside everything they had heard, read, and seen about me, prior to the time they came into the courtroom and were sworn as jurors... and that they would evaluate the evidence solely upon the evidence introduced in court, the testimony of the witnesses – the typical evidence introduced in court.

"Yes, that was the undercurrent. Anyone who can recall speaking to me about my predictions concerning the Leach trial knows very well (voice breaks) that my belief has been – for at least six months, maybe longer – that there would be a conviction in the Leach case... but that this conviction would not be based solely on the evidence... which came out of the courtroom.

"The conviction would be a combination of the information the jurors had been exposed to prior to the time they came into the courtroom in conjunction with (voice breaks) the evidence they heard.

"I'm not saying I'm clairvoyant. I'm just saying that any reasonably perceptive person would see, would know – based upon the way our minds operate, based upon the way we assimilate information, the way in which we recall past events – that the jury selected in this case, no matter how sincerely they believed that they could judge the evidence presented to them in court; no matter how much they might have wanted to do this, the reality, the manner in which we process information, record it, memorize it, and then retrieve it, would render the task impossible.

"Certainly, these observations of mine derive from a somewhat biased point of view. After all, I *am* the defendant. And, notwithstanding my attempt to... on occasions to step back and *objectively* look at the State's case, I found myself increasingly drawn in to the intense process of (sigh) preparing and presenting my defense.

"Implicit, I believe, in immersing myself in my defense, along with my attorneys, was the belief that we would succeed, even though, once again, in the back of our minds, perhaps – on occasion in the forefront of our minds – we *knew* that we were at an extreme disadvantage.

"Always in attempting to protect myself from the harsh eventuality of conviction, I repeatedly told people that the outcome in the Leach case... there would be a conviction. I said this again and again. And my opinion was not only shared by myself alone. Certainly, many people who approached me expressed the same opinion.

"I guess what I'm trying to say is... while for at least six months I had prepared myself in every way possible for a conviction, this defense mechanism began to slowly disintegrate once I became involved in the active conduct of the trial. I guess there are several factors which *forced* me, which influenced me, to play a role. To play the role of the defendant, who had every hope and expectation of being acquitted of a crime of which he knew himself to be innocent.

"Certainly I don't mean to say I was simply playing a role. What I'm saying is that the role I was playing required... and I become, uh, became... become (voice breaks). It's hard for me to put words together right now. That I had become so enamored by the strength of our case and the weakness of theirs that that undercurrent of hope that I would be acquitted began to surface, slowly. More gradually. Until it was not a vague and improbable outcome, but a real and possible consequence.

"I must admit, however, that I relied throughout most of these proceedings on the defense mechanism I alluded to earlier. That this trial really didn't make any difference; that the outcome was preordained... (voice breaks) that there was nothing we could do. Virtually nothing, no matter how effective or how sensational or how persuasive, that we could do to convince the jury that I was not guilty.

"I remember saying, during closing arguments, when we went back into the office, to Vic, Lynn, and Don (his defense team), that... we made a bet... *I* made a bet... that the jury would be back in three hours with a guilty verdict. Again, I was attempting to protect myself. Insulate myself from the terribly harsh consequences of a guilty verdict. Trying, perhaps, in a more personal way, to preserve my own spirit. To preserve my own desire to survive. To keep on struggling. To not be defeated. Rendered helpless by such an outcome.

"I can recall that we paid close attention to the reactions of the jurors... noting how close they paid attention to certain parts of the testimony, or how they might have disregarded other testimony. It's inevitable that you develop a hope, an optimism... that you're succeeding. That your point of view, arguments, and strategy are not being disregarded. It's inevitable that you come to believe that you're actually convincing people that what you say is right.

"Daily, throughout the trial, I would find myself immersed in the ongoing preparation of the defense. I engaged myself wholeheartedly in assisting my counsel in analyzing prospective jurors. And once again, once I became involved in this process, I required myself to believe in what I was doing. That I was doing it for a purpose. That this would not be a losing game."

After pausing for a tape change, he continued: "I was rambling on... don't know how much sense I'm making. Let me see if I can get to the point. And the point is that I became involved in the case for several reasons – not that I am enamored with or greatly enjoy the criminal trial process. Not as a defendant, but as someone who appreciates the law, appreciates the skill of trial attorneys, and the more and more involved I became, the more I came to play the role of the defendant.

"The defendant who expects the system to do justice – to search for the truth – in which the defendant expects to be free from prejudice, where the defendant expects the jury to depend only on the evidence. By degrees, I lost that overview.

That defense mechanism, if you will. This is just a game. The outcome is already predetermined.

"Pretrial publicity had so thoroughly contaminated *every* community throughout Florida, there was no hope. "And even now, I am most fascinated with – and angry at – myself for falling into that role. 'cause as my pessimism diminished, my optimism increased. My hope that I might be acquitted or there would be a hung jury began to increase. *Still*, periodically through the last four weeks, all I knew about how things worked could not dominate my innate enthusiasm.

"I've been tempted, on occasion, to call or to characterize this spectacle, this trial, as a *game*. And it's not really a game. It certainly isn't. The subject matter in this case was terrible and tragic, but the game was that both myself and my attorneys and perhaps all the participants of the trial, including the jurors, the press, and the judge, began to believe that we were actually engaged in the process of seeking the truth.

"How ludicrous the criminal trial is! Particularly in cases of this type where the evidence is complex and where the evidence takes place over the course of several weeks, involving a hundred witnesses or more. And how equally ludicrous it is when the evidence is of such a complex nature that it is presented before jurors, each of whom expressed during voir dire that they were aware that I had, in the past, been convicted of murder.

"I suppose that all this rambling I've been doing on this particular tape has been gone over before. I'm almost certain we've discussed it before. But I bring it up now in reference to what occurred in the last couple days.

"Beginning with closing argument: We all paid attention to the effectiveness of the State's closing argument, versus the effectiveness of Vic's closing argument. We paid attention to which jurors were sitting forward, who paid attention to which portions of which closing argument. All of us, but myself considerably more than the others, would be drawn into this whirlpool of that deceptive process which we call a criminal trial.

"How many times have I said before that in spite of the fact we took copious notes of what occurred during the trial, that in spite of the fact we had the benefit of police reports in front of us and depositions of the various witnesses and the exhibits that had been introduced – despite all this – we were often confused as to what was said by which witness and which exhibit was introduced and for what purpose.

"Lynn, Vic, and I have become well acquainted with the manner in which evidence is produced at trial. And if we have all the advantages of refreshing our memory with the statements of witnesses and the evidence on a daily basis, how in the world can we expect lay people to sit there on the jury – without the benefit of reviewing the evidence and without the ability to take notes – to sift carefully through what they've heard and weigh and analyze all this and get the truth?

"The final conclusion is we cannot expect them to come up with even a reasonable approximation. Yet, in spite of our better judgment, we fall into this trap of believing we are convincing jurors of the validity *of* our point of view. Think about the term 'reasonable doubt.' Is there a more vague phrase in the English language? And yet, is there a more crucial phrase used in the criminal trial process? Nowhere in the instructions given to a jury, and I believe nowhere in all the legal literature, is there an adequate definition of what a 'reasonable doubt' is.

"Reasonable doubt. What is it? Is it a doubt with a reason, you know? If one accepts that kind of interpretation, then any reason (sobs), no matter how slight, may suffice. All that I've been saying on this tape – and I've wondered about trying to recapitulate my criticisms of the type of criminal trial I've just gone through – has been a preface (sic) to what has occurred here these past couple days.

"I mentioned earlier the closing arguments. Following closing arguments I solicited the opinions of a number of people. Was Vic effective? Was the State effective? Did we win any points? Did people really think the State had a case? Did we? Of course, that population of people, that subgroup of individuals to whom I have access, were uniformly telling me that the State's case was weak… that they didn't have anything but circumstantial evidence.

"Now, somewhere in my mind I knew that that didn't make any difference. As deliberations began last evening, we (the defense team) sat back in our little office, just down the hallway from the courtroom where the jury was poring over the evidence. Just sort of relaxing. Believing it would be *some* time before a verdict came out. Even though I must confess I bet Vic $20 and Don $10 they would come back with a guilty verdict within three hours. I must admit I was wrong. By three hours; they came back in six. I consider my error to be slight, under the circumstances.

"But, it took a lot to make me a believer. I *finally* bought it that no matter what had happened, who had testified… and what they might've said, I had had it. I was doomed (pause and sobs). And I think this was despite the fact that Vic and Lynn did a marvelous job. True, they could have been more eloquent at times; they could have been more forceful. They could have been better prepared on certain points. True, their cross examination could've been more crisp – that they would not have opened the doors to some things which allowed the prosecution to embarrass us. We put on some witnesses who weren't particularly effective. But I think that occurred on both sides.

"I was not overly impressed with the prosecution, either. So the jury began to deliberate… and Vic and Don played gin rummy while I made phone calls, and waited, that first evening. And about forty-five minutes into the deliberations, they asked for a tape recorder. Again, I fell into that trap – believing or accepting the most favorable interpretation – that they were interested in (C. L.) Andy Anderson (a prosecution witness who testified he saw Bundy, driving a white van, abduct Miss Leach) and that they wanted to resolve doubts about his testimony. We had maintained, of course, that his testimony was *critical* to the case – indispensable. And based on that request, we felt cautiously optimistic.

"But about nine-thirty we had to go back to the courtroom, where the judge was to dismiss the jury for the night. They had been deliberating in that courtroom, and evidence – documents, pictures, maps, and so on – was tossed all over the place. It looked like they were really studying *everything*. Once again, my heart gave this lurch. Could it be? But something gnawed at me. As we watched the jury file in, I noticed that almost all of them were laughing, playing around.

"That is, with the exception of three women, Mrs. Murphy and the two women who sat directly behind her. On her face was this expression of deep concern, worry, doubt – it's hard to tell. Clearly she was not happy. Her expression was in stark contrast to the others. (Pat) Walski (the jury foreman) seemed to be in the highest spirits. Something about *that* put goose bumps on me.

"But call it what you will, I put it aside and actually got a damn good night's sleep. At *least* they're not completely sure. At least I have a chance, I thought.

"And then a strange thing happened. The judge (Wallace Jopling) invited us into chambers and said to me, 'Mr. Bundy, I'd like to have this on the record. Do you consider that you've received adequate counsel in this trial?' Vic had told me the judge was going to ask me that and I told him that my response would be, essentially, 'Well, I don't know. I don't know everything that's gone on.' Anyway, I told the judge, 'Well, from what I know, I *think* I have, but I don't claim to know everything that's happened.'

"Vic promised I could come down (to wait in the defense office) this morning at nine and I was pacing like the proverbial caged animal when they finally got there, some time after ten-thirty. I kept muttering, 'I hate this waiting! I hate this waiting!' It's the worst part of the trial; I can't imagine how I slept so well. When I awoke, I felt like a man who knew he was going to be struck by lightning but didn't know if it was going to be in five seconds, five hours, or five years. I just couldn't sit still!

"The bastards kept me waiting... a long time. I called Vic and he said he thought I was on the way already. The sheriff's people said there weren't enough bailiffs. I could have slept this morning. Hell, who am I kidding? After a reasonably serene night, I woke up with a start about five a.m., as the breakfast tray came around. Then took a cat nap after breakfast, then a shower.

"While I was waiting, the captain in charge of this unit brought me a letter from the director of corrections, telling me that I wasn't qualified to get married in Orange County. 'Not in the best interests of the inmate,' it read. Actually, I knew we had alternate plans, so that didn't bother me that much, but when it's all written in stone, put it down that this was less than a wonderful day for Theodore Bundy!

(Very quietly) "I keep rambling on how I believed I might get a fair trial, but shit, there aren't any fair trials for someone like me. They just want to put me away – for good. I don't know why I was so buoyed up four, uh, five hours ago, when I went downstairs. As I walked along, a couple guys down the hall mumbled good wishes, and one said, 'Hey Bundy, you gonna be okay, man. You got a good chance.'

"Good chance, shit! I *never* had a good chance."

Part Two

Bundy was sentenced to death, again, for Kim Leach's murder on February 12. Because of the time required for the prison to reprocess him back onto Death Row – thirty days prescribed by law – we had to wait a month before beginning the next planned stage of the interviews.

All his anecdotes and Ted's occasionally searching recollections of his past had been useful; we had his whole life story to cover. But once he was returned to Death Row it was time to talk about the killings. His letter of the previous November notwithstanding, we had to confront him about his crimes. We intended to hold him to his pledge of complete disclosure.

The balance of our interviews with Ted were all conducted inside Florida State Prison near Starke.

March 18

We decided to start him out with Kim Leach, who disappeared from her Lake City junior high school, about 100 miles east of Tallahassee, on the morning of February 9, 1978. From the available evidence, it seemed certain that Kim had been a victim of opportunity, a twelve-year-old who had just happened onto Ted's path while he was hunting. The day before, he had tried to lure a different young girl into his stolen van in Jacksonville.

TB: Uh, why did I go to Jacksonville? (long pause.) Well, some time in that latter part of January... I really wasn't sure *where* I wanted to go. I still felt I had to get out of state (following the Chi Omega slayings), but I had very little traveling money.

Jacksonville represented the closest large town to Tallahassee (about 170 miles east, or 70 miles past Lake City).

SM: Uh huh.

TB: It was possible to get there without spending a lot of time on the road or spending money. So I decided to check that out. The newspapers looked good. There was a lot more work in Jacksonville than Tallahassee (where Ted had tried, and failed, to get a day-labor job).

SM: How'd you get there?

TB: I drove.

SM (laughing): Is that a fact?

TB (laughing): Yeah.

SM: What did you drive, Ted?

TB: Uh, I drove a van.

SM: *Did* you?

TB: Uh huh.

SM: Which van did you drive?

TB: A van I had stolen on the streets.

SM: It wasn't the FSU van (the stolen Florida State University van Ted was identified as driving at the time of Kim Leach's abduction)?

TB (softly): No.

Bundy told his first lie just one minute into the interview.

SM: Did you steal the keys to the FSU van?

TB: No.

SM: You were never in the FSU van?

TB: No. I wasn't ever in the FSU van. Uh, I hesitated there because I've seen it so much. I thought that (pause) the only possibility would have been… uh, uh, uh, being taken to it. But, uh, I was never taken to it. The only thing I was ever shown was the photographs of it.

SM: What van did you take?

TB (long pause): A van.

SM: Are you trying to recollect or are you just being silent? (Ted says he is just trying to remember where he had stolen the van from.)

TB: I think it was on Monroe Street. I'm not sure. But there's a Salvation Army store there and a number of gas stations and businesses. In any case, there was a van there – and I checked it out several times.

SM: What was the make and year?

TB: It was, uh, white. It was a Chevrolet, I believe.

SM: Do you remember the year?

TB: No, I don't recall the year. And I kept my eye on it; that, and several other vehicles. I wasn't necessarily plugged into a van.

SM: Uh huh.

TB: I'd checked out a lot of the other places in town… for just any kind of transportation. Like, you know, auto stores, tire stores, where people take their vehicles in to be fixed and leave the keys in them.

SM: When *was* this… when you started looking?

TB: I don't remember the date, but on this Friday or Saturday I decided to go to Jacksonville and went looking again. I saw it there on the street… with keys in it.

SM: Was it at night?

TB: Yeah.

SM: Do you recall anything about the (van's) interior?

TB: I believe the seats were red. The dash was red the floor was bare. It didn't have a radio.

(I assumed Bundy was telling a half-truth. He probably did contemplate stealing a white Chevrolet van at some point. But it was the white FSU van that was found with fibers from Kim's football jersey and Ted's blue blazer in it.)

SM: Did you have more than one vehicle boosted at any one time?

TB: Yeah.

SM: How many?

TB (swallows loudly): Well, this was on the last day I was in Jacksonville – uh, Tallahassee. Technically, I had several.

SM: *Technically?*

TB: I mean, I wasn't driving several at a time. On that Sunday I picked up one and drove it and it didn't work. And then I picked up another. And it wasn't to my liking. So I got a third.

SM: These were all vans?

TB: Miscellaneous vehicles, with keys in them.

SM: This was Sunday, February 5?

TB: No, it was the Sunday before I left, February 12,

SM: The 12th? That's after you returned (to Tallahassee) from Jacksonville. Which means you took this white van the week before.

TB: Uh huh.

SM: What day did you take it?

TB: I believe it was Saturday night. I'm not sure.

SM: Well, it'd be Saturday night the 4th.

TB: Okay.

SM: When did you leave for Jacksonville?

TB: Not until Monday or Tuesday, I believe.

SM: Tuesday the 7th you have a charge at the Gulf station at the intersection of I-10 and 441, just north of Lake City.

TB: That would have been the day I left.

SM: Okay, and you ate at a Holiday Inn at Orange Park.

TB: Uh huh.

SM: Where did you stay that night?

TB: At a Holiday Inn in Jacksonville. I got in town there Tuesday afternoon.

SM: And you stayed in Jacksonville how long?

TB: Well, I stayed there (pause) the next day and then started back in the afternoon – back toward Tallahassee.

SM: So what did you do? Did you just look the town over?

TB: Uh huh.

SM: You bought some gas at a Shell station that day.

TB: Uh huh.

SM: The night of the 7th, which is Tuesday night, you were in Jacksonville. You bought gas at a Gulf station on Roosevelt Boulevard.

TB: Yeah.

SM: The *next* day, you bought gas at a Shell station in Jacksonville, but then you bought gas *again* on that same day in a Gulf station. So you had two on the 8th, one on the 7th (all with stolen credit cards). So, I guess, you gassed up when you got there and drove around Jacksonville for a day. Then you gassed up again and got as far back as Lake City, the Holiday Inn there, on the night of the 8th.

TB: Uh huh.

56

Stephen G. Michaud and Hugh AynesworthStephen G. Michaud and Hugh Aynesworth

SM: Why didn't you drive all the way back?

TB: I was very tired. And it rained very hard that night. (Ted probably *was* tired – from hunting for victims and from drinking. He was correct about the rain.)

SM: Okay. You had dinner at the Holiday Inn the night of the 8th. Do you remember the guy you had drinks with in the bar?

TB: Only vaguely. I couldn't describe him.

SM: What time did you leave the next day?

TB: It's hard to say. It rained very heavily that night and was very cool the next morning. And I started to have breakfast there at the Holiday Inn about seven or eight o'clock. As I started walking toward the main building where the restaurant was, I noticed there were one or two highway patrol cars parked there. So I decided to avoid that. I didn't even check out. I just got in the van and started back for Tallahassee.

SM: You didn't go back to Lake City Junior High School?

TB: No.

SM: Did you kill Kim Leach?

TB: No.

SM: You went directly west on 90? No stops for murder?

TB: 90 is not the freeway – 10 is the freeway.

SM: So you went on up to 10 and drove back to Tallahassee. Where did you get rid of the van?

TB: Uh, there's a high school there. What's the name of it? Uh, Leon High School? I believe there was a residential district with a parochial school. Somewhere between those two schools I parked the van.

SM: Did that ever show up in any of the police reports?

TB: Not that I'm aware of.

SM: And that was the only white van you stole?

TB: Yeah.

SM: Well, tell me more about that van.

TB: It had a flat front on it – unlike the later models where the hood seems to go out a little bit. It had a bald spare tire. No jack.

SM: Did you know who owned it? Did you check out the registration?

TB: No.

SM: Did you check out the name of the business in front of which it was parked?

TB: No.

SM: Did you leave the keys in it when you parked

TB: I believe I left them.

SM: Did you do anything to change that van at all?

TB: No.

SM: What about Leslie Parmenter (the teenaged daughter of a Jacksonville police detective Bundy approached in Jacksonville the day before he killed Kim Leach)? What was all that about? Was that *you?*

TB: No.

SM: What about her license-tag identification?

TB (belches): Well, I don't know.

SM: Was that manufactured evidence?

TB: Manufactured or something! I'm not sure. I stopped asking those questions a long time ago. I don't think I ever, uh, figured that out. I saw the Parmenters twice – once at a hearing in Lake City and again in court. And they seem to be, uh, fairly sincere. Genuine, whatever.

SM: That license tag, Ted. They got the right number. They did. And they reported it *before* you were even known to be in Florida.

TB: I have no explanation for it.

As far as we know, Bundy never directly acknowledged Kim Leach's murder to anyone, except to tell FBI agent Bill Hagmaier of the Bureau's Behavioral Science Unit that the little girl was not a preselected target. She was the final victim of what he called his final, "disorganized" phase of murder begun twenty-four days earlier with the slaughter at Chi Omega.

Bundy saved that disclosure for the final weekend of his life. In the spring of 1980, nine years before, our questions about the Leach case had yielded nothing. When Hugh and I spoke on the telephone that night, we concluded that we weren't going to get anything like a confession from Ted for any of his crimes. It was time to consider abandoning the whole project.

Another interview with Ted was scheduled for the following week. We discussed telling him that we were walking away from the story unless he started telling the truth. Bundy, we surmised, would hold the door for me.

But then it occurred to us: What about giving Ted the chance to talk without also overtly implicating himself in the murders? Why not offer Bundy the opportunity to speak in the third person? If somewhere inside him there was an urge to explain himself – and we believed that to be the case – then perhaps he'd be comfortable "speculating" about the killer. It wasn't a brilliant thought. We had no idea if it would work. Then again, there was nothing to lose. After nine months of effort we were stuck, and our editors in New York were growing restive.

March 26

SM: Ted, your recollections of the Leach case don't conform to reality.

TB: Sure they do.

SM: No, they don't. (Bundy looks wary.) So Hugh and I have come up with another approach to this.

TB: What's that?

SM: Well, no one knows the story better than you. Remember writing us? "I may not have *all* the facts, but I have the ones which count!"

TB: I do. I did.

SM: You haven't shared them, though. What you can do, however, is analyze the whole thing for us.

TB: Huh?

SM: You're the expert, Ted. You know the cases. You know the investigations. You're the suspect. Who else is in a better position to pull this all together?

TB: I've told you everything I know.

SM: You've told us *some* of what you know. What you *could* tell us, though, is what sort of person you think might have committed the crimes. Assuming it was a single person, he must have a personality and motives that you could infer from the evidence – and from your own background in psychology. (Ted had an undergraduate degree in psychology from the University of Washington.)

TB (sounding interested): You mean, for me to tell you what this guy... or guys... is like?

SM: Yeah, but not like some shrink. We want the person who knows absolutely the most about this story to tell about it. We're after an explanation here.

TB: I'm not copping to anything but theft!

SM: We realize that. What we need to know is who he is, and what he's like. Not Ted Bundy, suspect, talking to me in the first person.

TB (after a thoughtful pause): I think your idea may have some merit. I'll have to think about it.

March 27

Bundy had made up his mind. With minimal explanation, he took the tape recorder and cradled it in his arms, closed his eyes, and began an abstract soliloquy on stress and its effect on "this personality." Very soon I was lost, so I interrupted him.

SM: Your description of stress – it seems vague to me.

TB: Well, stress is a very ambiguous word in that it includes both the physical being and the emotional self. With respect to this personality, stress influenced development over a number of years. The stress doesn't just appear. It's present in its various forms for a long time and, as a consequence, certain alterations in the personality take place.

I guess what is stress to you might not be stress to me. An individual in this sort of circumstance would not recognize the demands to perform well academically as stress. But ultimately this guy starts to wear down. If you just see it as "God, I gotta get this paper in today. I gotta get to class today. What am I doing here? Am I doing well enough to go where I want to go?" Those type things. The long-term effect of this is something you don't recognize as a stressful thing.

Obviously, everybody doesn't react to these environmental influences in the same way. It has a peculiar, individualized effect. A lot of people would not have a bad reaction to the stress in a university setting. Stress is just a word; it's nothing that pops up every morning out of the toaster. And there are continuing kinds of stress, things that can be looked at as continuing events. Whether it be career demands, or money problems, or relationships.

SM: What kind of shocks or stressful events would you say this personality encountered?

TB: It's not an easy matter to isolate things. I mean, incidents which themselves could cause pressure or stress, be unpleasant to one degree or another or have a disorienting effect. You have to see it in its unique effect on the unique individual. There are no broad generalizations or predictions you can make. You just can't predict behavior like that.

Society wants to believe it can identify evil people, or bad or harmful people, but it's not practical. If someone does something antisocial and deviant, that is a manifestation of something that's going on inside. Once they do something, *then* they can be labeled. Predictions can't be made until that point is reached.

There are no stereotypes. There are no family backgrounds or personality types or life-styles that are, themselves, predictors. There are probably any number of persons in this prison whose family backgrounds were a large factor in putting them here. Family is very important, I believe. I've met many persons who have explained their adolescent years and their home life in such terms that it seemed inevitable that they would end up in trouble with the law. Robbers and burglars and what not.

When you talk about persons who end up here charged or convicted of murder, that is slightly different – depending on the homicide. What we don't understand is why someone would murder a person for apparently no reason. Not for monetary gain, (or) a crime of passion. We understand crimes of passion – where a man gets mad at his wife, or vice versa, and picks up a gun.

But what we're talking about is a hybrid situation. What is the motivation for it? What is the cause? We know what the effect is. We just don't understand the cause.

SM: The family in this instance is neither a force for stability or instability?

TB: I think you could say that the influence of this person's family history was positive. But not positive enough – not enduring, perhaps not strong enough to overcome the urges or compulsions that resulted. Most people think of attitudes being developed in the home. What I'm saying…in this instance, the influence of the family and the environment in which the person grew up were positive, but not so positive as to prepare this individual to totally avoid failure.

Everyone has to expect a certain amount of failure. It's trial and error out there. I don't care how good your family background was.

The thing is, some people are just psychologically less ready for failure than others. Some can handle failure in a positive way; others cannot. It would be too simplistic to say that because a person had trouble dealing with a career choice or a relationship with a coed, that this goes back to some defect in the way he was raised.

Parents can do only so much for a child. If they offer a stable, loving home life, where there is little apparent friction, the model of sobriety and responsibility and so on and so forth… then you just can't make those assertions that the family caused the aberration with any reasonable degree of probability.

Other things come into play – a whole host of other things. They might be escapist kinds of behavior, drinking or watching television even. There is the effect of pornography, for example; not suggestive, but more illicit or expressed forms of pornography that's in print or on film. Nothing is ever as simple as it seems on the surface.

We sent men to Vietnam and they were able to kill, because the tactics taken by their leaders was to depersonalize the enemy. You're not killing a man; you're killing a "gook," a Viet Cong. Under those circumstances, men kill very easily.

Certainly the situation we're discussing does not have the legitimacy or the atmosphere of war. And yet, the same psychological mechanisms are used by a person who kills indiscriminately – except he is not killing a person. He is killing an image. Or gaining some sort of gratification – just as some people might for bowling a perfect 300 game.

It's not an easy thing to visualize, to accept intuitively. This was a difficult thing for me to try to understand. There are no pat answers. If anybody's looking for pat answers, forget it. If there were, the psychiatrists and psychologists would have had this thing wrapped up long ago.

Perhaps it can be done this way: You take the individual we're talking about – a unique personality with certain defects, if you will – and then you subject him to stress. Stress happens to come up randomly, but its effect on the person is *not* random; it's specific. That results in a certain amount of chaos, confusion, and frustration. That person begins to seek out a target for his frustrations.

The continued nature of this stress this person was under – the nature of the flaw or weakness in his personality, together with other elements in the environment that offer him a logical target for his frustrations or escapes from reality – yields the situation we're discussing.

That's a broad overview. The real critical point of analysis here is why would a person with this kind of background, subjected to this kind of environmental stress, or this kind of environment in toto, seek out as targets for his dissatisfaction, frustration… call it psychopathology. I hate to use labels that are psychological or psychiatric because there are no stereotypes, and when you start to use those labels, you stop looking at the facts.

You can say, "Okay, this guy passed through this kind of a life. All this stimuli went into a black box in his mind and it came out in a variety of ways. But in one area, it came out this way.

In an apparent indiscriminate matter, this man ended up killing, murdering people. What happened in that black box? How can we say what stimuli were significant and which are not? What were those things that person saw and heard and felt and touched that resulted in this kind of behavior? And which do we just disregard? And then, why did that black box twist it?"

I'm not sure anybody has the answers to these questions – least of all myself.

I would say that if we took this individual from birth and raised him in the Soviet Union or Afghanistan or in eighteenth-century America, in all likelihood he'd lead a normal life. We were talking about the peculiar circumstances of society and of the twentieth century in America. There are a host of things to which a person is exposed which he would not be exposed to in a simpler culture, a more restricting or puritanical culture.

What is inexplicable, I suppose, is why that predisposition is there in the first place. I think that's what is inexplicable. For instance, why is this propensity activated and started to develop? I guess one analogy would be that some seem to prosper in a given soil and not in another. The soil we're talking about is our culture in this country. We're talking about the manner in which this propensity stops being something latent and starts being active – and develops into something which, for lack of a better description, is psychopathology.

And not just *a* psychopathology, because there are a lot of people who are sick in the head who don't act out. Or whose acting out does not become antisocial – or not as antisocial as the act of murder.

What we're talking about here, also, are those microscopic events in the mind – indistinguishable, undetectable events, like the melting of a single snowflake. I guess we know a great deal more about what makes a snowflake melt than the development of behavior that produces murder.

SM: In this person, there are no identifiable shocks, traumas?

TB: No... and none associated physically with women. There is really no trigger. It is truly more sophisticated than that.

SM: Describe in more depth what you called turmoil, chaos.

TB: You mean, how do I visualize it? I guess it is probably no more or no less than any young person would experience today who is going to college or just growing up. Nothing special, nothing peculiar, and nothing that is peculiarly related to the ultimate conduct that we are interested in. We could be talking at this point about anyone. A lot of things he understands and a lot of things he doesn't. A lot of things make him happy; some things make him sad. That's basically the kind of things I am trying to get across.

I don't have all the answers. I have never sat down and discussed this behavior before with anyone. So it is very hard to verbalize something which, by its very nature, is not only complex but often so subtle we can't immediately put our finger on what's going on – especially in its early stages.

This condition is not immediately seen by the individual or identified as a serious problem. It sort of manifests itself in an interest concerning sexual behavior, as sexual images. It might simply be an attraction such as *Playboy* or a host of other normal, healthy sexual stimuli that are found in the environment.

For most everyone that would simply be a sign of healthy interest, normal. But this interest, for some unknown reason, becomes geared toward matters of a sexual nature that involve violence. I cannot emphasize enough the gradual development of this. It is not short term.

The individual does not particularly see himself as the actor where the violence is directed toward women. But he is fascinated by this kind of literature that depicts this kind of action.

It is perhaps not so inexplicable when you understand the position of the women in the United States as they are marketed and used to sell things. Seen as objects of perfection, et cetera. Now, this is on a different level than this individual would deal with women every day, and not in the context of the sexual condition, because that is over here someplace, like collecting stamps. He doesn't retain the taste of the glue, so to speak, all day long. But in a broader, more abstract way, it begins to preoccupy him.

He has no hatred for women; there is nothing in his background that happened that would indicate he has been abused by any females. The only explanation would be that there is some kind of weakness that gives rise to this individual's interest in the kind of sexual activity involving violence that would gradually begin to absorb some of his fantasy.

And while he would not visualize himself as an actor, he would begin to fantasize about these situations. Once again, he was not imagining himself actively doing these things, but he found gratification from reading about others so engaged. Eventually the interest would become so demanding toward new material that it could only be catered to by what he could find in the dirty book stores.

In a pornography shop you can find a variety of perversions in sexual conduct, from homosexuality, to abuse, to lesbianism, et cetera. People who market pornography are dealing with a special-interest group. Anyone who walks into one of these places is not just interested in a Great Dane humping someone or two men engaging in sexual activity. It is just not the way it works.

But it does offer variety and different kinds of literature, and a certain percentage of it is devoted toward literature that explores situations where a man, in the context of sexual encounter, in one way or another, engages in some sort of violence toward a woman – or the victim. There are, of course, a whole host of subsituations that could come under that particular heading. Your girlfriend, your wife, a stranger, children, whatever. A whole host of victims are found in this kind of literature. And in this kind of literature, they are treated as victims.

(Bundy described that part of him that was fascinated by sexual violence as "the entity," or "the disordered self." It was the "Ted" that fantasized schemes, at first purely as an exercise in imagination, for isolating victims. He "posited" that "the entity" led "this personality" to experiment with disabling automobile distributor caps or letting the air out of tires. Then the girl or woman would be alone and in need of help, grateful for the appearance of a friendly stranger. Apparently, Bundy actually went so far as to attempt these approaches but discovered "that instantly one or more others always showed up to help her." At this stage, he said, the hunting was all mental, a game. Then he started to describe an actual attack and stopped. For some reason, he wanted to skip over this stage in the development of "this personality." Instead, he went on to explain voyeurism.)

TB: Say he was walking down the street on one occasion, one evening, and just totally, uh, by chance looked up into the window of a house and saw a woman undressing.

And it just occurred to him that, perhaps not in terribly dramatic terms but as if in a revelation, that there was a viable alternative to this nonsense of the flat tires and distributor caps. Certainly a less, a more acceptable one, one that put everybody in less jeopardy – would... might be realized by indulging in a form of voyeurism.

And he began, with some regularity, with *increasing* regularity, to, uh, canvass, as it were, the community he lived in. By peeping in windows, as it were, and watching a woman undress, or watching whatever could be seen, you know, during the evening, and approaching it almost like a project, throwing himself into it, uh, literally for years.

These occasions when he would, uh, travel about the neighborhoods that adjoined his and search out candidates for... search out places where he could see the things he wanted to see... uh, more or less these occasions were dictated... still being dictated by this person's normal life.

So he wouldn't break a date or postpone an important, uh, event or whatever. Wouldn't rearrange his life in any significant way to accommodate his, uh, *indulgence* in this voyeuristic behavior.

He gained, you'd say, a terrific amount of... at times... a great amount of gratification from it. And he became increasingly adept at it – as anyone becomes adept at anything they do over and over and over again.

SM: It sounds to me like he wouldn't get enough sleep; that he'd be continuously exhausted.

TB: Oh yes, I think this is fair to say... but what I think we can say... what began to happen was that, uh, important matters were not being rearranged or otherwise interfered with by his voyeuristic behavior, but with increasing regularity, things that were postponable were postponed or otherwise rescheduled to, uh, work around, uh, hours and hours spent on the street, at night and during the early morning hours.

SM: A while ago you envisioned that one night this person was walking by this bar. He sees a girl coming out of a bar or walking down the street from a bar. Could this have been a crystallization? Or something snapped at this point?

TB: Well, I think that's overdramatizing it. I think this personality we're talking about... uh, what's happening is that we're building up the condition and what may have been a predisposition for violence becomes a disposition. And as the condition develops and its purposes or its characteristics become more well defined, it begins to demand more of the attention and time of the individual.

There's a certain amount of tension, uh, struggle between the normal personality and this, this, uh, psychopathological, uh, entity.

There are all kinds of words. Malignancy is not exactly a proper metaphor, though I suppose that if malignancy means sickness of a serious sort, it would be apt.

SM: In the sense that tumors sometimes grow and expand and...

TB: Yeah, certainly that's an analogy that could be used here. Although it's not satisfactory in that one has no control over, uh, over a malign tumor, and yet, one would think that an individual would have control over the development of something purely psychological. It develops very, very slowly – and the person's aware of it, and, uh, essentially, the only steps that are taken are to, uh, initially conceal it and not let it interfere with normal things.

But basically, however, as this condition develops and becomes more distinct, there's pressure, a sort of contest, as it were. The tension between normal individual, uh, normal consciousness of this individual and those demands being submitted to him via this competing… this condition inside him seems to be competing for more attention. Okay? And it's not, it's not an independent thing. One doesn't switch on and the other doesn't switch off. They're more or less active at the same time. Sometimes one is more active, you know.

SM: What about that attack?

TB (sighing): Oh, I wasn't going to comment on that. What I was going to do was just to agree that there was a point where, probably… agree that a point would be reached where we'd had all this, this reservoir of tension building. Building and building. Finally, inevitably, this force – this entity – would make a breakthrough.

Maybe not a major breakthrough, but a significant breakthrough would be achieved – where the tension would be too great, the pressure would be too great and the demands and expectations of this entity would reach a point where they could not be controlled. And where the consequences would really be seen for the first time.

SM: How would this personality, having seen a woman that night in the neighborhood and having been aroused by her, have reacted? Would he have returned again and again to the house until there came a time when he saw her there alone?

TB: I think you could make a little more sense of much of this if you take into account the effect of alcohol. It's important. It's very important as a trigger. When this person drank a good deal, his inhibitions were significantly diminished. He would find that his urge to engage in voyeuristic behavior or trips to the book store would become more prevalent, more urgent. On every occasion when he engaged in such behavior, he was intoxicated.

SM: There was no alarm on the part of the dominant (personality)?

TB: It was as though the dominant personality was sedated. Not, now, to the point of unconsciousness, but to the point of being unable to fully control.

SM: (This self) was somewhat less arbitrary in its demands?

TB: Less domineering; still very vigilant. Anybody… the more they become intoxicated, the less cautious they become.

SM: What was it you found objectionable or unsatisfactory about the scene we started to discuss?

TB: Well, I'm not. I don't find it unsatisfactory. I just thought it necessary in thinking of… describing such an incident… it might make more sense to describe the state of the individual – by indicating that on every occasion when he engaged in such behavior, he was intoxicated.

SM: Right.

TB (long pause): And we can say that the, the... on one particular evening, when he had been drinking a great deal... and as he was passing a bar, he saw a woman leaving the bar and walk up a fairly dark side street. And for no, uh, we'd say that, something seemed to seize him! I was going to say something crystallized, but that's another way of looking at it. But the urge to do something to that person seized him – in a way he'd never been affected before.

And it seized him strongly. And to the point where, uh, without giving a great deal of thought, he searched around for some instrumentality to uh, uh, *attack* this woman with. He found a piece of two-by-four in a lot somewhere and proceeded to follow and track this girl.

SM: How great a distance?

TB: Oh, I don't know. Several blocks (pause). And when he reached the point where he was almost, uh, driven to do something – there was really no control at this point.

SM: Uh huh.

TB: And the situation's novel because while he may have toyed around with fantasies before and made several abortive attempts to, uh, act out a fantasy, it never reached the point where actually he was, uh, confronted with harming another individual, or taking possession or abducting or whatever – which really is ultimate, I suppose; one of the ultimate antisocial acts, as it were.

And so it reached a point where he... he'd gotten ahead of this quarry, this girl, and was lying in wait for her, as they say. But, uh, before she reached the point where he was concealed, she turned and went into her house!

SM: Uh huh.

TB: Okay? And yet the... the sort of revelation of that experience and the frenzied desire that seized him, uh, really seemed to usher in a new dimension to the, that part of himself that was obsessed with, or otherwise enamored with, violence and women and sexual activity – a composite kind of thing. Not terribly well defined, but more well defined as time went on.

This particular incident spurred him on to, uh, on succeeding evenings, to, uh, hunt this neighborhood, uh, searching (for others).

I mean, he had, in the months and years previous to this, frequently passed women in alleys, women in dark streets, women alone on any number of occasions, as he was making his rounds and looking in windows. But it never occurred to him, ever at any point, to use this as an opportunity to do anything. It just never occurred to him.

For some reason, this particular – the sight of that woman under those circumstances on that evening and given the condition he was in – sort of signaled a breakthrough. The, the breaking of the tension – making a hole in the dam.

Not bursting it down, but again, we begin to see the cracks, as it were.

On succeeding evenings he began to, uh, scurry around this same neighborhood, obsessed with the image he'd seen on the evening before. And on occasion, on one particular occasion, he saw a woman park her car and walk up to her door and fumble for her keys. He walked up behind her and struck her with a... a piece of wood he was carrying. And she fell down and began screaming, and he panicked and ran.

What he had done terrified him. Purely terrified him. And he was full of remorse and remonstrating with himself for the suicidal, uh, nature of that activity – the ugliness of it all – and, you know, he quickly sobered up, as it were.

SM: Fear of discovery, too.

TB: Fear of discovery, sure. Fear of a number of things. He was horrified by the realization that he had the capacity to do such a thing, or even attempt – that's a better word – this kind of thing. He was terribly fearful that for one reason or another he might be apprehended.

The sobering effect of that was to... for some time, close up the cracks again. And not do anything. For the first time, he sat back and swore to himself that he wouldn't do something like that again... or even, anything that would lead to it.

And he did everything he should have done. He stayed away from... he didn't go out at night. And when he was drinking, he stayed around friends. For a period of months, the enormity of what he did stuck with him, and he watched his behavior and reinforced the desire to overcome what he had begun to perceive were some problems that were probably more severe than he would have liked to believe they were.

SM: Yeah.

TB: Uh, he had… within a matter of months, slowly but surely, the impact of this event lost its, uh, deterrent value. And within months he was back, uh, uh, peeping in windows again and slipping back into that old routine.

It was clear to him, I think, that the course of conduct that he had engaged in on that first, monstrous, occasion, as it were, was totally inappropriate. Fraught with danger, badly thought out. And so, the repulsion that had seized him at the moment he knew what he had done, that repulsion began to recede. As he slipped back into his old routine, something *did* stick with him. That was the incredible danger: by allowing himself to fall into spontaneous, unplanned acts of violence.

It took six months or so, until he was back thinking of alternative means of engaging in similar activity, but not… not something that would be likely (to) result in apprehension… or failure of one sort or another. And, uh, as I said, this took place over a period of months.

Then on *another* night he saw a woman walking home – late at night, or early in the morning. He followed her home, looked in the window, and watched her get ready for bed. And he did this on several occasions, for this was a regular kind of thing.

Eventually he created a plan where he would attack her, in the house. And early one morning, uh, he sneaked into the house, through a door he knew was open, and entered the bedroom. And implementing a plan based somewhat on fantasy – based, you know, on anything but personal knowledge – uh, uh, he jumped on the woman's bed and attempted to restrain her. But all he succeeded in doing was waking her up and, uh, causing her to panic and scream. He left very rapidly.

And then he was seized with the same kind of disgust, repulsion, and fear and wonder at why he was allowing himself to attempt such extraordinary violence.

But the significance of this particular occasion was that while he did the same thing he did before – (he) stayed off the streets, vowed he'd never do it again, and recognized the horror of what he'd done, and certainly was frightened by what he saw happening – it only took him three months this time to get over it.

SM: The urge became more and more persistent.

TB: Uh huh, and then the next incident... he was over it in a month – until it didn't take him any time at all to recover from what always was the horror and repulsion and disgust. Whether it was, you know, fervent desire and a serious attempt to suppress this kind of behavior. Whatever. But now what happened was that the, the, this entity inside him was not capable of being controlled any longer – at least not for any considerable period of time!

SM: Can you describe the mood as it would come over this person? Is it predominantly like anger?

TB: No.

SM: Lust?

TB: No. It is going to be difficult to describe. I don't know how you describe the taste of a, uh... how do you describe what a quiche tastes like? Or what the juice of bouillabaisse is like or why it tastes the way it does? Some people taste clams and some people taste the, uh, mullet and the mussels and whatever else is in there. And so it's difficult for me to sit here and perceive what the mood would be like. It wouldn't be anger necessarily. It would *definitely*, at a given point, I think, well… let me regroup here. I said that initially the spark that was there that ignited the subliminal juices was not one born of anger or hostility toward women or anything of that particular nature.

It somehow evolved basically along… was stimulated, you know, by cultural kinds of mechanisms, but a point was reached where this entity – this condition, as it were – began to try to justify itself, to create rationalizations for what it was doing, perhaps to satisfy the rational, normal part of the individual. One element that came into play there was anger, hostility – what have you. It would be hard to describe it, but I don't think that… it was not an overriding emotion or feeling that was present when he would go looking or hunting, or however you would describe it.

Let's say it was more of a (long pause)… on most occasions it was a high degree of anticipation, of excitement, of arousal. It was like an *adventuristic* kind of thing. Perhaps people who go out deer hunting or fly fishing have the same feeling when they get up in the morning, you know? But it was that kind of thing – if you're following.

SM: Uh huh.

TB: However, with increasing regularity, what was once just a high state of arousal, of anticipation, became an almost frenzied desire to be, uh… to receive the kind of gratification that was being sought. And it was just an escalation of the desire to fulfill.

SM: Was this vengefulness... because the most important prerequisite was...

TB: We're talking about images... and it's a terrible thing to say. Sure we're talking about images. We're talking about anonymous, abstracted, living and breathing people... but the person, uh, they were not known. They were just, uh, uh, symbols. To a point they were symbols, uh, but once a certain point in the encounter had been crossed, they ceased being individuals and became, well, uh (sighs), you could say *problems* – that's not the word either.

Threats. Now, once a certain point in the encounter was passed, they ceased to have any symbolic value at all. And they ceased also to have... at that point, once they'd, once they became flesh and blood and once they ceased being an image or a dehumanized symbol, uh, that's when the rational self – the normal self – would surface and, and, react with fear and horror, and so on. But, recognizing the state of affairs, would sort of conspire with this other part of himself to conceal the act.

The survival took precedence over the remorse... with increasing effectiveness. When, in fact, it would almost seem this individual, recognizing the emotional trauma... the guilt and remorse he had... on it *and* on the normal individual, began to condition mentally, condition out guilt; using a variety of mechanisms. Saying it was justifiable, it was, uh, acceptable, it was necessary, and on and on.

SM: Necessary?

TB: Attempt... using really false mechanisms to condition out guilt.

SM: Would the violence generally be very quick or prolonged?

TB: He received no pleasure from harming or causing pain to the person he attacked. He received absolutely no gratification from causing pain and did everything possible, within reason – considering the unreasonableness of the situation – not to torture these individuals, at least physically.

The fantasy that accompanies and generates... the anticipation that precedes the crime is always more stimulating than the immediate aftermath of the crime itself.

April 2

TB: I'll bet you'll never forget these conversations.

SM: No, I won't. I was thinking about this model, this creation. But there are things I do not understand, right? Your opinion is that violence is a subtheme, or sub-subtheme, of what you call "depersonalization." And I don't understand possession.

TB: Uh huh.

SM: We also said that in this instance the victims would be images and symbols. But images of *what?*

TB: Of *women!* I mean, of the idealized woman. What else can I say?

SM: A stereotype?

TB: No, they wouldn't be stereotypes, necessarily. But they would be the reasonable facsimile to women – as a class. A class not of women per se but a class that has almost been created through the mythology of women and how they are used as objects. Of course, that's just one explanation.

SM: Would there be a standard of beauty or attractiveness?

TB: Well, I suppose, standards. Everyone has his standards.

SM: From the outline we're working with, there seems to be... there are semispontaneous effects and a number of events that were planned or organized and went under the... I'm trying to get some idea about the stimulus and response, or if there's a feeling that puts this person out in the community, uh, when an object-symbol is there, and there... then the process begins.
Would it be possible that a distinctly unattractive or homely woman would be walking the street and this person would come upon her? Would it matter to him that she was not physically attractive?

TB: Oh, I'd say it gives the model, it's an absolutely indispensable criteria (sic).

SM: Okay, can you elaborate on that?

TB: Well, I think that if you – for the purposes of our analysis, and for no really understandable reason except for practicality, this person's interests – looking for victims – were initially focused on his peers. The person's criteria would be based upon those standards of attractiveness accepted by his peer group. Of course, the styles have changed and because, overall, styles and therefore standards of beauty change, but... not dramatically, so.

SM: What role, in this instance being attractive, would the victims play? I'm talking about *before* they were accosted. Did you notice them seeming vulnerable? Was there anything about the way they moved, acted – or anything like that – that made them more likely to be victims?

TB: I don't know. I think that anyone who has studied the problem or the phenomena (sic) of people who appear to have a propensity for becoming victims would have trouble coming up with the exact "why." Outside of the fact they've made themselves available in some, perhaps, unconscious way. What we're talking about here is just opportunity, as opposed to more discreet factors that would be exhibited by the person.

SM: What, also, is your opinion that violence is not a "goal," that in itself is not a "game," and that, if I understood you correctly, is actually more of a tool to achieve a separate goal? That of physical possession. Why is it that in certain circumstances... why wouldn't there be a simple knock on the head? Why do certain circumstances require more elaborate violence than others?

TB: Well, it's not an easy question, but I think that this kind of person would be in this state of mind at this particular time, but he would not remain in that same stage in five or six years.

So you're asking… you're assuming that the personality is stagnant and doesn't change. The way we've been approaching it, we've been discussing it in chronological fashion – the state of mind or the state of development of this condition.

And it does *not* remain stagnant. So you ask me, if this person is capable of this or that at a given time, why the mode of operation changes several years later. Because, well, people change. Let's look at it another way. Any person's circumstances change, and changes result in study or changes come from experience – or just because time has elapsed. For no particular reason.

I think that we've established that this kind of individual – as a consequence of just indulging himself in the literature of the day – would have accumulated a great deal of information about crime and its detection. Take, as examples, notorious defendants like Albert DeSalvo or the Hillside Strangler individual. And you can see, based on what you can read about the investigations of those crimes, you can see that hysteria and public tension was drawn to this series of crimes because they were so unique and sensational.

And they occurred in a relatively short period of time. And, of course, in every instance, shortly after the alleged commission of the murders, another thing happened that insured such public hysteria and consequent police activity: the discovery of bodies.

Without a body, a crime is sometimes cleared through speculation, but the public's horror is not fixed on it. And so it'd be easy for this person to study that kind of reaction, public or bureaucratic, police reaction. And to make certain alterations in his modus operandi. This would tend to decentralize attention and to avoid the cooperation of several investigative agencies.

To provide varying M.O.s and spread them around, as it were, so as not to arouse the same type of unified reaction.

But another terribly critical factor is this: We look through this person's eyes and study the situation, and it may be that he felt that one of the things that seemed to arouse – one of the principal things in arousing the public and the police – was the discovering of the body. And if you *had* no body, then essentially you didn't… you're eliminating a moving force behind the police investigation.

And you're reducing publicity, you're slowing suspicion, limiting the possibility of witnesses coming forward – and keeping somewhat in control of the situation, as it were.

April 4

Bundy was extremely hesitant to discuss specific cases. Finally, I nudged him into a description of Lynda Healy's abduction on January 31, 1974. The twenty-one-year-old coed and ski announcer for a Seattle radio station had vanished from her basement bedroom in the middle of the night. Over a year later, her battered skull was found with those of three other victims at Taylor Mountain east of Seattle, one of Bundy's northwest dump sites.

TB: He had seen the house before and for one reason or another had been attracted to its occupants. Then one evening, just being in the mood, so to speak, he checked out the house (and) found out the front door was open. He thought about it. What kind of opportunity that offered. And returned to the house later and entered the house and explored it.

SM: While everybody was asleep?

TB: Yeah.

SM: Was this some days later?

TB: No, that same evening.

SM: I see.

TB: Then he went around the house and found a particular bedroom door that he opened – really hit and miss. Not knowing who or what, not looking for any particular individual. And that would be the opportunity. This was late at night. And presumably everyone would be asleep.

SM: Would he have some sort of knife or club so there would be no noise?

TB: I don't really know. If he struck the woman she would have probably left a large amount of blood. Or if she was shot there would have been a quantity of blood; if she was stabbed there would also be blood. So it pretty well eliminates the alternatives.

SM: There was, I believe, a small quantity of blood found on the sheets.

TB: I suppose you would have to go into the physiology of strangulation to determine what kind of hemorrhaging was going on.

SM: How would this person have proceeded from there?

TB: Well, you can put yourself in that position. You have the young lady in the middle of the night. And we know that at some later time the remains were found somewhere in the Cascades. So obviously she was transported up there.

SM: I guess you would have to dress her yourself?

TB: In that kind of situation a person who was alert enough to be able to dress would not be afraid in terms of struggling or crying out. So it would be unlikely that any attempt was made to clothe the girl.

SM: Then she was unconscious?

TB: Well, walking out under her own power at that hour of the morning would not necessarily be the soundest kind of approach.

SM: Would she have regained consciousness by the time they reached their destination?

TB: Well, that certainly is a possibility.

SM: A mighty curious feature in the bedroom was the fact that the bed had been made, but apparently not by Lynda herself, because of the type of fold that was put in the sheet.

TB: It was an attempt to cover up her disappearance.

SM: Would she be bound with rope or some kind of restraint?

TB: (That) would be the way it would be done.

SM: Would there be words exchanged?

TB: I doubt it. He would have gagged the person.

SM: Where would you guess they'd drive to? Where would be their destination?

TB: Some place that was quiet and private. His home or some secluded area.

SM: My assumption is that once the abduction had occurred, the person knew what else they were going to do.

TB: It would depend upon the condition of the girl. It would depend on the traffic. It would depend on a number of things. It would depend on a person's state of mind. How calm or how excited or excitable he was under the circumstances.

SM: How calm do you think he would be?

TB: This was one of the first instances that he'd abducted a woman in this fashion. He was extremely nervous, almost frantic and in a panic, trying to attempt anything. There you are – what do you do with the situation?

SM: Having crossed that barrier with contemplation and action...

TB: Uh uh. That barrier had been crossed before. But now it had gone a step or two further.

If he was intoxicated just prior to when the crime began, then he would likely regain his senses when he knew that (he had) exposed himself to a great deal of danger.

SM: Would she be bound and gagged? Unconscious? Would he just throw her in the back seat of his car, or would she be seated next to him?

TB: He'd probably put her in the back seat of the car and cover her with *something*.

SM: Then what?

TB: Let's say that he decided to drive to a remote location that he just picked out. Once he had arrived at this point where he didn't have a fear of alarming anyone in the neighborhood with shouts or screams or whatever, (he'd) untie the woman.

SM: And what then?

TB: He would have the girl undress and then, with that part of himself gratified, he found himself in a position where he realized that he couldn't let the girl go. And at that point he would kill her and leave her body where he'd taken her.

SM: Would he just stab her or whack her on the head or something swift or…

TB: We've established the infliction of violence was not something that this individual craved. It would be quick.

SM: Would there be any conversation between the two of them?

TB: There'd be some.
Since this girl in front of him represented not a person, but again the image, or something desirable, the last thing we would expect him to want to do would be to personalize this person.

SM: Would (he) have her undress? Would there be a sexual assault that would precede the actual (killing)?

TB: The sexual gratification probably preceded the point where the final decision was made to kill the individual.

SM: I see. In this instance, there was no confrontation within the assailant, or confrontation of the fact the victim had to be dispatched, until fairly late?

TB: A certain amount of the need of that malignant condition had been satisfied through the sexual release. That driving force would recede somewhat, allowing the normal individual's mental mechanisms to again begin to take hold. To control the situation, or more so than previously. You'd expect a certain amount of debate, or regret, as it were, that it was faced with a situation...

SM: Would there be a period of internal debate? Or would this happen fairly instantaneously?

TB: It would vary depending on the strength of the normal self in its responses. For instance, just how the sexual needs have been gratified. It could last a matter of hours. It could last just a few minutes.

SM: What would you (say) in this matter?

TB: It's impossible to say. Assuming, however, that he drove directly up into the wilds, and assuming a fairly continuous progression of events, it probably would have been a little more than a few hours.

SM: There must have been a lot of care taken to make sure that no items of clothing or anything else were.

TB: Well, you can expect a combination of things. Whatever her name is, Healy?
(There'd be) a considerable degree of remorse over the killing, and also a high degree of concern over detection, capture, whatever. But furthermore, we'd expect a great almost panic because of the novel nature of the situation. The panic, initially at least, would interfere with the ability to be meticulous about it – i.e., the cleaning up, and so on.

SM: I was interested that the body wasn't buried.

TB: Well, of course, if you understand the individual in a state of panic in the middle of the night. More likely than not, attempts to dispose of the body itself would have not been terribly innovative.

SM: What happened inside his mind as he left?

TB: A nominally normal individual who has become somewhat subordinate to bizarre desires and abducts a woman and kills her finds himself in a great deal of panic. And all he wants to do is put distance between himself and the result of his activities. Having done that (there would be) a fair degree of relief, so to speak. At least relative to the high state of anxiety that he was in when he was actually in possession of the body.

SM: There is, as you say, relief.

TB: No, I mean relatively speaking. In the days and weeks following (a) killing of this kind, there would be that undercurrent of anxiety that comes with wondering just what was seen, what was found, what was or was not missed.

SM: What about reflecting upon the incident itself?

TB: Initially, the person probably (was) totally preoccupied with whether or not any link would be established. Or what if any significant evidence the police had. So it would not be an occasion to reflect on consequences apart from practical consequences.

It's not a time to reflect, but a time to look. It would be a time for observing, and then there'd be that period of time when the normal self would be exerting its control and convincing itself that it now could be in total control and this wouldn't happen again. That would be the period of remission. At that point, I suppose, there would be some reflection about the satisfactory nature of the crime.

SM: You speculate that he could find the actual event unsatisfying?

TB: We'd expect that. Yeah. And this would be especially true – even more so – in the hours or days subsequent to the commission of the crime.

SM: So there would be an unsatisfied urge together with a dominant personality that is screaming for care and caution. There must have been tremendous tension.

TB: The organism always seeks to do things that relieve tension in one form or another. Defense mechanisms. They say any number of psychological disorders are the result of the attempts to diminish anxiety or tension or stress. Escape.

SM: Would he be able to deal with the tension?

TB: Well, the tension was concentrated principally upon the progress of the police investigation. (If) nothing of any significance was disclosed in the newspapers, then that would be one way a great amount of the tension would be reduced.

As far as remorse over the act, that would last for a period of time. But it could all be justified. The person would attempt to justify it by saying, "Well, listen you, you fucked up this time, but you're never going to do it again. So let's just stay together, and it won't ever happen again." Why sacrifice this person's whole life?

And so, the focus then became on surviving and modifying behavior. A sort of optimist. Sort of finding the silver lining, you might call it. Or in some way justifying what had taken place.

But this did not last for very long. A matter of weeks. We go first into a state of semidormancy, and then it would sort of regenerate itself, in one form or another.

SM: How would it reintrude into the mind?

TB: It's a regrowth, a reassertiveness (that) would be gradual in nature. Almost as if it was a reservoir for all tension or dissatisfaction. It would seem to grow and in that fashion sort of nurture itself on certain negative-type things.

But no one thing. It was no one thing you could say that would trigger him off, or anything like that.

I don't think we've covered the question about contemplation or introspection. I think we'd expect a person not to feel much remorse or regret for the actual crime – or guilt in the conventional sense for the harm done to another individual. Because the propriety or impropriety of that kind of act could not be questioned. If it was, then, of course, there would be all sorts of internal turmoil.

This one side of the personality, I believe, either intentionally or unintentionally, would condition out that kind of guilt or remorse. The guilt and remorse were most prevalent, if they were prevalent at any time, during that period when the individual was uncertain about the results of the police investigation. Once (it) became clear that there was going to be no link made or that he would not become under suspicion, the only thing which appeared to be relevant was not exposing himself to that kind of risk of harm again.

Not thinking about the nature of the act, of the death of the individual herself. The approach is, say, "Don't ever do it again." But as time passes, the emphasis is on "Don't get caught."

SM: Are there any effects on the work-a-day, everyday existence?

TB: Not ones which are detectable. Perhaps a great degree of irritability, or perhaps people would describe the person as being preoccupied with something, or not fully concentrating on the here and now.

SM: No difference other than what you would expect of anybody who had something on their mind?

TB: Yeah. No more than that. No more significant than mood changes in anyone who might be preoccupied with a job situation, or schoolwork, or whatever.

SM: When does he begin to analyze the mistakes, or the more dangerous aspects of the episode?

TB: You have that period where he swore to himself that he'd never do it again. That was the end of it. That he felt he had it under control. It was the deceptive fashion, you might say, in which that psychopathology withdrew into this dormant stage that (led) the individual (to the) erroneous belief that he got it out of himself. And this wasn't going to happen again.

As a consequence of that new attitude, the individual would throw himself into normal activities with more vigor. Just try to get a second wind. I don't know how to describe it. But he would try to indulge himself in normal activities. Almost as if he was welcoming himself back to a life-style, a state of mind, that was without the fear, the terror, and the harm.

But slowly, the pressures, tensions, dissatisfactions which, in the very early stages, fueled this thing, had an effect. (Yet) it was more self-sustaining and didn't need as much tension or as much disharmony externally as it had before. It sort of reached a point where this condition would generate its own needs, wouldn't need that reservoir of tension (or) stress that it seemed to thrive on before. Gradually, as I say, it would reemerge.

This individual would say, "Well, just one trip to the bookstore. Just once around the neighborhood." It did this kind of thing.

And then, gradually, it would become more active, more demanding, as it were.

SM: There would be a recapitulation of the whole history.

TB: Hmmm-mmm.

The individual would reflect on the quality of the act, to a degree, but not a great deal of reflection as a means of preserving it for the sake of gratification. Because it wasn't a totally satisfying experience, you know. Once the condition began to reassert its force, it didn't look back. It looked forward. Didn't want to dwell on the preceding event, but began to plan, anticipate, contemplate the next.

Of course, things would be learned. Experience teaches in overt and subtle ways. And over a period of time, there would be less panic, there would be less confusion, there would be less fear and apprehension. There would be a faster regeneration period.

SM: More self-confidence?

TB: Well, yeah. I suppose we'd expect more self-confidence, surely.

April 14

Roberta (Kathy) Parks, twenty-two, had been abducted from the campus of Oregon State University on May 6, 1974. Her skull was later discovered on Taylor Mountain.

As he discussed her, it was clear that Bundy had come to the prison interview room stoned.

SM: Why Oregon State? Why did he go to Corvallis?

TB: It would be an attempt to commit a crime without it being linked to other crimes. And there… again… increasing the intensity of the investigation as well as generating additional publicity.

SM: Is there a way to distinguish the personality? The characteristics of the personality at that time?

TB: Parks disappeared in May and (Brenda) Ball disappeared on June 1 – which is just a little less than a month (later). Georgeann Hawkins disappeared on the night of June 11, which is just a few days after the Ball disappearance. So we can see by the short period of time that elapsed between the disappearance of Parks and the disappearance of Ball (that there would) not be a great deal of change in the state of mind of the individual.

The M.O. is somewhat more sophisticated than the one employed in the Healy case. He may have approached her and asked her if she'd like to go to Taylor Mountain (laughs). How about that (laughs again)! Just a friendly little get-together up there!

SM: Would she be walking across campus? Or she'd be sitting in a bar, maybe?

TB: She could have been sitting in a library studying. She could have been sitting in a cafeteria studying. She was supposed to be depressed or lonely or something.

She might seek out company just to take her mind off her problem or loneliness – depression. Let's say she was having a snack in the cafeteria and (he) just sat down next to her and began talking, representing himself to be a student there, and suggested they go out somewhere to get a bite to eat or to get a drink. Either he was convincing enough or she was depressed enough to accept his invitation.

Of course, once she got in the car, then he had her in a position where he wanted her – and could then assume control over her.

A jog down to a local tavern in Corvallis would probably be the farthest we would expect her to accept as a plausible kind of trip.

SM: Would he be patient enough to go to the tavern?

TB: It's unlikely. He wouldn't want to be exposed to a situation where he would be seen in her presence. Certainly no more than necessary.

SM: He's still in a stage where alcohol is involved. If he had been drinking, wouldn't it be evident to her?

TB: It's odd that some people are more able to detect the effect of alcohol on people than others. Someone who meets a stranger who's under the influence of alcohol... outside of the fact that it might be on his breath... subtle changes in his behavior wouldn't be that evident. We're not talking about some stumbling drunk.

SM: What would transpire once they're in the car?

TB: He would not want to confront her in the car and in an area where a struggle could be witnessed by anyone just casually strolling down the street or something. So, once he had gained her confidence, then... on the way to this tavern they were going to go to, he said that he had just remembered that he had to pick up the finished copy of his thesis or something from the typist – and then drive out to a remote location.

At that point, he would accost her without any fear of attracting any attention.

SM: I'm interested in the mechanics of accosting somebody in a car.

TB: Oh, oh, you are (laughs)? Maybe you want to do it yourself, you know! I don't know about you.

SM: It could be. You told me I had it.

TB: Yeah. You have it in you. I mean, I think it's there. Just needs a little, uh, a little development (laughs).

SM: What I'm saying is, What is the most effective way? Pull a gun?

TB: Wouldn't need a gun, necessarily. This guy pulls up in a cornfield somewhere, you know, fairly abruptly.

And this girl – let's say that as he travels further and further away from a populated area, she probably is becoming uncomfortable. But she still wants to believe in the face validity of the situation her would-be abductor had created for her (clears throat). And, of course, by the time he pulled up and stopped, there would be virtually nothing she could do about it.

In that instance, virtually all that would be necessary would be for the person to get out of the car, ask her to get out of the car – and if a struggle had ensued, he would easily overpower her. And, recognizing the disadvantage of the situation, she would submit to whatever instructions he gave her. Out of fear, and out of whatever.

SM: You say, whatever instructions.

TB: At that point, he would have to tell her something. To be quiet, to do what he told her to do, et cetera.

SM: Would he typically want the victim to remove her own garments? Or would he prefer to do it himself?

TB: I don't know, uh, uh… Let's say that as a result of his voyeuristic activities where he had frequently watched women undress… let's say he had a preference to watch the victims undress.

SM: And then what?

TB: There would be a sexual assault and then... Let's analyze it a bit. With this kind of psychopathological condition, following a sexual assault of the kind that occurred in the case of Parks, there would be an immediate onslaught of self-recrimination, fear and apprehension over being detected – and almost a perplexity as to what to do.

At this point (he) would begin to almost debate with himself the desirability of killing the victim.

If this person's only goal at the point following the sexual encounter was to dispose of the person, then he wouldn't have gone to all the trouble of transporting the body back to Washington. For several reasons. Foremost, it would increase the chances of some kind of fluke detection – a car accident or something.

This burial site, or whatever you want to call it, where all these other girls were found. The discovery of the Parks body there would heighten speculation that the same person or persons had committed *all* the crimes.

Had he killed Parks in Oregon, he would have left her body in Oregon. He wouldn't have undergone the extreme measure of transporting a corpse several hundred miles! I mean, we're not talking about cross-town, or from one small town to another within a small geographic area.

She was taken to Washington while she was still alive. That's the most reasonable explanation.

SM: I wonder if the reason for her being transported alive to Washington derives from indecision as to what her ultimate fate should be.

TB: We're not looking at the reasons. The question you asked was, "Was she alive or was she dead when she was taken from Oregon to Washington?" The reasons why this girl would have been transported that amount of distance while she was still alive is another question entirely.

And, you're right. It certainly could have been a result of that indecision or conflict within the individual. Between that part of him that thought it was necessary to kill his victims, versus the part of him that did not – that found it to be extremely reprehensible, disgusting.

The humane, moral, and legal approach to the alternative of killing would be not to kill her at all. Even in comparison to murder, the act of rape is somewhat less severe.

We're not talking about rational and normal thought processes. A combination of desire to continue that possession, in addition to the indecision about murdering her, would result in the rather extraordinary act of transporting her that great amount of distance. You know, I mean… we've, we've arrived at these conclusions, uh, observations, based on all kinds of things – fact and parafact.

And it would seem, also, that the act of murder, as a… as a means of covering up a crime again, is, uh (pause), an extraordinary act. Extraordinary, uh, fashion of covering up.

SM: Would he ever think of an alternative to snuffing out their lives like that?

TB: What he thought about alternatives? The only alternative to not doing away with a person, it would seem to me, would be to release her. To let her go free. That seems the only alternative. And not a very fancy one for him, you'll have to agree, uh, under the circumstances.

SM: I asked a question earlier that I'd like to explore further. You said we had to posit that this individual's thinking processes were not exactly as logical at this time as when not confronted with an encounter, and that there raged this battle, this inner turmoil, about what to do with her. Could it have been, at least in part, that he wanted to keep her with him – sort of continue that possession back home for a while?

TB: That's, that's a possibility also. Or a combination. There was this time… you know, nobody is so simplistic all the time that they only do things out of, uh, a need to satisfy one particular desire or otherwise reward a particular motivation.

SM: Hmmm.

TB: Or to bring to fruition a particular motivation. Often times with anyone we see a number of different things acting upon that person at once. And perhaps on this occasion, we can figure it to be a combination of desire to continue that possession, *in addition to*, uh, the indecision about murdering her. That combination would result in the rather extraordinary (pause) act of carrying her so many miles.

SM: Would you take the precaution of rendering her unconscious?

TB: There certainly wouldn't necessarily be the need for it. We still have to remember that the individual – at least not on a conscious level – has no desire or implements no design with the goal of terrorizing or torturing the person. And he ordinarily would not want to inflict any unnecessary violence or pain to the girl. So it wasn't necessary to render her unconscious. He would have had only to tie her up.

SM: What would you say would go through his mind on the drive to Seattle? He must have been in a state of agitation, knowing what kind of cargo he had in there. A cop could have pulled him over for most any reason, you know.

TB: I don't know what you mean by "cargo." He didn't have any cargo in there. He had a body!

SM: Body, okay.

TB: You've been listening to too many (earlier police interrogation) tapes.

SM: Uh oh!

TB: Yeah, yeah, see. That was unconscious.

SM: I sometimes get this hypothetical person mixed up with myself... and others I have known. Sorry about that.

TB: Well, I've been known to carry cargo in my car. Such as lawn mowers, books, bookshelves, stereos, and the like.

SM: Plants.

TB: Plants, yes.

SM: Ted's Moving and Storage.

TB: Yeah. Well, back to your convoluted question. Cargo! Indeed! Okay... you've got this young woman who's been sexually assaulted tied up in the back of this person's car. If he's going to make a five-hour drive back to the Seattle area, he's going to be nervous. Very nervous. He's going to be thinking about what he's going to do.

SM: How long would it take him to resolve that?

TB: In a way, he'd probably view the driving time as a luxury – giving him time to think, as opposed to a constant state of agitation and anxiety. And (he) would not really make the final decision until he was back in the Seattle area. When he was really *forced* to, you know, I mean, really *forced* with facing the fact – "Well, what are you going to do? You're here now. What are you going to do?"

SM: Would there be a second assault on her before she was killed?

TB: Well, given the amount of time they would have had to have been together, it's likely.

SM: Would he need to start drinking again?

TB: Uh, he may, he could. But the barrier had been bridged, as it were – and the girl was in his possession. And it was something he had to deal with, drunk or sober.

We have to realize that he also had his normal obligations to school, to family and friends, and work and what not. If he had to be at work the next day, he could hardly leave the girl in his house the whole day, without concern that something might happen where she would be discovered. So, depending on what his schedule was, we could expect for him to either take her home or to take her directly to where he planned to dump the body.

SM: Where would she actually be killed?

TB: It would depend on whether he took her home or, uh… If he had taken her home that night, she would have been killed there, in the apartment. If he took her, uh, decided to take her right to the mountain… whatchacallit? – Taylor Mountain? Then, uh (swallows), she would have been killed there.

SM: Was he organized enough to have more than one residence, more than one safe-house, as it were?

TB: Probably. Uh huh.

SM: And, I assume, he would have known of other residences that might have been vacant for certain periods of time. So when you say "take her home," it could be actually to his home or another place that he deemed safe.

TB: A dwelling, yeah. He could have taken her home… or somewhere else just as secure.

SM: What are the times we're talking about here?

TB: It doesn't say here (looking at clippings), uh, what time she was last seen.

SM: Well, what I mean is, was it real late?

TB: I don't know what *real late* is. But was she last seen at seven o'clock? Eight? Nine? Later? Even if, let's say, it was early in the evening – say as early as six p.m., or so – you figure five hours. A five-hour drive back to Seattle would make it late, eleven o'clock or thereafter. Assuming no in-between time. Of course, you have to figure the time, that the original assault took place – the time that required.

So the time the guy took in getting back to Seattle it must have been after midnight.

SM: What more do you think can be said about the time from the arrival in King County to her arrival on Taylor Mountain?

TB: At the Taylor Mountain crime scene?

SM: Uh huh.

TB: …whatever it is. With reference to, uh, what's her name (giggles)?

SM: I think it's Parks.

TB: Parks. Terrible with names… *and* faces. Can't remember faces. You asked me something about going to Taylor Mountain?

SM: I asked you what happened from their arrival in King County (Seattle) until when she ended up on Taylor Mountain.

TB: You asked me to speculate.

SM: Didn't I say "speculate"? All right, I asked you to speculate.

TB: (laughs) I've gone through this for hours with other people. Pardon me, but I'll be very meticulous about the wording here. You asked me to describe what happened. I can't tell you what happened. All I can do is just assist you with my educated guesses.

SM: I'm so silly.

TB: Well, you know, I'm not trying to put you down. That's not my intention. I'm just... I'm concerned about wording and I'm going to correct the record for that purpose.

SM: All right. About Taylor Mountain. You *did* speculate there probably would be another sexual assault before or at the same time she was killed.

TB: It's a distinct possibility, since they were obviously together for an extended period of time. One would expect that the person became sexually aroused for a second time.

SM: I'd also guess that if he went through all that trouble, why not.

TB: Give it another lick (laughs)?

SM: Yes.

TB: You're really gross, Michaud (laughs).

SM: I keep wondering if they're going to let me out of here.

TB: This will probably be one of the most memorable periods of your life.

SM: Well, whatever.

TB: But I'm wallowing here (laughs). Poor Miss, uh... what's her name? Parks. I hope no one ever listens to this. They might think I was approaching a serious situation in a frivolous mood. That's not entirely true.

It was established quite early in that case that her body had been ravaged by wildlife... you know, coyotes, foxes, field mice, birds. A whole variety of wild animals, both big and small, feed on carcasses.

This might give us one clue as to why this person returned to that site on at least several occasions. Perhaps it was discovered that when a body was left there, and later when the individual would return to check out the situation, (he) would find that it was no longer there! And concluded that the animals in the area were doing, you know, his work for him, as it were.

And (he) would continue to go back there simply because he had his own garbage disposal. A whole bunch of little beasties who would, in effect, destroy every last shred of the victim.

SM: Hmmm.

TB: We can also see a considerable amount of the destruction of the bodies in the case of the Lake Sammamish victims. And that has been attributed, as I understand, to animal destruction. There's no reason we can't use the same explanation for the condition of the remains at the other site.

With that in mind, we can say that Parks was taken directly to the vicinity where the other bodies were found – and at that point he killed Parks. Either in the car… or marched her off the road and killed her in a more secluded location.

Damn, I need something to get fired up. I'm going to bring some dope down here some time… and we'll just smoke it.

SM: I figured you'd like the white powder better.

TB: What? Coke?

SM: Yeah. What does it do to you, TRB? Make you silly?

TB: Cocaine? I've never used it.

SM: Then why are you shaking your head?

TB: I was just thinking… uh, when you mentioned white powder, I thought you were talking about those tranquilizers I used to get in Orlando – *alleged* tranquilizers I used to get in Orlando. And it… it was white powder.

SM: Oh.

TB: I've never tried cocaine. I think I might have tried it once and got nothing out of it. Just snorted a little bit. And I just don't mess with it. It's too expensive. And I suppose if I was on the streets and had enough of it, I might get into it. But I'm strictly a marijuana man. All I do is… I *love* to smoke reefer. And I haven't, uh, never have tried anything but reefer. And valiums. And, of course, alcohol.

SM: Would the murders be essentially the same – knives, heavy instruments, strangulation?

TB: The means of dispatching someone? It would never require any instrumentality. A gun, for example, would not only make a lot of noise but would leave ballistic evidence.

SM: You said that this person would try to avoid, or minimize, the actual pain to the victim.

TB: Hmmm.

SM: You have no comment?

TB: I think we've just about covered it for today. Gimme a cigarette.

April 15

Bundy would not confront the extreme violence he practiced against his victims. He had obviously sanitized his descriptions of the murders of Lynda Healy and Kathy Parks, as he would for twenty-two-year-old Brenda Ball, who was last seen leaving a Seattle-area beer joint in the early hours of June 1, 1974. Ball may have been strangled, as Ted indicated, but her skull was also brutally fractured.

SM: What about the girl from the Flame Tavern? Brenda Ball?

TB: He was interested in varying his M.O. in such a way as not to continue to fan the flames of community outrage, or the intensity of the police investigation. This is why this Ball girl found herself to be the next victim.

SM: What would be a reasonable reconstruction of that night?

TB: Of course, I don't know, but we could say that he picked her up hitchhiking and they got to talking and she had nothing to do. He would ask her if she wanted to go to a party at his place and take her home. At this point, he would exert an influence on her which would be especially effective if she was under the influence of alcohol.

SM: He'd take her home?

TB: Sure.

SM: It would seem terribly risky.

TB: If you live with someone. But he had his own house.

SM: I see. What is going on in his mind on the way to his house?

TB: Conversation. To remove himself from the personal aspects of the encounter, the interchange. Chatting and flattering and entertaining, as if seen through a motion-picture screen. He would be engaging in the pattern just for the purpose of making the whole encounter seem legitimate.

SM: Uh huh.

TB: And to keep her at ease.

He didn't want this girl to get second thoughts about going with him to his place. And also, he was afraid that if he started thinking about what he was going to do, he'd either become more nervous or lose his concentration or in some way betray himself.

SM: So there's a very delicate balance between being cool and the excitement?

TB: Well, it's a critical balance, not a delicate balance. It became almost like acting a role. It wasn't difficult. The more an actor acts in a role, the better he becomes at it, the more he is apt to feel comfortable in it, to be able to do things spontaneously. And get better, as it were, in his role.

SM: So they go to his place?

TB: He'd have to explain why there isn't all the activity going on. It was probably not the first time she'd run into that kind of situation. Maybe it was. But in any event she was somewhat wary of the situation and yet bored enough, or intoxicated enough – or both – to just not really consider it threatening to her. They'd drink until she was exceptionally intoxicated. A dramatic departure from the Healy situation. In part, it is because of design. But in part it is just because of circumstances.

SM: The longer the conversation would go on, the more likely she would emerge as a person?

TB: Well, drinking has an effect on both parties. On the one hand, the more intoxicated he became, the more he repressed his normal codes of behavior. And the more she drank, the more she would lend herself to stereotypes.

SM: How would he proceed?

TB: The initial sexual encounter would be more or less a voluntary one. But one which did not wholly gratify the full spectrum of desires that he had intended. And so, after the first sexual encounter, gradually his sexual desire builds back up and joins, as it were, these other unfulfilled desires – this other need to totally possess her, after she's passed out, as she lay there in a state somewhere between coma and sleep, he strangled her to death.

SM: Seems to me there'd be some kind of logistical problem of getting her out of there.

TB: There wouldn't be an urgency, since she was in a place that was private. Ultimately, he'd have to bundle her up in some fashion and take her out to his car, when it's late some night, and drive her up to the mountains.

SM: What would he do with her until then?

TB: Just leave her in the bed, put her in the closet, you know. I mean, no one's coming in.

April 22

SM: Tell me how I should describe the feelings of "this person" during the approach... the interview, when a soon-to-be victim is located. Is he cool and detached, analytical... or is he frantic?

TB: You could expect a great deal of anticipation, mixed with a lot of tension... before... in the period preceding the abduction or whatever you called it.

SM: Is it hours before? Or...

TB: Well, whenever the individual commands himself to one degree or another. To actually attempting to carry out something. Hmmm.

SM: Then that length of time preceding the event would vary? In your guess, it could vary?

TB: Uh huh.

SM: About how much?

TB: Oh, I don't know. Once he'd made his contact – and it appeared he was going to be able to carry it through – he became very calm and analytical about the situation he was in. And then when... he's got a period of relaxation, which would likely continue until the time came for him to kill the victim – at which point he would become torn apart as to the correctness of his conduct.

But he'd still have the overriding need to dispose of the victim, and, of course, once it was done, he would usually go into a state of panic.

Suddenly it would seem as if his dominant, or formerly dominant... uh, predominant, normal self came back into control in a horrifying way. Or one that is presented with... conceived with panic and confusion. The enormity of what lay before him! Fear of being captured or discovered. And feelings of regret, remorse.

The hours fall and the individual is more likely promising himself he'll never do it again – and so on and so forth.

SM: You said earlier that the dominant or the more rational, the more normal part of this person, would actually be in a fit and would organize the killing – because at that point it was necessary for survival. That the other part would engineer the abduction, or whatever happened, but that when it was over, the rational self and the instinct of survival would take over. Do I understand that correctly?

TB: It was more or less a collaboration between the two, the malignant condition having more or less been satisfied for the moment... and receded in this activity to the point where he's almost, uh, in dullness... left the situation. Then the individual's normal, rational, moral, and law-abiding... uh... Well, a normal self would undertake these actions initially and the surface justification is, "Well, it's never going to happen again." And that way you can do it – but only if it never happens again.

But of course, gradually time would pass and the... whatever factors nurtured this psychopathological condition would start to build up again. To its capacity or need to act.

SM: Then it was almost cyclical.

TB: Yeah, in that fashion. You could say it was cyclical.

SM: So what happens next?

TB: I would envision a continuation of this kind of collaboration... between that one part of this person's self, which demands certain gratification, and the more dominant, law-abiding, more ethical, rational, normal self – which was sort of forced to become a party to that kind of conduct. Basically, you might say there was a shared division of responsibility.

This came as much from evolution as from conscious choice, because the ultimate goal... no, not the ultimate goal, but certainly an important consideration... for this malignant side of the person did not want to be captured, did not want to be detected. And...

SM: Would the other side?

TB: No, the other side wouldn't.

SM: Would this personality ever consciously, or even unconsciously, whatever, actually put itself in a circumstance where the idea is to be caught?

TB (adamantly): Well, not for the one we're talking about here!

SM: What's a...

TB: It's a popular theory, but... Over the years I've read a lot about how certain types of killers like to leave clues and have themselves caught. They enjoy the limelight. We do have an incidence of individuals like that, like "Son of Sam" because of the kind of news-media attention they generate. I think you'd be astonished at how many virtually anonymous people have been linked with more murders than "Son of Sam" or even John Gacy, which is not... He (Gacy) never got in a position where he could become publicized. They caught him, convicted him, and put him away with a minimum of flurry, as I recall. It wasn't like chasing a killer across several states, or, uh...

SM: You've talked at some length about how the abnormal "entity" took over – with increasing regularity, forming a sort of partnership with the more normal part of him, the part that had to deal with the day-to-day activities. And I guess the enthusiasm to be very active during this period was a way of protecting the other.

TB: "Concealing" is a better word. I don't want to overwork the simple analogies, but because a man becomes an excellent tennis player doesn't mean he cannot go out and do his business. Or become absorbed in tennis, parachuting, or whatever; it may be a terribly important part of himself. Using a slightly different analogy, homosexuals – at least in the past – concealed a certain part of their lives. They didn't bring that activity and those desires into the business place so that they could function.

Of course, straight people felt that homosexual school-teachers were standing in the classroom all day thinking about abusing the little boys in the room. It was, however, only a part of their lives. As we know, sex and even interpersonal relationships are just part of our lives.

Well, this particular activity is just a small, small portion of what was predominantly a normal existence, which *continued* to be a normal existence, not only at the will or whim of this antisocial pathological mental condition. It was just a *different* part – just as the homosexual would have a different part. Or the sailor would have a different part of his life he would not share. We don't share every part of our lives with everyone we run into.

SM: We are, then, talking about modes of existence, rather than two different minds?

TB: Yes. We are *not* talking about two different minds.

SM: We are talking about two different behavioral patterns?

TB: Yes.

SM: One of which is the predominantly public self?

TB: Yes, the public self – normal self, which is not necessarily latent but which would certainly have its latent phases.

SM: Would there be contempt because the public person bore a grudge or hatred for the other?

TB: You would expect that. But I doubt it. Seriously doubt it, in this case...

SM: Is that a measure of how integrated the mind would become?

TB: It is indicative of the state of coexistence. This person could still be very much in favor of law and order and the police... and be very much genuinely shocked by crime in the newspaper. And very much moved by people who suffered the death of loved ones. Complete, genuine responding in a normal fashion. Willing and able to help police. He would have a real feeling in those regards. Not out of desire to protect or hide. These were just normal responses.

It was almost as if he said it was wrong for all these things to happen. "It is wrong for me to jaywalk. It is wrong to rob a bank. It is wrong to break into other people's houses. It is wrong for me to drive without a driver's license. It is wrong not to pay your parking tickets. It is wrong not to vote in elections. It is wrong to intentionally embarrass people."

The uniqueness of the whole situation is how this condition pertained to such a narrow spectrum of activity. The inhibitions that would normally prevent a person from acting that way were specifically excised, removed, diminished, repressed... in such a way (as to) not affect all the other inhibitions – or to result in the deterioration of the entire personality. But only in that tiny, tiny slice!

SM: In other regards, then, he was socialized.

TB: Possibly. Oh hell, yes... let's face it.

SM: Did this person contemplate the future? Was there any sense that the string must run out at some point?

TB: (He) contemplated his future. I suppose it caused him to be more concerned with normal, everyday things. When this individual contemplated the future, it was in terms of acceptable, *normal* goals. He was not preoccupied or worried about his ultimate capture, *if* his number would come up – or that time would run out.

On the other hand, he would have a combination of fear of capture or of remorse for having exposed himself to that kind of situation. Yet that was not the kind of worry or concern that was pervasive. There was no thought given to the long-range consequences of this kind of behavior.

SM: Have you found any credence in the notion that there could have been two people that worked at virtually the same time in Seattle?

TB: Two different individuals? Oh, sure.

SM: What are your thoughts on that?

TB: I think there are probably a good dozen people in King County right now who are capable of the same thing. And are probably at one point or another engaged in conduct that will lead to that. It's a frightening notion. But it's as true and real as this trashcan.

There are any number of people capable of that. Somebody that was truly shrewd – with a little money – could probably escape detection indefinitely. It has always been my theory that for every person arrested and charged with multiple homicide, there are probably a good five more out there somewhere, following along a path – maybe not the *same* path, but a path that would eventually lead them to the same place.

We're seeing greater and greater opportunity for this kind of behavior to manifest itself – continuing right on down through the family, continuing right down to morals, increased cultural liberating… "do your own thing" kind of atmosphere. Greater mobility is a factor, too. Certainly, greater chaos on the social level. And economically. You see lots more kids on the run, on the move.

Women's liberation is another extraordinarily interesting thing, because women have a great deal more freedom to move here and there. They are no longer stuck in their homes. They are not watched over. It seems that it is happening in a geometric fashion. The more they expose themselves as victims to this potential behavior.

The more you erode traditional means of conditioning people to behave in certain ways, the more kinds of individuals are going to be exposed – who have this kind of weakness. They are going to be more successful more rapidly at it because they are going to have many more prospective victims.

The police are becoming less and less capable of detecting this kind of behavior, because you have this great body of young people on the move. You can listen to any television program talking about how we've got so many missing teenagers we don't know what to do. And that's going to increase all the time.

SM: Society won't tolerate that kind of mayhem.

TB: You'll tolerate it because you won't really know what's happening. You know, this fifteen-year-old girl disappeared. We assume she ran away. She had run away before. But what they don't know is that she's in a ditch somewhere. And they may *never* know it.

I read an article in the newspaper not long ago. A story about a well-dressed woman found dead in an orange grove – and there was no way to identify her. The (body) obviously wasn't all there. Just one of hundreds of missing people's bodies they cannot identify. This is just one, one particular factor that would interest a particular kind of individual. Not all of these individuals are going to be interested in hitchhikers and transients.

I think people should be aware of the extraordinary potential in this area. And it is only going to increase, notwithstanding a rather cataclysmic change in the way society functions. I suppose in an all-out war of some kind or even a strategic war would calm society down and tighten it up. Increase traditional forms of control or authority. Decrease anonymity, decrease mobility. Maybe something that would censor a lot of the licentious, sexually stimulating material on TV and the sexual literature shops.

I read this article recently, written by a woman. It's fictionalized, but millions of gullible women are reading this. It says, "My biggest thrill is to go out to a bar and pick up somebody I don't know and take them home with me – and get it on with them." And she goes on about Charlie and Johnny and Alfonso and his Mercedes-Benz – and what a trip it is. No entanglements. All you have to do is pick up somebody attractive and get it on.

That kind of message just isn't in the romantic novels anymore. Look at the TV shows that promote nontraditional, almost radical departures from the norm.

This Jim Jones thing. Now, we are supposed to recognize that Jim Jones was a fanatic, some sort of a nut. They portrayed him in the beginning as a normal, nice young kid who grew up wanting to be a preacher. And became a preacher. And then became more and more ambitious. Started taking drugs, got paranoid, and went to Guyana. Blah, blah, blah.

But sitting there, watching this horror unfold in the comfort of your living room, makes it much less horrible. It showed what had been my experience for the first rime, seeing a male kiss another male on the screen, followed by a simulated sexual encounter.

We are talking about breaking barriers... but it happens constantly. I can think of a half-dozen sitcoms where kids are being brought up by single parents – where the themes are broken homes or how to deal with broken homes. I am tired of ranting and raving, but what I'm saying is (that) as the culture declines, as people are cut loose and don't know what to do, they are floating around without the protection of the family, without protection of experience, tradition or anything. They become more vulnerable to people who want to exploit them.

April 23

SM: The evolution of this personality – all these cases seem to differ dramatically and substantively, and it seems there is not a linear evolution, as it were. At least, if there is, you haven't explained it. How has this person changed in time since the first "transaction"?

TB: Well, I think we'd expect that after the passing of a period of time, his psychological condition, as it were, or part of that individual's self – that which seemed to be the root cause of the behavior – would reach a state of maturity. I mean, it's growth would become somewhat diminished.

But even in adults, of course, we notice changes. In grown people we see a change in routine, so on and so forth. But, uh, and that would also be this condition – would also be less likely to – less unstable perhaps – less likely to shrink into a state of dormancy upon the commission of the crimes.

It would be relatively stable in the regard that it was inactive – but still, with respect to the amount of time this growth took place, the normal personality, the normal self, had a pretty good understanding of this condition. Learned, uh, how to tolerate it.

And perhaps, as a symptom of this matured state of development of the condition, uh, uh, we'd expect this individual wouldn't need to drink to overcome his inhibitions. That particular kind of behavior, if for no other reasons than the particular inhibitions that were aroused by the kind of conduct we're talking about, uh, didn't exist.

SM: So they had been wiped out.

TB: Yeah.

SM: How would that kind of development affect the, uh... the personality's approach to victims? Would it become more systematic?

TB: It wouldn't... uh, change materially. You couldn't expect it to.

SM: Well then, what would be the other effects... apart from the fact alcohol is no longer necessary as a trigger?

TB: Probably no other effects, except the ones I've described – like the decrease in recovery time. There wouldn't be *any* recovery time.

SM: Well, did it result in the compression of time between incidents, so that instead of maybe once every three months, it would be once a week, or...

TB: No, no.

SM: So it doesn't affect the spacing?

TB: As I described to you earlier – I think in relation to a slightly different topic – I can't, uh, remember exactly, but something about (pause). The timing factor would be entirely dependent on – *would not* be dependent on this individual's state of mind alone.

In the early stages of development, it was to a certain degree, you know, but as there was less and less time needed to absorb the trauma, the shock of the commission of the crime, uh, there were still other factors to contend with which regulated the time factor.

Such things as publicity, opportunity, and so forth. So, as I said before, you find a state of diminishing returns normally – where this person can only engage in that kind of behavior so frequently.

Not for psychological reasons but for reasons related to detection and the like.

SM: About this physical possession: Do you surmise that the victim would have to be alive, or conscious, or would the feeling of physical possession be met, if you will, or satisfied or whatever, if the victim was unconscious or dead?

TB: Well, it would be – in dealing with the kind of profile we've created (coughs) as I've stated before, nothing is clearcut and nothing is simple. I guess the parameters of the notion of possession were somewhat ill defined.

I think that initially this individual perceived just the bluff… where the victim would be under his control, as it were. And the killing of the victim, we would expect, would have seemed a rather extreme act – but one that the individual considered necessary to eliminate the possibility of his getting caught.

I think we see a point reached – slowly, perhaps – where the control, the possession aspect, came to include, uh, uh, within its demands, the necessity… for purposes of gratification – the killing of the victim.

Uh, then using – examining that kind of attitude – that perhaps it came to be seen that the *ultimate* possession was, in fact, the taking of the life. And then the purely, the physical possession of the remains.

SM: Uh huh, I see. How does the sexual component fit in with that? What I'm asking is, would the sexual assault – the sexual aspect of it – necessarily have to precede the killing? Or was there a development that way as well?

TB: I would say that, uh (coughs), that it wouldn't be significant. And that furthermore, the sexual act – in the larger scheme of things – was sort of obligatory conduct. Not in itself, you know, the sexual act was not the, the… the principal source of gratification. Being satisfied. There's no denying there's a sexual aspect to it, uh, but it was less – the sexual aspect was less than actual sexual conduct and more directed toward the sex of the individual and other attributes possessed by that individual's appearance… that we talked about.

SM: What I'm trying to understand is, if we have a victim who is an object, or a symbol or image, how is sex related to… Is sex confined to an act? Sex is usually between two people. Maybe "sex" is actually the wrong phrase for the sexual component here.

TB: I'll tell you. We were talking about sexual activity versus the larger universe of behaviors that are sexual in nature but are not intimate or directly related to sexual activity. Whether it's the way someone dresses or the way they carry themselves, or the body language or what have you – that convey sexual messages, uh, often in more subtle fashion… but nevertheless, you know, that's all I can say.

SM: It has to do with mastery and ownership, uh, possession.

TB: Well, you know, talking about ritual in its most general form, part of the ritual between men and women when it comes to close relationships or whatever is sex. Uh, sexual intercourse.

SM: You were talking about the sexual component and we've determined to call it "possession." Now, you said sex was almost obligatory.

TB: Well, it's ritualistic, almost. For a lot of people the fantasies about sex do not live up to their original expectations, okay? And most heterosexual persons – homosexuals, whatever – would probably agree that the most satisfying sex is that which is had with responsive, willing partners. That is also clear. So I think it would be fair to say that engaging in an act of sex with a person who is injured or frightened or whatever – or conscious or whatever – would not be satisfying sexual contact, okay?

SM: Right.

TB: So if we apply that to this individual, we can see that the act of sexual intercourse, as it were, or any kind of sex act committed upon the victim was again something almost... would be considered obligatory and not designed to elicit a great deal of mutual satisfaction.

Uh, with respect to the idea of possession, I think that with this kind of person, control and mastery is what we see here. A profile of an individual who has decided possession is somewhat truncated, not very sophisticated, not very elaborate.

In other words, I think we could read a book about the Marquis de Sade and other people, who take their victims in one form or another out of a desire to possess and would torture, humiliate, and terrorize them elaborately – something that would give them a more powerful impression they were in control.

But with this person, we don't see that kind of act. Again, it's a sort of a simplistic kind of desire.

SM: What about the evidence of mutilation, the suggestion of mutilation, in some of the cases? Use of foreign objects and that sort of thing?

TB: Well, I think that, assuming this personality was capable of, you know, committing a whole spectrum of crimes, you'd expect that he would – in the course of this behavior – experience aberrations. They're going to perform some sort of aberration, which may not be significant of anything – except just something spontaneous.

SM: Well, the key to that question is that if penetration, if you will, or sex as we've discussed it is obligatory, then anything, basically, that you can do...

TB: I suppose that if we searched the files of a large homicide bureau, we'd find a number of cases where that's the way guys got their kicks – by using foreign objects and things – but I think we have to say that more often than not in *this* kind of circumstance, that that kind of act would not be the desired one.

SM: Yeah. I don't think I can grasp well enough or try to describe or convey the *mood* of this person in the midst of, and immediately after, an incident. I mean, I can infer some things, uh, from physical evidence. I can infer from the model we've created, you know... but I can't *really* understand it well enough to tell.

TB: Well (sighs), I'll try to review it with you.

SM: I'll give you an example. There is the suggestion from physical evidence of extreme – certainly connected in the mind with extreme rage – absolute, towering rage. And yet you say that rage is not a component of this personality – that rage is not a word to be linked to describe this process.
So how can we...

TB: I don't know what you're referring to – what cases you're referring to.

SM: Well, the Chi Omega case suggests a towering anger of some sort. And some of the skulls found in Washington had big dents in them. From the medical reports, the forensic descriptions, all one can imagine is blind fury and all the words that come to you to suggest vengeance, anger, you know... that kind of vignette. You claim this person does not feel those things.

TB: Hmmm.

SM: Give me some descriptive insights here.

TB: I can only review what I was talking about yesterday and perhaps see if there's something we left out. We talked about the excitement, mixed with anticipation – the looking for the victim. We talked about the next stage, where a state of almost... like an actor in a role... approaching the victim... playing a role, absorbed in a role.

We talked about that period after the individual had gained control over the victim, which was, we could say, would probably be more often than not in a state of semiconfusion. And, uh, kind of eagerness to, even get it over with, uh (pause).

We talked about a perfunctory sexual act – and then, a state of panic, uh, or fear, over the necessity of carrying out the next phase – of killing the person.

We talked about the overwhelming panic, confusion, and regret that followed and the process of covering up – the shredding of that condition to a state of dormancy. And the period of – a kind of period when the person sort of recovered from what he'd done.

Not rage, as you described it... because I don't see it entering here. The act, for this person the act of – more often than not the killing of the victim – was done out of, sort of... On the one hand, that act would be, uh, accomplished because of his perceived need to reduce the probability of detection. Another factor was that this was a means to an end – that is, of accomplishing ultimate possession of the victim, so to speak.

More often than not the act was basically done because this person had already performed the sexual act with them and was inclined to feel remorse. He wished he was not in this position, was scared and was debating within himself the possibility that maybe this person could be released and that... and so on and so forth. It was kind of turmoil, as it were, until it was – again it was, you know, the decision was invariably made to kill the victim.

April 29

Bundy's boldest act before the Chi Omega killings was the July 14, 1974, double murder of Janice Ott and Denise Naslund, whom he lured away from Lake Sammamish, near Seattle.

TB: Well, again, assuming that we know what we're talking about here – that it's the same person we described in the Healy and Ball cases. Then he shows up at Lake Sammamish. So we would have to reflect back on what presently we know about this entity and compare it to what seemed to happen at the lake.

In that, uh, light, the Lake Sammamish cases don't *fit*, you know. Obviously don't fit the Healy or Ball M.O., for example. And it apparently happened in mid-afternoon, in broad daylight, with a large number of people in close proximity. Beyond that, however, there is not a lot known.

And, of course, the girls were killed. I guess that's known. Outside of that, very little.

It's clear that the Lake Sammamish incident was either the result of the venting of a great amount of tension or frustration that had accumulated over a long period of time.

Or it was an attempt to indulge in a different M.O.

SM: Could both be at play here?

TB: Look at it this way. The individual had contemplated that kind of scheme before, realizing its obvious drawbacks. (He) would not have ordinarily attempted it, but his reluctance to engage in that kind of scheme was erased or otherwise overpowered by the need to seek out another victim.

SM: Or victims.

TB: Well, or victims, yeah. And it was daring because it, uh, I mean for courage or something of that nature, but I say "daring" in the sense that he took a great number of risks to carry out this scheme.

SM: It was very nervy.

TB: Well, that might be one way of describing it. Or desperate or whatever. Uh, huh.

SM: How many days prior to the event would this person have anticipated doing it on that day?

TB: Well, it'd be hard to do. I don't think we can really say. It could've been planned or he might have just turned on the radio and heard that a big crowd was to be at the lake that day. Things just came together, you know, like the soft spot in the dike. All of a sudden there's that opportunity and that pressure. And the dike breaks.

SM: That's what you would guess?

TB: That's one explanation. That's all I have to say right there.

SM: A radio broadcast. Things just fell together. A speculative reconstruction here...

TB: I can only offer based on what I've read. Uh, I haven't seen any of those police reports, and, uh, what I know is what I read in these recent publications that have, uh, recapitulated, in a sense, that publicity and perhaps some of the behind-the-scenes statements from investigators. Furthermore, the first publicity I was exposed to, uh, was more than six years ago.

SM: Yeah.

TB: Six years... whatever. We assume, based on reports in the newspapers, one of the girls was approached by someone, and there was some kind of a report that he had a cast or a hurt arm, or something of that nature. And from some witnesses,

I don't know, uh... it's somewhat confusing... there seem to be several persons who saw somebody with a sling. So it's all fairly nebulous.

Assuming those reports are fairly accurate, they all tend to support the theory that it was one individual, using a ruse of some kind; appearing to have a handicap. That's just what we would expect, uh, if his intentions were to abduct a girl in such settings. It would be clear that in a crowded area, he just couldn't walk up and do it. The alternative was some kind of ruse.

It would be clear that he had as his goal to get the girl away from the large crowd to a secluded area. It's hard to say exactly what pretense was utilized to gain their confidence. (He) would not be able to drive a great distance without arousing the suspicions of the girls in the car. And so he would choose a secluded place, a secluded area, within a fairly short driving distance of the Lake Sammamish area.

SM: Then he'd pull off the side of the road, a dirt road or something like that?

TB: Or get to a secluded area, whatever that required. Driving up a road. Somewhere where there were no cars, no traffic or whatever.

SM: What would be the nature of the conversation between the two of them during the drive?

TB: (He'd) be acting a role. Talking about the weather, reinforcing the ruse, just chit-chat. He had a house somewhere in the area and took them there, one girl to the house, and came back and got the other one. In order to do that, the person had to be very secure that no one would enter the house or disturb it – or that no one else lived there or would be expected to come there.

That's one hypothesis. Another would be that he killed the first girl and returned later to search out a second individual.

SM: Right. So you regard it as unlikely they would have been killed at the spot where they were later found. (Bundy nodded.)

I see. The house, would it have been where people were on vacation or something like that? Was he aware this house was empty?

TB: That's possible.

SM: In this instance of the first girl (Janice Ott), how does he press ahead with his plan to insure she does not become a personality to him?

TB: I think we discussed before that we'd expect this kind of person wouldn't want to engage in a great deal of serious conversation. We talked about the role playing, the reacting, the kind of dialogue, the pitter-patter used to pacify or otherwise gain the confidence of the person. But once the individual would have her in a spot where he had, you know, security over her, then there would be a minimum amount of conversation which would be, you know, to avoid developing some kind of a relationship.

SM: What would be the method you'd expect him to use to incapacitate her?

TB: Fear. I suppose in such circumstances we could expect some sort of fear factor – a knife, a gun, anything to gain the attention of the individual.

SM: So the weapon is drawn or brandished. Then what?

TB: You could tie her up and try to calm her down. It's really hard to say. Once that point had been reached, he could sexually assault her, tie her up, or whatever.

SM: Would she be gagged?

TB: Well, she might be. If the surroundings he chose were secluded enough, then it wouldn't make any difference.

SM: How would he kill her?

TB (agitated): I don't know. Strangle her. Stab her... something.

SM: Did he anticipate getting more than one victim at the start of that day?

TB: Well, again, this Lake Sammamish incident would mark an extraordinary departure from the previous crimes attributed to this person. So then we would probably assume a number of departures.

In all likelihood, this individual knew about the criminal investigation process. If he had been acting more rationally, he would have realized that the disappearance of two girls in this fashion would yield a tremendous amount more interest and activity on the part of the police. So, normally, he would not want to generate this additional attention.

SM: But it's obvious he did.

TB: Yeah. It's possible he felt the first one wasn't satisfactory. Or, again, assuming this was an extraordinary departure – he's acting in a much less restrained manner – we might also suspect that whatever desires drove him seemed to be stronger than usual.

SM: Why did he go to the lake that day?

TB: It's hard to explain everything. There may have been other factors that had an impact on his condition that day – his need for gratification, the degree of it.
We talked about stress and the way passage of time would build up tension, but also he would suffer from periodic fluctuations that were more biologically or biochemically based than from any environmental explanation or psychological reasoning. It came as a rise in intensity, and these periods had no regularity.

SM: Would this have been the first instance of double murder?

TB: It would probably be.

SM: Would this second self... or other self... by this time be totally integrated into the person's being?

TB: The overexcited, overaroused, driven, compulsive state this person was in... could in no way be integrated with what we characterize as the moral, ethical, law-abiding part of the individual.

We'd probably be more accurate if we stated that this normal self had been repressed... to such a degree that even the encounter with the first victim did not sufficiently arouse it... so it could take predominance.

SM: How would this occasion, with its unusual and seemingly bizarre departures, affect the development of this unusual entity?

TB: Well, we would see... because of the drastic departure from the previous pattern, a resulting intense barrage of publicity and investigation. And, combined with his realization that he had taken excessive risks, we'd see the normal portion of him, again, making an even greater *commitment – resolve*, if you will – to never let it happen again. The absorption, the normal activity, and so forth.

SM: So there would be a moderate period of remission, inactivity, after this?

TB: Somewhat longer. But we're not talking of more than a month or so. That reminds me, a while back you were interested in his fantasies. I just remem... just came across in my mind some thoughts on it.

The fantasy phase is somewhat unworkable when applied directly to real situations. In his reading and his observations and what have you – in his fantasy world – he'd imagined, for some reason, people disappearing all the time. And he was aware of how people dropped out and became runaways and what not.

In devising his scheme or plan, he had taken this somewhat unrealistic conclusion that under the correct circumstances, he could select *any* person as a victim. And that there would be virtually no attention paid to that person's disappearance. Because people disappear every day! It happens all the time.

Of course, a lot of his activities were predicated on minimizing publicity, the tension, and what not. And he was always amazed and chagrined by the publicity generated by the disappearances he thought would go almost totally unnoticed. Of course, this was an unrealistic expectation.

SM: He was always amazed?

TB: Yes. And still, he would cling to that belief – that there would be virtually no furor over it. This was something that would cling to him for long periods of time, notwithstanding the fact that, based on reactions to the disappearances, he had been proven totally wrong. For some reason, it was a necessary way of looking at things. To say that perhaps this person won't be missed. I mean, there are so many people. This person will never be missed. It shouldn't be a problem.

SM: What is the affect of newspaper and TV accounts on this kind of personality?

TB: He studied the papers and watched the TV accounts – in addition to reading all the other material he'd read in the past. He concluded that the police and/or the news media publicized too much information about a case. That is, from the perpetrator's standpoint. That didn't *always* hold true, but more often than not it was the case.

This individual would read news accounts of that kind of official speculation with a critical eye. He knew more than the police. He knew when they were right. He also knew when they were wrong. The police, through the news media, would enter into speculation or advance conclusions that convinced this person, either, one, that they were on the wrong track, or two, they didn't know anything. More often than not, they didn't know much of anything. Often they were comparing apples and oranges.

Speculation about the progress of a police investigation is like anything – mostly inaccurate. Sometimes the correct theme comes through. But most of the time, it showed the police were flopping around, unsure, kind of lost, hoping for a lucky break.

SM: Do you think the *speculation* was inaccurate or that the police were just going the wrong way?

TB: Probably all of the above. The one thing that offers some insights is the conflict between various people and different agencies, along with the lack of skills some of the investigators displayed. Those on the front line started running every which way. That, you know, probably gave a better insight into what was going on at the time, especially from the murderer's viewpoint.

Since my name came before the police within a matter of weeks after the Lake Sammamish thing, I suppose they can be faulted for not actually coming out to talk to me. But on the other hand, they can't be faulted because they were working from a *huge* list. They had hundreds and hundreds of leads.

Which one do they pick? Do they pick the law student with no criminal background, who was probably even known by some of the prosecutors working the case? Or are they going to go after the types, you know, the guys in the files... the real weirdos? The guys going around exposing themselves or whizzing around in a Volkswagen saying, "Hey baby, you want to go for a ride up in the mountains with me?"

Perhaps the (lack of) manpower limits them. But for that kind of case, they would probably need a thousand investigators.

SM: Would the M.O. be the same with the second victim?

TB: Since published reports indicate that a number of women were approached in the same manner that day, and since the first one worked – since he wasn't acting with much restraint, I'd guess he'd figure a similar approach would also be successful.

SM: Would he change clothes?

TB: Probably not.

SM: Would there be any alteration in his appearance?

TB: Probably not.

SM: Would the second be taken to the same place as the first?

TB: Well, we're figuring this person had fallen into a kind of routine or pattern, and so we'd assume he took her to the same place. We can assume that because apparently, the bodies were found in close proximity to each other.

SM: Would the second victim see the first victim?

TB: Oh yeah, probably. In all probability.

SM: Would the other individual still be alive, or not?

TB: Well, had he been cautious, he would've probably killed the first individual before leaving to get the second girl, but in this instance since we've agreed he wasn't acting cautiously, he hadn't killed the first girl when he abducted the second.

SM: Would there have been any unique thrill or excitement from having the two of them there together?

TB: In all probability we're talking about an aberration here, a unique circumstance.

SM: Would the first victim be conscious?

TB: In all probability.

SM: What happened when they encountered each other?

TB: It seems there would be little importance attached to the arrival of the second individual. It seems the person would be more acutely interested in her own welfare and well being.

I suppose if you took two such individuals and kept them confined for days or months, they would certainly establish a rapport and be very concerned about each other's welfare. Here there was a good amount of fear and panic – most of us freeze under those circumstances.

We might surmise that in this case there was little interaction, as such. This individual would not want any interaction, as he did not want interaction on a one-to-one basis.

SM: What happens then?

TB: He'd follow the same pattern with the second girl as the first.

SM: In view of the other girl?

TB: In all probability, yes.

SM: After the sexual assault, he has two bound victims. What does he do now?

TB: Well, by this time his frenzied compulsive activity of that day has run its course. Then he realized the jeopardy he was in. Then the normal self would begin to reemerge and, realizing the greater danger involved, would suffer panic and begin to think of ways to conceal the acts – or at least his part of them. So he'd kill the two girls, place them in his car, and take them to a secluded area and leave them.

SM: Right away?

TB: Within a matter of hours.

SM: Would the killings be quick and as painless as possible? Or...

TB: The actual act of killing the victims was just a necessity. He would not linger or relish the killing, since it was only a means to an end, to avoid detection.

SM: There was speculation heads had been severed in some of the cases...

TB: Anyone knowledgeable about murder investigations knows you can determine a victim's identity easily from a head, so it's unlikely he would have decapitated them. Animals would have disposed of their remains. (We didn't know it then, but Bundy was masking his degeneracy again: He beheaded at least a dozen of his victims.)

SM: What would be the emotional aftermath?

TB: Well, later in the day this person would be exhausted. After going through what he went through, he wouldn't be in the mood to do much of anything.

SM: Sleep or eat, huh?

TB: Sleep.

April 30

My last one-on-one interview with Ted. We had decided to let him slip further back into the anonymous third person on the theory that what he might say, although impossible for us to connect to his crimes as we knew them, could reveal as much, or more, as his "speculations" on known murders and assaults.

SM: Would this killer ever pick up a girl and decide not to murder her, for whatever reason?

TB: We can posit that he was driving down a road one evening and saw an attractive teenaged girl hitchhiking. He picked her up and they engaged in conversation and, uh, she agreed to go to his house. And they spent the evening.

She got very, very drunk. They both got drunk. Throughout the evening they engaged in voluntary sexual activity, and throughout the evening he felt himself being tested, debating with himself whether to kill her or to just let the situation run its course normally.

SM: Would he keep her at arm's length? (a particularly poorly phrased question.)

TB: Well, not necessarily. He was in one of his reformation periods, (a laugh). He'd sworn to himself that he'd never engage in that kind of conduct again. That he wouldn't let himself be carried away like that. But when he was faced with this very attractive girl hitchhiking, it kind of presented a challenge.

He didn't look on it as a challenge but as an opportunity; it was sort of an ambiguous situation.

SM: It seems as if his normal self was responding positively to her.

TB: Uh huh. That would be fair to say. The sexual activity was very responsive and very energetic. Uh, at certain parts of the evening he felt himself on the edge of taking her life, just, just out of the desire to do so. But the justifications were not there. Nor was that malignant condition that active at that time. It was active, but not at high strength. But when morning came around and they dressed and he took the girl back to the area where she lived, he felt like he'd accomplished something.

He deluded himself at that point into thinking that he had really conquered those impulses. But within a period of time he discovered that that was an inaccurate conclusion. He didn't recognize then, or perhaps he did not want to recognize, that just the matter of a week or two later he probably would have killed her.

SM: What happens when the malignant part cannot be controlled or insists on gratification? At Lake Sammamish, for instance, there were great risks taken. But what if the urge is there and it can't, for some reason, be met?

TB (pause): In the wake of a particular crime, he was not in a state of remission. That is, he actively wanted to go out and seek a victim. But he knew that he could not afford to do so without creating an intolerable amount of more public frenzy and panic, as well as police activity.

But while driving one day, he saw a young girl walking along a deserted area. It was just too good an opportunity to pass up. So he exited his car and approached the girl and shoved her into a bushy field. Without any preparation. No planning. Without any disguise. Just an impulsive kind of thing. And then he was faced with the prospect:

What should he do with her? He'd have to debate a considerable amount. There had been an illegal act of rape. Yet he
refrained from harming her physically and left the scene and
returned to his car and drove home. Had it occurred a few weeks
later, he wouldn't have acted in the same way. Or a few days
later. But he did not want to create a great amount of public furor
because it would reduce the opportunity for victims later on and
it would increase the possibility of eyewitness reports. And he
knew enough about these circumstances that, in all likelihood,
it wouldn't be reported. Or if it was reported, nothing much
would be done about it. They wouldn't necessarily link it to the
other crimes. It would have been a simple act of rape of the type
that is fairly common.

(Bundy said that the act of rape alone did not satisfy "the
entity." But during the last segment of this last interview, he
described another scene in which, he maintained, the object was
rape. Two days before his execution, Ted told Dennis Couch
of the Salt Lake County sheriff's office how he had murdered
sixteen-year-old Nancy Wilcox in October of 1974. According
to Couch, the account Bundy gave of the crime matches this
story, almost verbatim.)

TB: As we've discussed before, frequently after this individual, uh, committed a murder, he would lapse, uh, into a period of
sorrow, remorse, et cetera. And for a period of time he would do
everything to overcome and otherwise repress the, uh, the overt
behavior. Indeed, on one particular occasion he went to extraordinary lengths to do this following a crime, and he felt that he had
succeeded, that the abnormal course of conduct had just sort of,
uh, extinguished itself. He became somewhat satisfied and secure
with the feeling that he had accomplished this.

But in this instance, the cracks in the facade, as it were, began to appear. He then would attempt to channel the desire within him into a different area, into something which was still, uh, improper, immoral or illegal, but something that was less serious, less severe.

Uh, and so he, in sort of a, uh, a compromise decided that rather than go out and inflict this mortal injury on a someone he would search out a victim in such a way that there would be no possibility of detection and he would not be forced into a position of having to kill. In essence he compromised into just going out and performing an act of rape, as it were.

So, he, uh, began to just go out driving around the suburbs, uh, in this city, uh, that he was living in, and one particular evening he's driving down a fairly dark street and saw a girl walking along the street. Okay?

SM: Uh huh.

TB: Because the area was dark and she was alone, he decided to select her as the victim for this intended act of sexual assault. He parked his car down the street, and, uh, then ran up behind the girl.

Just as he came up upon her, they were at a place where there was an orchard, or a number of trees or something. As he came up behind her she heard him. She turned around and he brandished a knife and grabbed her by the arm and told her to do what he wanted her to do. You know, to follow him.

SM: Yeah.

TB: He pushed her off the sidewalk into this darkened, wooded area, and uh, told her to submit and do what he wanted her to do.

She began to argue with him and he kept telling her to be quiet. She said she didn't believe he would do anything to her, anyway. Then he began to try to remove her clothes and she would, uh, continue to struggle in a feeble manner. And also voice verbally her objections to what was going on.

And then, uh, the significance, now, is that his intent with this victim was not to harm her. He thought this was going to be a significant departure; perhaps even a way of deconditioning himself, to climb down that ladder or, uh, I can't think of a good word, de-, *de-escalate* this level of violence to the point where there would be no violence at all. Even no necessity for that kind of encounter at all.

SM: I see.

TB: But he found himself with this girl who was struggling and screaming. Uh, not screaming, but let's say just basically arguing with him. There were houses in the vicinity and he was concerned that somebody might hear. And so, in an attempt to stop her from talking or arguing, he placed his hand over her mouth.

She stopped and he attempted to remove her clothes and she began to object again. At this point, he was in a state of not just agitation, but something on the order of panic. He was fearing that she would arouse somebody in the vicinity.

So, not thinking clearly but still intending not to harm her, let's say, he placed his hands around her throat.

SM: Uh huh.

TB: Just to throttle her into unconsciousness so that she wouldn't scream anymore. She stopped struggling, and it appeared that she was unconscious. But not, in his opinion, to a point where he had killed her.

SM: Right.

TB: Then let's say he removed her clothes and raped her and put his own clothes back on. At about that point, he began to notice that the girl wasn't moving. It appeared, although he wasn't certain, that he'd done what he had promised himself he wouldn't do. And he had done it, really, almost inadvertently.

Uh, so he took the girl by one of her arms and pulled her to a darkened corner of this little orchard and then, in a fit of panic, fled the scene. He got back in his car and drove back to his house, still not knowing if the girl was alive or dead.

But once he returned to the house, upon reflection he began to wonder. He didn't know if he'd left anything at the crime scene. He hadn't thought about publicity and physical evidence.

So he decided to return to the scene and if the body was there to recover it and take it somewhere else where it wouldn't be found.

SM: Is this the same night?

TB: Huh? Oh, yeah. But he faced two problems in returning to the scene. First, prior to the incident he was in a state of intoxication, and he didn't know the area that well. So he couldn't remember *exactly* where it was he had to return, couldn't find his way back, as it were.

But let's say, after a considerable period of time of driving about in the general vicinity, uh, he was able to locate the area. It was getting fairly late about this time.

Nobody was in the vicinity, so apparently she hadn't gotten up and gone away and the police hadn't returned to the scene. Or she was still there.

He parked his car at the curb in front of this small orchard and walked into it and saw that, in fact, the body was still in the same position he'd left it. So it was clear that the girl was dead.

So he carried the body to his car and put it in and covered it. Then he returned to the general area with a flashlight and scoured it to pick up everything that he may have left there – her clothing, et cetera. He placed that in the car and then returned to his apartment.

SM: Did he find everything?

TB: I don't know.

SM: Would he have worn a mask?

TB: No, I don't think so. I mean, he didn't… it was dark and he…

SM: Well, the reason I asked is that if the intent was not to kill the victim, you would think that there would have been some kind of measure taken to disguise his identity.

TB: In a way, it was planned, but in a way it was like a spur of the moment thing for this person. He figured the object was to do it in such a way that it would be done in a very dark scene. Eventually, he found that kind of opportunity.

SM: Why would he return to his apartment as opposed to just driving out in the middle of nowhere and dumping her there?

TB: Well, first of all, it was late at night. And as we know, he tries to secrete the body with some care. Rather than just driving off somewhere late at night and dumping it along the roadside, he needed time to think about what he should do – how he should do it.

SM: So he would take a couple days before he…

TB: Yeah, a day or two.

SM: How long might this person keep the bodies at his house? My impression is that Brenda Ball could have been kept there after she was killed for three, four, uh, five days – something like that.

TB: Uh, I don't recall exactly what I said about that. I mean that we could say that this individual would not keep the bodies any longer than necessary to determine the best way of disposing.

SM: So the idea really was that the residence was the safest place.

TB: Well, where else would he go? It would be the most logical place to go for him to take time to think. It was also a place where he had some privacy, too. Rather than go out and park in a drive-in restaurant or something. It's clear that there are only *so* many places he could go where he could feel safe and relaxed and think about the, uh, the situation that was facing him.

SM: Overall, the impression I get of this person and his career is that maybe the front end of the incidents would be planned fairly well, but the back end of the operation was not always so well thought out.

TB: That's not an unfair analysis. But on the other hand, let's (take) the facts of the Washington cases and try to draw some inferences from that M.O.

We assume that the bodies were disposed of in Washington the way they were to minimize publicity – to diminish the possibility that they would be located within a short period of time. Thereby diminishing the amount of investigative activity, as well as publicity. It's clear some thought was given to it and, in fact, this individual's approach to disposing of the bodies was fairly effective.

I mean, a person finds himself (with) a corpse, and what is he going to do with it? Ideally, he'd have an incinerator in the basement – and there wouldn't be any problem at all in that respect.

SM: Maybe the best way to put it is to ask the question this way: Would this individual have on his mind the disposal problem at the time he was in search of the victim?

TB: I doubt that there'd be a necessity to, because he had already thought about it – at least in general – prior to that time. The specifics of it would, of course, be dictated to a certain degree by the situation. Let's say, then, the case we just talked about: He hadn't said, "I'm going to take her just to Point A." In fact, he went back to his apartment and looked at a map and said, "That looks good." And (he) then drove to that area. The specifics of where he would dispose of the body would depend on access roads or whatever.

SM: There's perhaps a lack of sophistication on my part. Having to go in and out of residences with any large bundle would seem to be risking everything, no matter what time of day.

TB (laughs): You say that you're not sophisticated enough. But I think, Steve, with enough study and interest, that you, too, could become a fairly effective mass murderer.

Anyone has the capacity, and it (doesn't) take a great deal of skill or thought to do it. The very nature of the crime – since it's based on opportunity – it's a relatively easy kind of crime to get away with.

SM: Hmmm.

TB: This person taking bundles in, in and out of his house or his apartment. We say in retrospect, that was really chancy. But there were times when I think he… he almost felt as if he were immune from detection.

Not in a mystical or a spiritual sense or anything, but that on occasion he felt like he could walk through doors. He didn't feel like he was, uh, invisible or anything like that. But at times he felt that no matter how much he fucked up, nothing could go wrong.

The boldness was probably a result of not being rational. Of just being moved by a situation – not really thinking it out clearly, and not even seeing risks. But just overcome by that boldness and desire to accomplish a particular thing. Only in retrospect would he wonder how he managed to succeed in spite of some of those rash and bold acts.

SM: We've discussed the total depersonalization of the victims – that they become objects.

TB: That's one way of describing it. Now, clearly, they are people-flesh and blood. They have all the characteristics of human beings. It would be unfair to say totally – totally and absolutely – but they would be depersonalized sufficiently so that he was not able to muster that natural, normal ability to feel compassion for that individual to also place a high value on the sanctity of life.

Oddly enough, this person (in) normal situations would place a high value on life. And on the goal that people should be free from suffering and so on. But he would not allow himself to feel those emotions for the victim.

SM: As you explained, there would be the erasure of those key inhibitions.

TB: It would be very specific.

SM: What I was getting at was, could it be that there was a heightened sense of possession by taking a victim home?

TB: Not necessarily. It's possible. I mean, like that old cat bringing the mouse to the doorstep, you know. Such a person would do this not necessarily to heighten the sense that he possessed the person, although I'm sure that to some extent this might be true. But more often than not, I think we understand that taking a victim home was just one way of insuring privacy for whatever period of time the privacy was necessary. Not as a part of a ritual of, you know, like the cat bringing the bird into the kitchen in front of the master.

SM: Would he have anything further to do with the victim after the victim is brought home? Or just store her?

TB: The perpetrator wouldn't have a need or desire to do anything more at that point, other than dispose of the body.

SM: You surmised that this personality would be capable, under the right circumstances, of the kind of incident that occurred in the Chi Omega house.

TB: I don't know that I said that.

SM: That's what I thought I heard. Am I wrong?

TB: I don't know. I can't remember that we discussed Chi Omega specifically. You at one point were talking about injuries inflicted upon victims that indicated extreme, extraordinary rage and so on. If he committed the crimes in Washington state and also was responsible for the Chi Omega murders, we would have to say that it was something of an aberration in the way it was committed. That something, obviously, went wrong.

Part Three

June 21

Hugh takes over. This was the second part of a good-guy/
bad-guy interview technique. Bundy recognized that. What
he wasn't prepared for was hostile questioning which would
cut back and forth between his "speculations" and the facts
of his story.

HA: The cafeteria is closed for cleaning, so you'll have to
do with some potato chips and ice cream bars. Maybe today is
"lean and mean" day.

TB: Every day is that in here. But then I suppose the
Starke Hilton isn't so wonderful either. Did you get with
Carole last night?

HA: No, we met this morning, just outside the prison. She
sent some mail and some vitamin pills. You know, she thinks
you're getting ready to make a mad dash for the outside. She
notices that you're on edge and maybe even it's something
you've said to her. I don't know. I cannot quite get on the
same wavelength with Carole. She is so protective of you that
anybody else… almost… is a bastard going in.

TB: What do you mean she thinks I'm going? She doesn't…

HA: She thinks, or at least by what she says, it appears she figures you're going to make a try at it.

TB: Sheesh. (he peers out the window in the door where a guard saunters close every few minutes.) Not so loud. That's not very popular to discuss. Not even if you're not planning to travel. (extra loud) *And, I'm not!*

HA: Okay, okay. I want to talk about these stories that the victims all were physically similar. You know, long dark hair, parted in the middle, hoop earrings, et cetera. People have said that the killings were not random and the supposed similarities prove that.

TB: They had a tendency to just fit the general criteria of being young and fairly attractive (long pause) and alone. Too many people have bought this crap that all the girls were similar – hair about the same color, parted in the middle, close to same height, blah, blah, blah – but if you look at it, almost *everything* was dissimilar: time, place of disappearance, physical description... all of it. Physically, they were almost all different, but...

HA: But how would you know? Some of them look similar in the file photos. Other than height and weight, which did vary as much as anything, how could you be so sure of their differences... unless you were there?

TB (abruptly): You're trying to weasel in where there is nothing to gain. I *know* about these victims because I've been accused of killing them... uh, most of them... and so I read everything I can get my hands on about the various cases. How in hell do *you* know all about the victims? How do I know you weren't there, old buddy!

HA: Touché! Okay, let's dig in a bit more, mixing some fact, logic, and a bit of amateur psychology. Were most of these girls watched for long periods of time before the killer got the nerve up to hit?

TB: Well, one wonders how long someone watched that girl in Corvallis, Oregon. Or the girl over in Eilensburg (in eastern Washington). And I was never gone for long periods of time. Uh, if we'd consult our model, our personality profile, we'd recall that this person would *avoid* long periods of observation because it would increase the chances of an eyewitness confrontation. And that, we would expect, uh, that the abduction would occur, *more*, uh, primarily as a result of opportunity.

HA: Except, perhaps, at the beginning – when he followed the girl home, saw where she lived and later returned to her house, and...

TB: Oh, yeah, yeah.

HA: But that was way back in the beginning.

TB: Well, we're talking about opportunity also. There may not have been that many opportunities right away. You know, there are so many misconceptions of me. Let's put it this way: Law enforcement judges me and predicts my behavior based on what they think I know and what... how they think I act. Now, *clearly*, if they don't know how my mind functions – they think it functions some way other than how it does – they are going to predict behavior that I won't engage in. They're going to expect me to react in a way that I don't react.

I've never wanted publicity… and yet there are those, most people probably, who believe that I needed it. I've never liked it, needed it, or wanted it.

I *have* used it to my benefit. When I wanted better digs in jail or some consideration that most human beings have, I used whatever publicity I could to get it. When I wanted to put pressure on somebody or something, why not? Every little game like that has been used to dehumanize me these last five years.

I'll probably use the press again – not for money. God knows, I've been offered a lot of money to do things, make appearances on TV and the like. What's that going to get me? Maybe some better reefer, maybe some unneeded enemies in here. No help on the legal front. But there will come a time… and I'll be calling *Time* or *Newsweek* or CBS news. And they'll come, gladly, mark my words.

I may have to defend myself publicly. You have more of a chance to describe me and explain this whole sideshow because you don't have to start with clips from the newspaper and cops' often-ridiculous imaginations. Like this guy said recently, "He's an emotional robot, nothing inside." Boy, how far off can he be! If they think I have no emotional life, they're wrong. Absolutely wrong. It's a very real one and a very full one. Another misconception.

They see me as *part* of a human being, so they don't know what the other part is capable of – and that's terrific. They won't be able to anticipate.

HA: You always get angry or upset when we talk about Liz and what she meant to you at one time. Some call the relationship a "love-hate" situation. Others claim you humiliated her until you almost forced her to turn you in.

TB: Well, that's not true. As I've discussed earlier, while I'm not trying to fix blame and I have understood totally what has occurred between Liz and I over the years, it *was* Liz on at least two occasions that went out with other people while we were dating. I don't call that humiliation, necessarily, but it has a profound effect on... Now, I may have caused her to feel badly on several occasions. It wasn't a conscious, intentional attempt to make her feel humiliated. Going out with other women wasn't an attempt to humiliate her because I always *hid* the fact when I went out with other women.

HA: Until you got to feelin' guilty about it and told her.

TB: Well, she would find out about it on occasion. She never found out about 'em all. She never found out about Marjorie (Ted's first girlfriend) and any of these other girls until the police investigation. So I didn't humiliate her time and time again.

HA: And you don't... still don't... blame her for calling the police?

TB: I think she had some real suspic... fears in her mind and these weighed heavily on her. And she didn't report me because she wanted to hurt me. And I *did* forgive her, because I loved her. There's *nothing* wrong with that. It was an understandable weakness, and I understand her desire to do her public duty. So *what!*

She didn't cause me to get caught. I got myself caught by the policeman – and that led to other things. That's all there is to it. And I *forgave* her and I never considered that she did it to hurt me. There's not that much to forgive her for. She is not responsible for me getting caught.

HA: Do you expect to ever see her or hear from her again?

TB (softly): No, no. I don't suppose so.

HA: There are those who say that Ted Bundy may fight for his life for five or six years, but that when the time comes… and you walk those last yards… it won't be the same Ted Bundy they knew. They think that prison will have beaten you down into conformity. That you will sink deeper and deeper into yourself. You *really* don't have that much in common with the ones I've seen on Death Row here, anyway.

TB: Well, first of all, you don't know what my life is like back on "R" Wing, but I suggest you compare notes with Steve and Carole and anyone else you'd like to, to get a perspective on me. I think you'll find that I'm as emotionally… have as much emotional and intellectual vitality as I've ever had.

Certainly, the effects of prison have taken their toll. But I don't think that anyone could say that I'm crushed and defeated and empty – and that I'm sinking deeper and deeper into compulsive madness. *Maybe* you'll have a suspicion, but I can guarantee you that the reverse is happening. I get stronger and stronger.

I don't know what your opinion of me is – and it *really* doesn't make any difference. I mean, not your opinion but your observations, as to, you know, if I'm an empty shell, ashes inside, uh, uh... going deeper and deeper into some emotional morass or some madness, or whatever. But, uh, what can I say? *I* know what I'm like, and I know... I, uh... I know what's happening to me.

HA: I don't *know* what's happening to you. I don't think any person can know that. But you seem pretty vital and strong... and damned alert to me. I don't know what that *means*. You might have always been that way. Whether you're stronger now, I couldn't judge.

TB: I feel... I believe I feel it – but maybe that's just something to hang onto. But I know I'm... my habits are better than they have been and I'm more controlled and more disciplined than I have ever been.

HA: Well, of course, most of that is *not* of your own doing. I'd like to move briefly to another area.

You've commented on how wrong some people have been in describing Ted Bundy. Yet they've generally only interpreted what you've promoted via your behavior.

You give people a feeling of being very cold, calculating, mocking. Cold hearted, very methodical. I think that at one time you probably hid behind this kind of a facade; it was *needed* by you when you didn't feel like you were a part of things and so on. I'm not playing amateur psychologist here, but it seems almost as though, to buttress this place you felt you were in, you formed a definite *contempt* for a certain part of society – law enforcement, lawyers, and the like... and I think that definitely shows.

You're arrogant. You're damn sick of a lot of things you've faced in society. A lot of things happened to you that you couldn't cope with, and, to a great extent, you got even!

TB: And this chain of events has made me a *cold* individual. And it's made me very *harsh* on particular segments of society – like you said. And I've adopted a lot of the opinions and attitudes that prisoners – uh, which I think are reasonable under the circumstances. It's necessary to adapt that way to survive. Uh, the people who are seemingly always assessing me – as to whether I'm cold or not or calculating or not – are more often than not people I – like psychologists or psychiatrists and reporters – for whom I have absolutely no need to come across as a warm, friendly person.

I am *really* a private person. I have very few close friends. There's no reason why, Hugh, and don't take this personally, (but) there's no reason for us, *necessarily*, to come across as (though you and I are) old, long-lost buddies.

HA: Sure, and I don't...

TB: I mean, we're sort of thrust together in a situation.

HA: I haven't tried to country-boy you.

TB: No, you haven't been soliciting my... soliciting me in that way. I mean it's just... I mean to say, "Well gee, why doesn't Hugh ever give me a detailed rundown on his childhood and his family life? What his kids are like? And his home? Is he *cold?* Is he calculating?" That's not it at all. That's not our goal here – to be, you know, long-lost...

HA: I'd tell you all that if you asked me, though.

TB: Yeah.

HA: But there's no reason for it to be that way.

TB: There's no reason for me to inquire into your love life or your domestic affairs. And yet, if I don't do that, people say, "Well, he's cold and *distant*." I'll tell that to some stranger who walks up and plops down a notebook and says, "Okay, tell me everything about yourself?"

Well this guy doesn't know me and he's not going to get to know me. I don't feel that it's necessary to develop a deep friendship with him, because in most cases they're my *adversaries* anyway. And I know the limitations of the field.

I've adopted some pretty harsh attitudes about society, uh, in recent years, but, you know, that's a response to what's happened to me.

HA: Well, you *seem* to… I probably wouldn't say this, but you asked me how *I* felt or what I saw in you. Very frankly, you are damned composed. If I had been accused… or somebody had even intimated… that I had killed a bunch of people – and I've seen it as high as thirty-six girls – I would be pretty damned upset. I don't know how I'd cope with it. I don't know if I'd be strong enough to cope at all. But you, uh, sort of sit back and make fun of the cops and their blunders… and point 'em out. It simply doesn't seem to touch you as much as I think it might me.

TB: Well, of course, I don't… you don't *know* whether. I thought I would – I told myself back in Salt Lake City – that

I would kill myself before I went to prison. Most people think that way. "I would die before I'd go to prison," I told myself. I was fright... uh, fearful of it, thinking I would be raped and so on. But I survived... though I went through some horrible periods. The *worst* was the time I spent in the Salt Lake City jail – that first four or five months.

Those were nightmarish times. I *cried* at night. I was, uh... I was a wreck! If I wouldn't get a letter from Liz for three days I would go to pieces. It was *rough*, really rough. But I got over it. I learned how to cope with it because I *wasn't* going to tear myself apart. I wasn't going to destroy Ted Bundy because of the accusations. I was going to survive. Transcend it, overcome it. I couldn't do that if I was tearing myself apart, feeling embittered and persecuted – though I felt those emotions. But I didn't let them destroy or control me, after a short while.

HA: That's what I mean. I don't know how you used to be, but you seem rather in control these days.

TB: You get used to those accusations if they're repeated and repeated as they have been for five years. You get immune to it. You see, I couldn't endure this humiliation if I gave up. I'm a survivor. And I poke fun at the police because they're damn... not incompetent... but they're so ineffective. They may be incompetent, too, but by and large, they're just not using their heads.

And they're *protagonists*. I shouldn't look at them as my friends. I don't. I don't think I should. Since they are the ones who are challenging me and accusing me, I've every right to criticize them.

HA: (You've) talked about justification and how it works on a killer's mind. (You've) discussed police and how they operate. And you talked about how you had to grab control of yourself. Much of this, particularly when you reach inside for the feelings – even though I feel that's part of the overall justification here – comes from a very intelligent man. I've had people comment how "brilliant" they think you are. How do you feel about this? How smart are you?

TB: Well, I'm not *stupid*. But I'm not... I'm far from a genius, too. People use the "terribly bright, terribly handsome" thing as part of the image process. I'm not exceptionally handsome. I'm not exceptionally bright. I may not even *be* bright by some people's definition – or *handsome*, for that matter. But it's part of creating the myth of Ted Bundy – which is separate and distinct from my reality.

Something that will shock people and make them wonder why, shake their heads or otherwise to make the story more sensational. You just... it just seems to be the theme that they've adopted in the Ted Bundy case. The bright, intelligent freak!

HA: But you told Stephen that you were getting smarter all the time.

TB: Well, I hope *everybody* is. I'm learning from my experience. And I'm mellowing with age and doing everything most people do – and finding that I enjoy my ability to *see* things and to move about and examine things much more now than I ever could before. Now I have frames of reference to understand why people behave the way they do. If that's "getting smarter," then it's true: I *am* getting smarter.

I enjoy my intelligence. I enjoy talking… enjoy trying to be articulate when I can, though sometimes I'm a bit embarrassed by the way I speak. I don't consider myself *smarter* than other people, but it… I always look at others as being at least my equal. Now if they show themselves to be dumber, then I guess I have some contempt for them.

HA: That reminds me: Stephen mentioned a fellow you told him about – an Italian barber in the Salt Lake City jail. He got out and was later caught in an armed robbery.

TB: He escaped. What he did was… he'd been charged with *several* murders, but he'd always managed to beat them. They finally charged him with murder where there was an eyewitness who saw him leave the scene. So he decided to play crazy. And he read books and we'd talk about it. And he'd tell me what he was going to do. He started seeing little green bugs and said he felt the air sucking out of him; you know, real crazy stuff!

He did this and he convinced a panel of psychiatrists that he wasn't competent to stand trial. He knew exactly what he was doing. The guy was the barber. He ran the store. Whoever runs the store, especially in the county jails, he has it all together. He gets around and sells stuff. He was a businessman, very shrewd, and somehow, he convinced them he should go to a mental institution.

He had confided in me that he knew how to get out of the state hospital because the inmates carried the keys. He was… here he was, getting out of a first-degree murder charge… and he was going to walk right out of the state hospital!

And that's what he *did!* He got the keys and sped away… and was later caught in LA.

HA: Does that memory and that association give you any thoughts? You probably know enough about psychiatry to toss some interesting tidbits (around). Have you ever considered it?

TB: I think I've made myself clear on that. Ted Bundy is not crazy, or anywhere near it. I have done some things I'm not proud of. Some of these things I may talk about; others I never can. But, just like I've told every lawyer I've ever talked to, forget any insanity defense for me. I'm not insane, by anybody's stretch of the imagination. Think about it a minute. I'm not crazy. Everybody knows that.

HA: Well, he's (the guard) gone now, so we can talk without you holding that microphone under your arm. Why is Carole thinking you're aiming to try to get out of here? And are you? What would you do on the street? You'd be recognized everywhere you went.

TB: I don't know why anybody would think I would want to leave this country club (laughs). Yeah, people here think about it all the time, talk about it, but only with those they trust implicitly, but it's damned hard to do.

I'm not going anywhere. (Bundy would plan an escape four years later, in 1984.) Sometimes they act like they hope I would. A smart man can make it, I think... but that's a subject for another time. Listen, I've just admitted I'm as smart as the average guy and I'm not crazy. So why would I slip my white ass out of here, only to get it blown to smithereens by some of those rednecks who don't get to shoot often? I'll take my chances. (he lights a cigarette) But I guess anybody who's already escaped from a couple jails always thinks, maybe, maybe...

HA: If you got out, where would you go? Most of your friends probably wouldn't care to take the heat of hiding you out. Where would you get any money?

TB: Oh, I'd have to go somewhere where nobody knew me – that means Australia, South America, China. I'd have to travel at night, to a port town, and stow away on a ship. I'd never, *ever* contact family or friends. Couldn't afford to. I trust my family, but there's been too much heat on them already. And my friends might have read too much to remain objective about me.

I've studied a bit about makeup and how to look like somebody nobody would be looking for, but…

HA: So, you got out and ran away. There's nothing in prison of a therapeutic nature that would change your habits, your inner problems. So, I assume, you would kill again – and pretty damn quick. Right?

TB: Wrong! Wrong! We're not dealing with me anymore. Let's not take liberties here. We've created this individual, so we must use him. If the type of individual – the one who, we know, has killed numerous young women – were to be on the streets after a lengthy incarceration, we can assume that, yes, he would kill again. He's received nothing – absolutely nothing inside a prison to help him sort out that sickness.

Speaking about taking the heat… did I tell you about the trick I played on Don Kennedy's (the defense investigator at the Leach trial) wife while we were waiting for the Leach verdict to come in?

HA: No.

TB: I was in the lawyers' room there and I was making some phone calls, and I called Don's house in Lake City and his wife answered. I said, "Is Don there?" I knew he wasn't. I had seen him an hour before. I said, "Well, he's supposed to pick me up here, in front of the courthouse. I'm out here and waiting. Do you suppose you can find him?" She said, "Who is this?" I replied "Ted Bundy." The phone clicked and I damn near laughed my ass off. When Lynn (Thompson, another lawyer) came in later, he asked me what I was laughing about... Did I know something he didn't?

June 24

HA: Let's look back at what we've discussed. It seems to me that in talking about justification, he justifies as he murders. Justifies the attacks and the victimizations. Later, in retrospect, he realizes that these justifications and rationalizations are not legitimate.

Is there *any* kind of feeling of remorse there that... maybe even though these people were nothing to *him*, they have families and loved ones and it might be of some value to let the people know where the bodies are – if it didn't bother him or hurt him. What do you think he'd think about that?

TB: He *might* think just like you said it here, but again, we've seen that almost six years in some cases have passed and no clues have turned up. No anonymous letters, uh, no information of that type. So for at least six years, we can see that *whoever* he is, he hasn't (been) detected or found the need to reveal the, uh, locations of the remains.

I would imagine that in the event that this person – or a person like this – were ever able to, uh, *conquer*, or eliminate from his mind and his behavior the need to act out in that fashion, then he would have to be so situated that he could do so without *scarring* himself.

If, all of a sudden, in some way he was able to rediscover or rebuild those inhibitions, uh, that prevent most of us – that prevent most people from committing murder, uh, *overnight*, and the guilt that we would associate with the breaking of those kinds of taboos and inhibitions, then, *if* the cure would be as bad as the disease, he would be creating a situation where he would be living in a nightmare.

So, if he were to put himself back together, he'd have to do so in sort of a *prospective* fashion, rather than a retrospective fashion – and then how he felt about killing would apply only from Day One on forward. And he would have to cut off the past and let it float away.

There's *nothing* this man could do to bring back the persons he killed. There's nothing he could do to decrease the anguish the loved ones have been through. So, uh (long pause)... that would be one way of explaining it.

HA: You don't think that he would realize that letting the families know where the bodies were would ease their burden?

TB: I don't know. Personally, I don't, uh... I don't know how I would feel if I were someone whose – who had somebody close to them disappear under suspicious circumstances. Would I feel better knowing they were a pile of bones somewhere? Or *worse*? I mean, I just can't... it'd be difficult to say.

But whether or not *that* would actually be the case... like being at least partially irrelevant to – again, this individual would still be thinking about *survival*, and it would be inopportune for him to be sticking his neck in a noose, uh, in that fashion anyway.

I mean, if the goal for putting himself back together again was to live and to minimize or *eliminate* his threat to others – toward innocent people – and to lead a healthy, productive life, it would be contradictory for him to go about confessing to crimes because he, uh, perceived the need on the part of those who knew the victim to know, in fact, that the victim was the victim. Does that make sense?

HA: Maybe to a psychopath. It gets a bit convoluted, doesn't it? Well, let's move on. Suppose this person was caught. Would his main thrust be toward survival first?

TB: Say the person *wasn't* caught. I mean, caught or not, I suppose the individual... The goal is survival. Everyone I know of, their primary goal is to survive. Sometimes in different ways.

HA: Would this person ever really want to change?

TB: Well, we, we... uh, described this individual and found that his behavior, which was becoming more and more frequent, was also *concomitantly*, – I love that word, *concomitantly* – occupying more and more of his mental and intellectual energies. So he's facing a greater, uh, more frequent *challenge* of this darker side of himself to his normal life.

It was actually draining off – it couldn't keep the distinct – the one was demanding so much that it was going to interfere with his, uh, surface validity, his normal appearance.

So clearly, he would have to make a *choice*. Now, assuming that he was capable of making the choice, he would have to weigh the future consequences of continuing along this course of action, and, of course, the conduct of murdering in such senseless and incomprehensible fashion, or return to a normal life.

It would be clear that there was no longer a choice. It would either be one or the other. Now, if he was captured, it'd be clear that this conduct was *seriously* interfering with his ability to not only survive but to live free and so on. And so he would have to. There's clearly motivation there.

And he'd know – we *all* know – not only is the act of murder, of the kind we're talking about, senseless, inhumane, and cruel, it's *also* illegal! And people lose their freedom when they engage in that kind of behavior.

So, understanding – if he was capable of understanding – the dimensions of the problem that seemed to grip him and the consequences in concealing that kind of behavior, and if he was capable of making an intelligent decision, he would probably find a way to extinguish the motives as well as the behavior. Looking behind the behavior of killing as well as the art of killing itself – and all points in between.

It would be a real choice. If he failed to do that, I mean, there's no in-between. There's no middle ground. If only he could realize this. If he couldn't, then, of course, he wouldn't… uh, wouldn't do anything about it. But if he's capable of making a choice, he'd probably try to understand the problem – what his independent variables were and how to eliminate them, how to deal with them in some fashion. Eliminate – not just reduce or suppress – but *eliminate* the need, the underpinnings of his, uh, criminal behavior.

HA: Well, you've been convicted in the Chi Omega case. You pled innocent but were convicted. Could we examine the evidence in that case in relation to the man you've just described? Could we look at this case and see what's valid and what isn't? I think we have to get into that.

TB: Well… that case doesn't fit (laughs). There you *are!* We've done a lot in one sentence. See how easy it is to take care of that in the book!

HA: Yeah, but…

TB: We've created a model that doesn't fit the real-life situation.

HA: Well, let's examine the differences then.

TB: Sure.

HA: From the M.O.s on through.

TB: Yeah, but in that case…

HA: There's not a *complete* difference in M.O.s. Some of the cases in the northwest had girls assaulted in their rooms or apartments.

TB: Well, it would seem the difference between the individual responsible for those in the northwest and the Chi Omega sorority house were considerably, significantly different. You can find similarities. Yes, you can sit here and talk about similarities – where the victims were young women, *true* – but the M.O. is strikingly different.

No attempt at possession. No attempt to kidnap the victims. No attempt, it appears, to have sexual intercourse with the victims. The victims were not just knocked unconscious; they were brutally beaten. And you might make the conclusion – based solely on the autopsy photographs and the medical examiner's reports…

There were bite marks. There was a kind of, uh, residence involved and in none of the northwest cases except the Healy case was a whole *houseful* of young women the target of this kind of attack. And in no case were there simultaneous or multiple kinds of attacks that occurred almost… in a very short period of time.

And we'd assume that, somehow, Lake Samamish – because we've been trying to compare the Lake Samamish situation – we're talking about the difference in time, and… so the differences involved here…

HA: But you said yourself that this person would probably alter his type of attack to meet a certain opportunity or situation.

TB: Well, first I meant… occasions would alter or he'd otherwise attempt to conceal himself in such a way that there wouldn't be a connection made, or to alter – you know – to alter by throwing police off the pattern. It's conceivable, you know. People do this.

HA: But would Chi Omega be a buildup of a tremendous pressure that just exploded all at once? It wasn't something carefully thought out. Maybe it was a spur of the moment thing. This person had so much pressure built up, that he was like a time bomb, waiting to go off.

TB: Well, that's... that's a possibility, but then again, the, uh, facts in the case would indicate that there's *absolutely* nothing known about how the individual entered the house – not withstanding the discussion about whether the lock on the back door was... there's considerable controversy.
There's no sign of forced entry. If the door was locked then, *most* of these girls that went in and out of that house that evening... that door was locked. Now, one might have found it open. There was some discussion about it sticking open, but...

HA: Did they allow the delivery of food in there?

TB: I don't know. I mean, I don't know. I imagine they had to deliver food.

HA: I mean, if they called the Pizza Hut, would somebody come over with a pizza?

TB: Oh, yeah. They had those things running around all over.

HA: There are all sorts of ways for a man to get in.

TB: Yeah, but there's nothing to support that. So either it was an *absolute* shot in the dark (long pause), a totally chance occurrence, or it was a highly planned thing. And it does not sound like it was a highly planned, uh, attack. But the fact still remains, there's some question about how the person got in there.

It would take *some* thought. Somebody *knew* the door was sticking. Somebody knew the combinations, was in the house and stayed, didn't leave.

HA: Don't you think that was the more obvious of the alternatives?

TB: What?

HA: That somebody was in the house earlier and stayed?

TB: All the girls swore they didn't give the combination away, so it's... there's nothing to support it, that somebody was in the house. We assume, well, we're led to believe that they had interrogated everyone who lived in the house at the time. But they didn't come up with a strong suspect.

That doesn't mean anything, because if somebody was Mr. Clean Jeans, uh, a good sociopath or whatever, you wouldn't suspect him. Or her. Outside of that, I don't... I recall the houseboy's saying something about that was *his* favorite theory. In fact, a couple of the houseboys and one or two of the girls said they thought there were any number of places a person could've hidden in the sorority house.

But it's the gaining the entrance at *any* time... whether it be earlier in the day or whatever. What would be the pretense and what would be the point of entry?

HA: You tell me. He'd have had to know the name of somebody in that house. Or would he have just met somebody from the house who gave him important information – about the door or habits of some of the girls?

TB: (We've observed) the planning of the attacks was not all that much planned.

HA: A lot of people hung out in that bar nearby. It would have been fairly easy to find out the names of some of the Chi Omega women.

TB: Sure.

HA: It's like knocking on the door when you're a burglar. If nobody comes, you go on in – if you think nobody's home. If somebody comes to the door, you ask for somebody else.

TB: Hmmm.

HA: Would it be something like that?

TB: Yeah, except when somebody comes to the door... you knock and somebody comes, they'd have remembered that individual.

HA: Yeah.

TB: Yeah... and yet these attacks occurred early in the morning, so anyone who... He was not seen knocking at the door at two or three in the morning. That doesn't work, because it's clear the girls were attacked in their beds.

HA: Would this man be adept in finding out information by telephone? You can find out most anything by that telephone.

TB: Oh, you're right there.

HA: Would he have that ability?

TB: Not that I know of.

HA: You could call a sorority house and find out who's out with whom, who's gone and where, who's home, who's in, and anything else. I'm just trying to figure it out.

TB (laughs): I *know* you are!

HA: Maybe he just met a girl at the bar next door and was rebuffed by her... and when she left, she went home – to the Chi Omega house. And maybe he followed her. Maybe he was, as you indicated he often was, under the influence of alcohol. Was somewhat out of control. How does this scenario strike you?

TB (laughs): You're working... but...

HA: Well, okay, the M.O.s are different. What does that say to you? Why would it be different? Give me a couple good reasons why you think it would be different.

TB: Different person (laughs). Well, I mean there, probably there are hundreds of cases every year, coast to coast, that fit the M.O. of a young woman found nude, beaten, and, uh, sexually violated, along a deserted highway. Uh, that doesn't mean that they're all committed by the same person.

So what you're trying to do – what you're wondering – is how can we apply this hypothetical personality type to the facts of the Chi Omega case, and in what way would we have to alter that, uh, personality type to similarly explain it... to account for the manner in which the crimes were committed?

HA: Well, we're talking about *no* possession – but, actually, it *was* a kind of possession. Certainly during the act of killing there's possession, brief though it may be. This man couldn't *always* take 'em home. I would assume that's the ultimate possession, to kill someone.

TB: Well, we saw that, initially, the killing was not possession. It was the cover-up, the, uh, although it may have had some other significance. It seemed, though, that the primary purpose, one at least we picked or would suggest, was that of eliminating a key, if not *the* key, witness. Now, both of these girls were, in all likelihood, killed in their sleep, so it was not the witness factor.

HA: Do you think this was definitely an aberrant situation?

TB: We would have to – with this personality type we would have to conclude that it was very clearly an ex-... *extreme* aberration, a change of character, a change of [long pause]...

HA: Is there something in Chi Omega we're not seeing? That I'm not seeing? Because there *are* resemblances to the other killings. They were young girls, alone in their place, asleep. They were certainly possessed, if only briefly.

TB: Well, the two girls who were beaten but not killed weren't alone. They were with each other. Matter of fact, every girl in the house was alone. Despite the fact she was alone in her own bed. Most of the rooms had two occupants. The two girls who were killed were alone at the time, but the other two were both in their beds. They were both in their rooms at the same time but were in their beds.

It could be… an aberration, caused by a great deal of pent-up frustration… of rage or whatever. It's, it's… it varied at points.

HA: Frustration. Rage. The pressures of the moment. Sometimes sorority girls can be quite snobbish. When people aren't too gregarious or sure of themselves, sometimes people get hurt… or extremely angry. Could this man have been insulted, put down, or ridiculed by one or more of the girls in that sorority house?

TB: Could be. Uh [long pause]…

HA: This crime almost seems like somebody was getting even for something – the extreme rage. Do you understand what I mean? More of a revenge-type murder than the others. Do you see the possibility that there was some *contact* between the murderer and these girls before the crimes?

TB: You mean, other than the victims?

HA: Yeah.

TB: Well, I think that's *possible* but unlikely, for no other reason than, if we assume the victims weren't the ones who did it, but somehow the perpetrator focused on that house, then we'd expect his approach to be more well thought out and planned. Uh, because obviously it would seem to me that not just *anybody* can walk up and get into a sorority house with forty occupancy... and do what was done there.

HA: So, you think he planned it [for] quite some time.

TB: Well, I do, and I don't. The method of the murders suggests that, uh, they *weren't* planned out. The method, the entry, suggests that *something* was known about the sorority house. If, for example, had one of the girls, among those killed or beaten, in fact, insulted him or something... then he might've had a lot of knowledge of the layout of the house – and the exact location of the room of the intended victim. That would have been possible, but *only* if he had a great deal of knowledge about the house. You only have to sit back and envision how difficult a complete stranger or a workman or something like that would have had it that night.

HA: How do you think he got in?

TB: Well (long pause)... all the evidence points to the back door. But how he got in the back door? The, uh, pieces of bark on the carpet, which could've been easily tracked in. However, there's a possibility the door may have been, uh, stuck open, although most of the evidence that night found it to be locked (pause). I'm having difficulty getting into the Chi Omega case myself. It's the, uh… it's 'cause it is… it's not unique, it's just… it's on appeal and I'm *here* and principally because of that case. And, uh, that's kinda poor.

I don't know how to approach the case and speculate about it extensively without in some way jeopardizing the appeal or a retrial or whatever. I mean, a lot is known about it, okay? And a lot can be inferred – if that's your desire – from what's known about that case. All the facts of the case and what's known about my, uh, living situation, uh, my activities during that period.

HA: Okay, let's veer off. Let's talk about something you're familiar with elsewhere, the Caryn Campbell case. Most people think the evidence there was very, very slim. There was no real eyewitness. Let's talk about how… What do you think happened in the Campbell case? How would a man like this… Would he approach her as she was going up to her room and talk to her… represent that you were a police officer and ask her where she was going? What? What? How would you do that?

TB: She had left her… the people she was with… had just returned from dinner with… and gone up in the elevator and was seen by another group of people who were attending the same, uh, uh, convention. It was… the elevator was not… was not far from where her room was – and something happened in a very short space of time. A very short, uh, physical space.

It is considered highly unlikely that she – I've seen the layout of the lodge and diagrams and what not – and it would seem unlikely that (she) would have been attacked or *physically* dragged away under those circumstances. Or was carried away or harmed. So it would seem that she met her attacker and went somewhere with him.

HA: Do you think she was told he was a police officer and needed her for something? His car was broken down, or...

TB: The problem there would be, first of all, according to her fiancé, the room was untampered with and they didn't have a car, so you wouldn't expect that the ruse that was used in the DaRonch case or one like it was used in the Campbell case. She didn't have a car, so he couldn't say, "Your car is stolen." If he had told her her car had been broken into, and she was a couple doors away from it, you know, she would have probably expected or wanted to look at it.

And in the course of getting her magazine, she never got the magazine. Her fiancé and his children were... she'd just left them, so she wouldn't believe the story that they'd been injured or in trouble with the police, so, uh, it *sounds* like the situation as we see it doesn't lend itself to that kind of approach.

HA: So you think it's more likely it was just a plain old man-woman approach.

TB: Uh, that doesn't sound likely, either. You know, there's a suggestion that she and her fiancé weren't getting along well. I say "not getting along well." I mean "not getting along right at that time."

HA: It was somewhat strained, I've heard.

TB: Somewhat strained. Those things happen. It does. It would not *appear* that she would up and... was the kind of person who would run off with someone, especially. That doesn't make sense either.

HA: Where does that leave us? With the old arm in a sling routine? Or a broken leg?

TB: It leaves us probably with as many imaginative approaches as you can think of to get somebody's attention, in, uh, gaining their assistance. The guy, whoever, could have feigned a heart attack or something... feigning illness. Asked for her assistance to get him to a hospital, or *anything*.

HA: But she didn't have a car. Could he have used *his* car?

TB: Or to get back to his... get back to his, uh, uh, whatcha-callit, his room. To help him to his room or help him to his car. To some place where he would have her alone.

HA: Would he have a room?

TB: It's not unlikely. I suppose they tried to check out everybody, but my recollection was that there were a few, uh, "anonymous types" whose names they couldn't follow up on. But I'm not absolutely sure of that. And my understanding, also, is that the police checked all registrations of hotels in the area – motels where a single individual was, uh, was staying. But what's interesting there is that it would seem that if a man was going to abduct a woman and take her to his room without being spotted, he would register for *two* people.

HA: That sounds logical.

TB: Perhaps that's a defect in their law-enforcement techniques.

HA: I see what you mean. It would also seem that if they had a suspect, they would check the handwriting on the room applications.

TB: That's true, assuming the person could write with only one hand. You can get locked into a lot of things sometimes. That's... that's what... is often the difference between success and failure. Sometimes people... we assume too much. We assume, again, patterns and routines. We don't assume, you know, the extraordinary case – the unusual case.

HA: Getting back... you described in some detail how it *all* began suddenly. It was months before the next time... then fewer months, then three weeks – until the demand became insatiable.

TB: Hmmm.

HA: How many people would this man kill? How many would you guess? Don't look at me that way. One digit or two? I'll hold up my fingers. I'll play (Norman) Chapman, (a north Florida policeman who interviewed Bundy just after his final arrest). He even got three, didn't he?

TB: Well, he got *to* three. I was waiting until he got to four before I nodded.

HA: Did you nod at three?

TB: I nodded three. I thought that was outrageous enough. Uh, no, uh... what's the digit? Oh, it's... I don't know (sighs, pauses), uh...

HA: Do you want me to turn off the machine?

TB: No, uh, the machine doesn't bother me as much as...
we're talking about a personality type, not a person. Who knows
how many persons there are like this... how many people they
kill. They've killed too many.

HA: But how many do you suppose he'd kill before he got
caught?

TB (laugh): Ummm...

HA: You've said you want this book to be pretty damn
accurate, haven't you? Without your having to...

TB: I want it to be. I want it to be informative. I want it to
be, uh...

HA: You also want people to pay attention to it – and so
I've got to get into this – and you've got to understand this. It's
sad, but...

TB: Yeah, but I think it's safe to... whatever the police say;
it doesn't make any difference. Uh (long pause), the importance
to me of this book is not how many, but...

(A prison employee walks by, carrying a sports referee's
striped jacket. Bundy mentions that he once officiated a
basketball game. Hugh allows that he had also been a referee,
professionally. The subject of victims is brought up again.)

TB: There's a certain amount of pressure on you to make the call. You're looking... you're there, and you obviously don't treat it like a lark. You won't sit down in the middle of the action, have a Coca Cola, and chat with the guys on the sideline. You've got a *job* to do and you're involved in it. And, depending on the different kind of game it is, you might depend on just how important your role is, uh, for a person who, who's...

For a person who's *committed*, uh, fifty or one hundred murders, uh, perhaps he'd view his role as being serious – that he had an important... or he attached some significance to it. But maybe not any more than you would attach to refereeing an important football or basketball game.

And I tried to make this clear when we were talking about the hunter, uh, somebody's going hunting. I mean, uh, at *each* stage of that process, the individual's feelings would be different.

And when he's fifteen. I mean, it'd be a much more mystical, exciting, intense, overwhelming experience... than when he's fifty. And when – even within that given hunting expedition – the feeling of sighting the animal would be different than shooting it or showing it to your buddy. Or putting it in the trunk and taking it home and butchering it and having it for dinner.

At each stage, there's a different set of emotions involved. And it's not to say that deer hunting may not be commonplace to some people, but some might say, "Oh God, it's hunting season again," and pick up the gun and go out with the kids.

And that's the way some guys may approach killing their fellow human beings. It's hard... I find it... to *accept* that.

HA: I don't know if it's hard to accept, but it's hard to understand. I guess – unless you've been in that position.

TB: How does a person... how does a soldier deal with war?

HA: Well, he has the justification built in, you see, there.

TB: So does the mass murderer.

HA: Really?

TB: The justification's built in, at least it would... that's one way to approach it.

HA: Could you expand on that a bit, because I *don't*...

TB: I'm trying to find some illustration that helps you.

HA: I think war would be a better example than refereeing sports.

TB: Well, I mean it's a different... it's more to the point.

HA: Now, you say the justification is built in. *What* justification is built in to kill another human being? For your own enjoyment? That's what it amounts to. What justification? You can't say, "Well, they deserved to die. They're not very nice people. I need this feeling." I just don't understand.

TB: Sure. Well, like *any* justification of that sort, let's consider the justification of a soldier who develops... "rationalization" is the word... that you'd develop to cope with shooting large numbers of his fellow human beings that he didn't know.

Well, first of all, he didn't know 'em. So what! In the urban masses... in our urban society, we don't know a whole lot of people, so, uh, uh, uh... now I suppose there's also (the rationalization) "He would have gotten me if I hadn't gotten him." Which might not fit into what we've got here, but on the other hand, uh, there might be some mass murderers who might say, "Well, she or he would have *hurt* if I hadn't hurt *them*." And they might also say, "Well, there's so many people, they won't be missed."

So what's one less? What's one less person on the face of the planet? What difference will it make a hundred years from now? Again, they are rationalizations, but not rational; justifications but not just.

That could apply to any number of different things, but it also applies to the persons who are able... who are trying to *cope* with their need to kill. They're not coping with what's really driving them to do that. Mainly, they don't *know* what it is. They can't see it. They don't want to see it – so they come up with those and other justifications.

And again, we're just throwing up any number of things to try to make some sense out of it... and I'd say... the victim was *luring* them or trying to arouse them, uh, in some way. They *deserved* it, you know, or, uh, all sorts of things like that. It's a common excuse on the part of child molesters, rapists, and the like, that, uh, that they would say that the victim lured them on or was trying to excite them or arouse them, when, in fact, that was probably not the case. But that's just the justification used to, uh, make some sense out of his crime.

HA: But that justification: Is that only before, or is it evident afterwards also?

TB: I would expect it to continue. Just as it is for the soldier in the field. Now clearly, as we know, the soldier in the field comes home, and some men are scarred psychologically because they're trying to *deal* with this. Many just never deal with it. I would venture that not everybody who came back from World War II or Korea or Vietnam is a basket case... because they just kind of – most of them – put it to rest over there.

Hey, I had a job to do! I *did* it. I mean, I didn't know those people. We don't find American tourists going over to Germany and shooting German men working in the field anymore, because... uh, the surface justification for that is no longer there. It's a very curious way of dealing with it, but...

(After a break for lunch, where Bundy scarfed down three ham and cheese sandwiches from the "store," the interview is resumed where it had broken off.)

HA: Where were we? Oh yes, we were discussing justifications.

TB: How would a person who was considered *partially* sane and had subscribed to society's norm – uh, rules, ethics, and morals, at least on the surface and probably deeper than that – I mean, how in the world could he live with the knowledge he has, somewhere inside his brain? That he *kills!* How do you deal with that? How do you cope with it? How do you square it with how other things are? With the way he is *supposed* to behave? With the way the rest of the people behave?

And you have got to come up with *some* justification. The guy isn't going to say, "Well, I'm a weak, sick human being." I mean, that's not justification for a person who doesn't want to perceive himself to be sick, a weak human being and one who has a maladaptive behavior. He's got to come up with *something* that is a little bit, uh, uh, less incriminating than that.

HA: But the more intelligent a person is, doesn't that make it harder to justify?

TB: No, it would be easier!

HA: Why?

TB: Because it would be easier to construct a more elaborate, uh…

HA: More imaginative?

TB: More imaginative, more elaborate, more free, uh, justification.

HA: But how long does this justification last? When he examines his behavior later on and he talks about it later, does this hold up?

TB: Certainly not, but (laughs)… that's not the point. We're talking now about… we're *both* looking at a person from the top of the mountain – in the clear, cold light of the morning. We're saying, you know, this guy's really not thinking clearly. We see how this thing is developing. We see what went wrong. Why didn't he realize this? Because he *didn't* realize. He didn't have time; the rat-race, so to speak.

Uh, he probably couldn't... certainly you can't... we cannot sit here and neither one of us are going to say that a person like this is justified in killing... in, in... we can't say "indiscriminately" because there was a certain amount of discrimination involved apparently, but justified, in killing young women because he said to himself, "Well, we're already suffering from a population problem."

Or they're trying to lure him, or, uh, uh, they deserve it... or any of these other things. It's totally absurd. We know it's not right. We know it's not reasonable or logical or justifiable. And yet, we have to, uh, by definition, this person's behavior was not grounded in serious self-examination. Nor was it rational.

If it had been rational, if *he'd* been rational, he would have realized what was generating, what was, uh... He may have looked at himself or had, uh, sought out somebody else to help him look at himself – and to find out what was actually the cause of his problem.

HA: But this individual... you said he *probably* thought he had dealt with this himself and had licked this situation. I recall one time you discussed the case of the woman in the orchard, where he *thought* he had whipped his urge to kill and was just going to rape the girl. And he accidentally murdered her.

TB: Hmmm. Hmmm.

HA: In dealing with this kind of thing, he's trying to perfect it by himself. These justifications must have been examined in great detail. And at some point, (they) must have been recognized for what they were... or he would probably have not moved ahead to try to correct it. Is that probable?

TB: Well, yeah – examining it in great detail. Let me see if I can come up with an analogy. It's like trying to examine what's in the medicine cabinet by, in great detail, examining what's in the mirror. Uh, he wasn't seeing through, perhaps, the morass of justifications and obfuscations that he'd created and indulged in – and what he was closely examining was the reflection in the mirror, not what was behind it. Not what was really going on. Uh, does that help at all?

And so, with that principal shortcoming in mind, he was... well, on the one hand he thought he'd looked at the *problem* and dealt with it. He had. But he was just sort of a... I hate to use the phrase "time bomb" because it's so frequently used, but he was just ticking away. Where he was just a problem looking for an opportunity, not looking *for* it, but, I mean...

HA: If he had the insights and the hindsight that you enjoy now, would he continue doing this sort of thing? If he had the ability, as you have, to examine this behavior, would he still be likely to kill and kill nevertheless?

TB: Well, obviously it's... I don't care if a man is a raving maniac. Let's start over. You're talking about a man who has a type of (long pause) what will we call it... "personality disorder"? I *still* don't know what in the world to call it. But if this person of maladaptive behavior – this part of him that is compulsive and uncontrollable – had the ability to truly look into himself, he'd recognize what it was that was causing him to think and act the way he was (long pause)... and *if* he was able to control, isolate, and identify those things about himself that gave rise, as it were, to this weakness (pause), I think there would be a high degree of likelihood that he would no longer engage in this kind of behavior.

Of course, we have to put out there any number of stipulations. We have to assume that this isn't a disorder of biochemical origin, uh, underpinnings.

HA: Or, as you also suggested, possibly genetic.

TB: Or genetic, or *something*. With the individual we're talking about, it's hard to say, although it appeared to be one of these environmentally based conditions, an aberration, as it were, almost. It's, uh, it almost has a foundation – and the interaction between the organism and environment, which could conceivably be reversed if we knew *what* the stimuli was in the environment that was arousing the organism – the human being – in the man's mind. *That*, of course, is the big test.

Now, behavior modification: I am very familiar with it and I'm *not* familiar with some of the other ones, like group therapy, individual therapy – there are a variety of them.

Ostensibly, there are probably as many effective therapies as there are effective therapists. And the same therapy could not be used by another therapist. At any rate, I didn't mean to come across like behavior modification was the end-all answer to all human problems. It's one I'm familiar with and it's applicable to a variety of disorders. It's no panacea. I was just using it to cite an example of how one could attempt to go about treating somebody for this kind of disorder.

HA: This individual, this killer… would vary his M.O.s as he became more adept, as he became more knowledgeable of what it took. How *much* variance would there be? You've said that in most cases, he liked to take the victims home, and, if possible, keep them as long as possible… reasonably possible. Now, this must have been damn hard to do. If the man had a full-time job… if he ever had any drop-by friends. It would seem almost impossible.

How often would he do this? And would it last for several days?

TB: What I said, was… that in those situations where he couldn't do it, he didn't do it. We've used our knowledge of facts and circumstances surrounding the cases in the northwest – some of them – to try to come up with an answer to that. And we really don't know for *sure*. We just don't know.

HA: But it was the *desired* thing! And whenever it could happen, it probably did. When all this was going on in this man's life, was there any struggle to try to *not* do this? Was there any attempt, say, to have a girlfriend that this person would go to, to try to keep himself somewhat level? Would he have a normal sex life with one or more ladies?

TB: Oh, surely. Again, I mean… we can see that this kind of person, *because* one of the primary reasons he did this… uh, committed the murders… was a search for a release of stress or feelings of low esteem or anger, hostility, resentment, whatever. It was channeled for some reason toward women. Young women – and in a particular way.

That does not mean that what he was suffering from was, in fact, a sexual problem or that he hated women. Uh (long pause), so we could expect that he had normal sexual relationships with, with a woman or with women – which would not be interfered with in any way with the other conduct. He wouldn't let it interfere.

HA: Is there other stimuli that might, like alcohol – extreme alcohol use – get the roles mixed up, causing him to actually try to murder one of the girls with whom he is having a "normal" relationship sexually?

TB: Anything's possible, and we'd expect that... well, boyfriends murder girlfriends all the time – and they're not mass murderers. So we'd expect that even in a fit of rage, that, uh, it might be possible for him to kill a girlfriend, but it would *not*, in all likelihood, be related to his other problem.

You see what I'm saying? Uh, but more likely than not, as we've witnessed the development of this darker side of this person's life, we'd expect to see how very closely controlled and separated this part of him became, and how he was able to keep it, uh, more or less, *from* those around him who thought he was normal. And because this separation was so distinct and well maintained, we would find it unlikely (that) the roles could get confused.

HA: This person, we assume, may be more clever than many of those who try to find and stop him. Would he ever have the urge to leave clues or toy with the police... write letters or something like that?

TB: Well, we're talking about – it's hard to say whether this person was, in fact, more clever than the police. And it's not necessarily so – talking in general terms now – that criminals that get away with lots of crimes are smarter than the police.

The *police* are actually at a grave disadvantage in trying to solve *any* crime, especially one that has been fairly well planned out and where the criminal is as conscious of what constitutes evidence and what doesn't and tries to minimize or totally eliminate traces of evidence.

A policeman could have an IQ of 200, or 180 and still not catch a knowledgeable criminal with an ordinary IQ of 100. It's just that the police are at a... How in the world, do you solve these crimes – I mean, unless you're some kind of incredible clairvoyant – if there's no evidence? It doesn't mean the cops are dumb.

It just means they don't have the tools. And they can't anticipate the crime. They can't – if the evidence isn't there, there's no way they... I wanted to use the word "manufacture"... it. They certainly *can* manufacture it, but only after they have a suspect.

Law enforcement – the solution of crimes – is, in my opinion at least, a random kind of thing. It's almost by accident. The way most criminals catch themselves is because they don't plan things out and they act impulsively. The police are just there to apprehend the criminal who has already caught himself.

There are some things that can be done to prevent crime, but by and large society is extremely vulnerable. Absent the police state, there's very little (the cops) can do. No matter *how* many police cars they have and how much and how sophisticated their equipment and how big their computers.

Now, as to whether or not this fellow would leave clues or write letters, I don't think so. This person did not want to get caught or take any chances to get caught. So why? Leaving even false clues is a problem. A false clue might turn out, somehow, almost by chance, to lead the police in the *right* direction. So *no* clues are better than false clues.

HA: But he has thought about leaving false clues, hasn't he?

TB: I can't imagine any person planning a crime not thinking a little bit about false clues, misleading the cops. If they're thinking about *clues*... about evidence.

HA: What about clothes? Where are all those clothes?

TB: What clothes?

HA: The clothes from the victims who were found without clothes.

TB: Oh, I see.

HA: C'mon now, Ted, do you think I think you didn't understand? Many of these girls were found without clothes. Predators might have destroyed some of the remains, but what about the clothes?

TB: Hmmm. Well, I couldn't tell you. He could have had a clothing fetish or something. But we've postulated... we've created the model of a criminal who, uh... whose prime interest was not leaving clues. So, on the one hand, he wouldn't expect to take the clothes and keep them, because that constituted evidence.

On the other hand, we wouldn't expect him to leave clothing with the victims, because clothing has... is, a collector of trace materials. So I assume he burned the clothing or threw it away.

HA: Probably whatever was expeditious at the time – to make damn sure it wasn't *there*. Would he ever have a reason, ever, to let someone know where some of the bodies of the victims were? To "account" for them? If they couldn't be traced back to him?

TB (long pause): Well, my understanding is that several... I don't know how many – "several" is the only term I could use to describe the number – several persons still missing in the northwest... and in Utah... pretty much prove that he didn't tell or show anybody.

HA: Now let's delve into an area that makes you cringe every time I get close – the numbers. When Stephen and I get this book moving – and it should be soon now – we have to deal in a straightforward way with the enormity of this crime. We are writing about Ted Bundy primarily; and though *honestly* we cannot say you killed twenty, thirty, or fifty girls, we have to have some kind of reference point to work from.

You told me your story was more important than the Boston Strangler's. Unless you give us something to explain the numbers – and thus, the relative importance – I cannot see your logic. He killed, how many? Thirteen? What makes you so important? A guy who stole credit cards and cars and says he didn't kill anybody.

If you sincerely want this book to be of some value, we've got to know what kind of a league we're playing in here. I know, generally, what you've done, but maybe I only know a third of it. We're not going to quote you; I realize that legally you have appeals that may last several more years, but...

TB (ignoring again the intentional use of the pronoun "you"): People who read this book will get some insight into how a particular kind of mentality that contributed to a multiple – may be responsible for a multiple-murder situation. They'll see how he got to *think* that way... and what makes... what factors in our society facilitate this kind of behavior.

And what is it about the human mind that makes this kind of behavior... to, to... carry it out – and if there's anything that can be done to reduce the possibility of a person who'd been predispositioned to this kind of behavior, uh, of actually engaging in it...

Now, as far as facts, figures, body counts that's *absolutely* the furthest thing from my mind. I realize, uh, the interest you've attached to it.

HA: And the interest of the reader.

TB: And the reader, oh sure. I agree, but what can I say?

HA: Well, we'd like to be able to be as correct as possible. Realistically, we're going to have to say *something* about the numbers that have been bandied about.

TB: Well then, you're going to have to... I, I think... I'm fairly sure that with the information you have at your disposal and the understanding you have about how the mind we're talking about works, you can separate the wheat from the chaff and come up with an accurate figure.

I'm not going to commit myself on that. It's an impossibility. Well, what we might do is... you bring me the names, dates, and places of all the alleged victims... (long pause). And that won't work because they are attributed to me and I'm not going to sit here and say which ones are, probably are, and which ones aren't (laughs). That isn't going to get me anywhere.

On the other hand, I'm not going to *strain* this fiction to the limit, saying, "Well, the person like the one we're talking about is probably responsible for X number." I mean, how can a "personality type" be responsible for murder? That's impossible. I mean, it's just illustrative of a class of people.

HA: Then from another direction... this type person... there's a possibility, I presume, that he has killed others that, so far, have not been discovered.

TB: Probably. That's a distinct possibility – because of the movability, the freedom people have, the hitchhiking, so, uh... I just hate to...

You can go as high as you want. The higher the number, the better. The more *horrified* people will be. The more they will read and the more interested they'll be in finding out what makes a person like this tick. And the more they pay attention. If you're truly interested in pointing out the facets in society that are concerned with this, then you... you make it up.

I'm not going to do it. I can't, you know, not... But you can. I don't know how you're going to try to do it, but you can sit there and go through it somehow – the list. This does and that doesn't, you know. I've never seen the names, photographs, and data on thirty-six, forty-two – whatever it is the respective police agencies are talking about.

When people come to me and say, "What about the Washington cases?" how many Washington cases are they talking about? I don't know. They're talking about Healy and Ball – I don't know how many others. And the Utah ones – and

Campbell? These are the ones that always tend to be associated with me… I don't know.

But I *can* figure the description, how the man operates, the M.O., planning, the strict need for secrecy, and so on. For every one that's *publicized*, there could be one that was not. It *could* be. Thousands of people are reported missing and are never heard from again.

HA: Would you remember… you say you can fill in the needed holes of motivation, planning, and detailed M.O… would you recall every one, publicized or not?

TB: Speaking of this *entity*, despite your eager phraseology, I imagine every one would stand out for some reason – perhaps, uh, oh, most certainly, for *different* reasons. As for myself, I remember everything I have ever done, right down to the nth degree!

HA: I don't have a firm feel for what kind of *release*, what kind of need, what kind of gratification is expected. Can you give me an idea of the expectations? Now, I realize that this is not rational… it is still something that can be stated.

TB (lengthy pause): Well, I don't know how to say it any more clearly than I've tried before. I mean, it doesn't…

HA: When you go out on a date, say, you go to a ball game, you know what to expect. If you go to a party, you know what to expect – usually. You plan to have sex, or you *have* sex, and you know pretty well what to expect. Well now, while his…

TB: What do *you* expect?

HA: Well, I mean, you know…

TB (laughing): I don't either.

HA: Well, you expect a *nice* feeling. You go somewhere where you're alone with a girl. You expect to give and receive pleasure… have a climax… after which you feel greatly relieved. You feel tender. You know. You know; you've had normal sex.

Uh, sometimes the factors are not right – things are not right – and it isn't as enjoyable. But what I'm asking: What would this person expect? What kind of feeling? What would he expect to *do?* That's what I don't understand.

TB: Well, I don't know… but I can, you know, speculate. They're all very difficult. I mean, when you get down to a certain level of trying to understand why people behave the way they do, there's just no explanation.

Now, why do people watch baseball games? It's a *stupid* thing, you know, watching somebody hit a ball and run around a diamond. But *why* do people watch that? What complicated explanation – knowing that *any* explanation at this level trying to explain human nature is not going to be totally understandable to everyone.

We can only say again, as I've said before, I believe that in the beginning – the act of killing – we would *not* expect it to be the goal. Remember, it was the *possession* of this desired thing, which was, in itself – the very act of assuming possession was a very antisocial act – was giving expression to this person's need to *seize* something that was... uh, uh, highly valued, at least on the surface, by society. Uh, sought after, uh, a material possession, as it were.

I mean, had he been raised in a different background, maybe he would have taken to, uh, stealing Porches and Rolls-Royces. As we said, the *killing* was probably as much of a necessity as it was a part of the attempt to gratify... the urge he had. The necessity of covering... of removing the witness.

HA: Well, that's partly what I meant. Further, I can understand wanting something that seems unattainable. But I'm trying to understand how you *feel*. Is this something that is always carried around? Or is it something that only comes up via some stimulus?

TB: When people have – are – unable to cope with some part of their life, the feelings of discontent, loneliness, alien-ation, self-esteem, or whatever it is, they usually attribute their state of mind to one degree or another to society at large. And they finally choose some way of venting what they have inside.

Or suppressing what they feel. I suppose they're either making an affirmative statement or they're just striking out blindly – and really didn't have an individual style. But you're right, you're right, it's... there is *not* that fulfillment there. I'm not saying there is. I've *never* said that!

HA: That's true.

TB: I've said over and over that there was this need to satiate the urge to possess in this particular fashion. These kinds of victims would drive this kind of individual *on*, hoping or looking for the pot of gold at the end of the rainbow kind of thing.

HA: But I guess what I was getting to, also, Ted, was that, in essence, we're saying that this person was "showing" society – that is, taking something that society valued.

TB: Uh huh, right.

HA: Well, surely Lee Harvey Oswald felt that way to some extent in killing President Kennedy, striking out at society, killing a beloved leader. But there's more of a sexual thing to a man who goes around killing young ladies. Uh, why not kill the Pope? Or the President? Or somebody like that?

TB (laughs): That's what I've been telling you! There's no *reason* why. It's just that you have an incident looking for a place to happen. There's no reason why. Nobody... there's no... that's where we err when we try to analyze human behavior. We cannot explain it. We can't explain every facet of it.

At some point we act the way we do because of the stimuli we're exposed to and the environment we live in. There's no one else in the history of this planet or living on the face of this earth who has seen and heard *exactly*, and felt exactly, the way *you* have or the way I have. And for that very reason, we can only predict, in gross ways, how people are going to respond. That's exactly what this, why this happens.

Why would somebody strike out in this way and not *that* way? Why wouldn't they go talk to their mother or a therapist or a girlfriend to try to find some resolutions? Why, why, why? You get to a point where you can't... there's just no answer to the question.

It just happened. It was *there*. You had a person, a type of individual who was not coping with some things. The natural tendency would be to express them, to release them in some way to try to resolve this conflict, this tremendous discomfort. And then... it certainly wasn't... we can't say that anyone has it programmed in his genetic material that he's going to sit down and read the newspaper and be affected by stories about violent crime.

Or it probably isn't part of our genetic makeup that pornography shops down in a particular part of town beckon. And individuals may go down there to see the, uh, those kinds of things. These *chance* happenings, those *offerings* that are out there in the environment. We can't say what... we can't say why a person might find them, in most cases, very attractive. He just does.

HA: I just looked at a few of my notes here and wanted to ask you: Did you or did you not go back to Pennsylvania a few years ago to try to find your father?

TB: I didn't.

HA: Haven't you ever wondered if he's alive?

TB: I've had that. *Sure* I've wondered, but it's not something that lingers on and that I think about much. I'm happy to be alive. My mother has never made the attempt – when I was growing up, never made the attempt to tell me. If she had wanted to, she would have. Since she didn't, I figured she didn't want to and there was good reason for it. It didn't bother me one way or the other. So, uh, it was never a source of any kind of problem.

HA: Aren't you curious?

TB: I couldn't say there's no curiosity, but on the other hand, there's a lot more, there are a lot more things that are more worthy of my curiosity. I mean, he didn't raise me. And I guess my particular view of the world is that, uh, we're probably *95* percent the way we are because of the way we were raised and where we were raised. That whatever genetic material we're carrying along with us, well, you know... It's just too hard to tell. Maybe it would be interesting to know if there was cancer in the family. Or about a rare blood disease. I mean, the way I am and the way I view society didn't emanate from my natural father. It's just not reflected in me in any way – so I'm not looking for anything.

I mean, I certainly wouldn't be looking for him to show him what kind of a person I was going to become, because I'm not going to *be* that kind of person. No way. He contributed absolutely nothing, substantially, to my, uh, development. So it's never been a problem to me.

HA: As I recall, you told Stephen that your mother at one time had volunteered information.

TB: I *believe* that's what she was trying to do. I don't know for sure. I, uh... This was after my arrest in Salt Lake City, back in 1975. I'd been in jail and was out on bond. There had been all kinds of published reports; they had, you know, pried into my background. And it had been the source of some public comment that I was illegitimate, blah, blah, blah.

I'm sure this topic had not been discussed by my mother and I. And so, it was sort of taboo, and I'm not *sure*, but I have

a feeling that even my brothers and sisters weren't made aware
of it – even though they may have, if they thought about how
I could have been their natural brother when my parents were
married when I was four years old. But it, it… we never talked
about it, my brothers and sisters and I.

So anyway, I get out of jail in Utah – and this would be
the first time I had seen my mother since all this publicity had
come out – uh, I can't remember the exact context, but my
mother said… and she had this real *concern* in her voice…
something in her tone indicated to me that she had something
real serious to talk to me about. She wanted us to talk alone.
I was just out of jail, you know, and I was knee deep in a lot
of trouble. I didn't need anything more right then. I didn't… I
didn't… I couldn't…

HA: Why would that have been troublesome?

TB: Well, obviously it was something that had troubled
my mother very deeply, or she would have told me long before
that.

HA: Perhaps it might have helped her to have told you.

TB: It wouldn't help me. I was, I mean, I had a lot to
deal with then. I had, uh, court the next day. I was in a lot of
trouble, and I *still* didn't give a shit. I didn't need any more
burdens. Right then, I had enough to carry. Now, we've seen
each other since then, and if my mother wanted to tell me,
that's fine. But under those circumstances, at that time, no.
The last thing I wanted to think about was any more deep,
dark secrets, problems.

I was fresh out of jail – and had a horror of jail. You just cannot – no one who has not been in there on a serious charge for several months can imagine how hard it is for those first few months. Once you... those first six months... after that, jail doesn't have any more effect on a person.

HA: You mean from a mental aspect?

TB: That's it. I mean, I'm used to jail. After the first six months, jail was no sweat. One of these days the criminal justice system is going to realize that. If you keep a man in prison past a certain point and he learns to adapt to prison, learns how to satisfy most of his needs, then the prisoner, in effect, becomes almost prison-proof. That's why, I think, there are so many recidivists. I don't care how harsh the prison is, past a certain point, incarceration dulls the sensitivities of the individual in such a way that in the future – when he's on the streets prison is less fearful, as a consequence, to criminal behavior.

HA: The inmate doesn't have to make the decisions. He's got safety, food, and doesn't have to fight for it, generally.

TB: It's no longer that horrible, unknown, threatening place. But anyway, getting back to the other thing, that was the occasion I mentioned to Steve... that maybe Mom was going to talk to me about it – and I don't know for sure.

HA: Your uncle, the college music professor... We have discovered that you were very close to him. It seems to me this man represented a sort of culture, sort of a style, a classy man. You were sort of reaching out to him in some way.

TB: Yeah, I mean, there was... I found something inherently attractive and compelling – I don't know what the other word would be, but certainly attractive – about my uncle. His demeanor, his intellect, his culture, and so forth. But, while he is probably our *closest* relative – I mean, one of the closest – I had really never spent a lot of time with Uncle Jack. We'd go out to their place on the Olympic Peninsula from time to time. I'd spend a couple weeks out there in the summertime. But, uh, I greatly admired my Uncle Jack and Aunt Eleanor.

HA: Have you heard from them lately?

TB: They stopped by on the way back from seeing my aunt. When I was in the Leon County jail, they stopped by. But I never... (clears throat) They were always sort of a different (again)... well, they lived in a different society than my parents did.

HA: They lived in a society you wished your parents were in, right?

TB: Well, yeah. I wished *I* was in, sure.

HA: And yet you couldn't quite attain it. You couldn't quite push your way in. You weren't quite *there*.

TB: Well, I was a *kid!* I couldn't pick up and leave home and...

HA: Sure.

TB:… and go off and find that kind of world. I mean, it wasn't feasible. It was impossible. But, uh, certainly I envied my cousin John and the advantages that, uh, *he* had… growing up in that kind of family.

HA: He's your age, isn't he?

TB: A little bit older. A few months older.

HA: Somebody told me when I first started questioning folks that John had always thought you were guilty – and expressed that to the family – and it caused some bad feelings.

TB: He never expressed it to me (laughs)… so for that reason, it doesn't bother me if he felt that way anyway. Again, I've… it wouldn't make any difference if everybody thought I was guilty. I mean, I've just *insulated* myself from that. So what? What's it going to mean to me? I'm in jail. What people think…

HA: It's not going to cost you a hell of a lot more.

TB: What people think of me is not going to do anything more to me. If I had a pin driven into my skin for every person who thought I was guilty, then I might start to worry about it, but I don't feel that way.

June 26

HA: You've never been religious, have you?

TB: Not… certainly not in the conventional sense. Not in a sense that I've envisioned the Bible as divinely inspired and *the* word of God. In the sense that I would attempt to pattern my life after, using principally the guidelines set down. In that sense, I'm not religious. In the sense that (pause) I'm something of a pragmatist when it comes to religion. I'm not a religious person in the sense that I'm a missionary or Bible-thumper or even a person who prays or dwells on Christianity or the existence of God. I'm pragmatic when it comes to organized religion. I think it's a tremendous, stabilizing force – a good force. And the lessons that it teaches, *when* it teaches them successfully… when you get past the hypocrisy… God knows there's a good deal of hypocrisy in practicing Christians, but organized religions are good for the society.

And I recognize that I might belong to a church and I don't look *down* on 'em, most of the religious people, even though I tend to believe a lot of them are terribly hippocratic… or hypocritic(al).

But nevertheless, it's a cohesive factor in the community.

HA: It binds *so* many people together. You've talked to Stephen about the decline of the family. Of course, the church has been the main, cohesive factor in a family. Many build their lives around it.

TB: Yeah, uh, church *does* require, uh, demand a certain amount of mediocrity and nonthought; don't rock the boat, you know. My mother and I used to have, not *bitter* arguments but very serious arguments or discussions in the late '60s and early '70s about the *failure* of the church – our church in Tacoma in particular – to take a stand against the Vietnam war. That was – clearly if anything was contrary to the doctrines of Christianity, or anything in the Old Testament as well, it would be the Vietnam war. I felt there was a glaring failure on the part of organized religion to really practice what it preached, so to speak.

HA: Well, also in the area of racial equality. You'd think that if there is to be racial equality, the church would be the one place to say, "Come, let's do it here!"

But you do believe in a Supreme Being, don't you?

TB: Yeah, well, I believe in a higher power or force, which is above and beyond, perhaps, even our comprehension. The gods of the religions around the world are real in that they represent something that a man reaches out for, that's larger and more powerful than he. Unfortunately, those who do not fully comprehend that power, attempt to create God in man's image and clothe it. Man's urges and desires and passions in God end up being, uh, a *personality*. Which seems totally foreign to reality.

HA: You have a way of deviating around a question if you don't like it. A few days (ago) we started to talk about your future, but, as usual, we wound up a few miles south. So I'm going to begin again, slowly (laughs). How do you characterize yourself? What do you think of Ted Bundy? What are your thoughts about eventually being put to death here?

TB: Okay, well, to the first part, I don't care about the great mass of people out there. I care about people I know and come in contact (with) and how they feel about me. You asked me how I'd describe myself, not how I would *like* myself to be. I mean, if I was to project any image, it'd be the image of what I *am*. And a lot of that... There's no way the essence of me can be communicated through *any* medium, other than through continuous and long contact.

However, if I were to describe myself, okay, or as I perceive myself to be... and not necessarily in order of importance... I would, ummm, I would have to say that I am a person who is *constantly* changing, but not in a state of flux, not in an unstable mold.

HA: What about the news media? You seem to have mixed emotions. You told me a few days ago you figured the news media had *cost* lives in certain kinds of cases. Would you elaborate?

TB: The public has a right to know. It's just a question of *when*. I mean, do they have the right to know facts that may or may not be introduced in the trial? Or may or may not be admissible? Before the trial begins? Does the news media have the right to contaminate the jury pool before trial with evidence that may not be admitted in the trial? Does the defendant, who often does not even go to trial, have the right to see his life produced and reproduced in the newspapers as a result of the access the news media has to the court system? Uh, I think the public has the right to know that a crime has been committed and the name of the victim of the crime. They have the right to know that somebody's been arrested – and the name of the person arrested. That's *all* they have the right to know before trial.

HA: That's similar to the legal-media situation in England.

TB: *Exactly* like in England. The public has a right to be present in the jury room and present in the courtroom. The cameras do not.

HA: Can you sit here and honestly tell me that you didn't play to the cameras in the Chi Omega trial particularly? That you didn't use *every* interview you've ever had to pry out some sort of advantage?

As for how much fact should be released before trial, it sometimes cuts both ways, like most things do in our justice system. For instance, if nothing but the accused's name was released before trial, what would that do to the person who had been unfairly charged with a crime? Haven't you seen cases where the media scrutiny on a case has freed innocent people?

TB: There may be some. I don't know of any.

HA: Well, I could refresh your memory. But it isn't important because you believe that your jury panel might have been tainted in the Leach case because of the fact your Chi Omega trial was televised all over Florida a few months beforehand. And, in that instance, you may, indeed, be right.

Let's examine for a moment how heavy media attention to a case can work in favor of the public. Suppose – we're doing a lot of supposing these days – we have a handsome young man who has allegedly killed three dozen or more young women in five or six different states. Since he's done several in one state... moved on to another and done six or eight more, and on and on, the states themselves didn't pay much attention to this man – didn't even know who he was – until he was captured in still another state. Suddenly there's an avalanche of publicity and people start recalling he was here, there, and over there. Witnesses suddenly appear. Even victims, some of whom got away, come forth.

Now, though this may be somewhat bitter medicine, don't you think that society has been served? And don't you think without the media, this man may have never been put away for good?

TB: Well, the press has the capacity for both good *and* evil.

HA: Agreed. Fully. But let's address the hypothetical I tossed out.

TB: Who's to say this man was really guilty of the three dozen or whatever number you patched together there? Maybe he didn't do them. Then look what harm was inflicted on this human being.

HA: I'll be the first to admit that law enforcement has, from time to time, stacked cases – given a killer credit for more than he's done, lumped a hundred burglaries on a guy who doesn't care because he's going away for life anyway. But I defy you to show me one case in the U.S. – no matter how long ago – where a man charged and convicted of several murders was *really* innocent.

I guess we're not going to get anywhere on this one. You used the press when it suited you: when you were involved in minor cases or in Colorado on what some cops considered a rather weak murder case. But then, when it all fell on top of you – and the press pointed to you like you were an animal – you didn't like it. I can't say I blame you, but frankly, I'd hope they reacted just as strongly in any such case.

What hurt you far more than any press coverage was the fact that you have never, *ever* been able – or, should I say, willing – to reveal where you were on the occasions of the three Florida murders or any number of others in the western states. I've asked you. I've begged you. You get this pout on your face, hunch up your shoulders, and refuse to say anything about alibi. What do you suppose the odds are that somebody suspected in three dozen murders or more has not one – not a *single* one – alibi that he was somewhere other than the crime scene?

TB: Is this an interview where I cooperate with you and Steve to try to explain how all these crimes happened, uh, probably, or is this going to be a crucifixion with Ted on the stake? I think Carole's judgment is correct. I don't think you're interested in the truth or a reasonable approach to digging beneath the surface here. And if you think I enjoy any of this, you are considerably off base, too.

If I want the kind of abuse you're giving me, I can get it, with ease, back on The Row. And probably make somebody happy inflicting it. I don't think you're having such a good time at it. If you want to… uh, find out the truth, Hugh, all you have to do is investigate in some of the cases.

HA: I've done that… And I think you know full well, I've done that. I started out believing that you might be innocent. There's always that chance. And your family and friends – and you – swore that you were. But after a few months of crisscrossing the country, I *know* what you've done. I don't know how many, but I know it's at least more than anyone has claimed.

TB: If you were a lawyer, I'd... No, I'm not about to share with you those salient facts that, uh... I'm just thinking here. Back to that thing you said about the press helping an innocent man: You said you could name some. Let's see if you can come up with something other than the conjecture I've been hearing here this morning. Have you ever helped free an innocent man? You've been a newspaperman for many years.

HA: No, I don't suppose I have, but I've seen numerous occasions. Like the Clay Shaw case of about ten years ago. Shaw walked free after two years and only one ballot by the jury. (And) Gene Miller, an acquaintance of mine on the *Miami Herald*, won, I believe, the Pulitzer Prize for winning the release of a man on Florida's Death Row when he proved him innocent. I don't think you...

TB: Those are completely different kinds of situations. One had all the publicity in the world and the other had virtually, I would assume, no publicity. It's not the case here.

I can see how it's possible for a newspaper to get on such a crusade and rescue someone. They *can* do good. But it's also possible for them, in their zeal to fill column inches and minutes on the evening news, to publicize in a sensational way the criminal justice system – and harm a defendant who has not yet had his day in court. And the harming, I think, is much worse than the occasional time they do something to help an innocent person.

Most defendants aren't harmed by excessive press coverage because the news media can't make their living off the run-of-the-mill burglary. In that case, usually all you have *is* the name of the victim, the accused, and a brief summary of events, right up to the trial. And even then there isn't much reporting done. So most defendants aren't affected.

But in the *hard* cases, where the pressure is on the judge and on the system to perform and the press comes in and creates even more pressure, it multiplies the chance for error.

HA: Well, we got off to a rather rocky start here today and I don't know whether we're going to get productive or not, but I'm going to run my list and tell you what I think. If you want to call it a day, I'll understand.

TB: You haven't touched me. I'm not affected by what you think.

HA: Tell me your thoughts on capital punishment.

TB: Hmmm. Well, we discussed this earlier, uh… Do you have a cigarette? Thanks. It is motivated solely and exclusively by this perceived need of the state, the prosecution, and the victim and his family, to – and in this case, obviously – to obtain revenge. To be fulfilled in that need for revenge, the measure for measure, an eye for an eye. There's nothing more.

It isn't a deterrent. In fact, in one of the books about me it says, "Why did Ted come to Florida?" Of all states, why to the state of Florida? Where they have this death penalty and all these people on Death Row. The inference was made, I recall, that I was *seeking out*, that I was trying to be self-destructive or something. But I've never gone to a state or researched the state's capital punishment laws to determine how many people are on Death Row. I didn't think of Florida in those terms. My opinion is that the law is, the death penalty is, of absolutely no deterrent value – and I think that's supported by recent crime statistics for the state of Florida, which shows that murder is increasing.

HA: Of course – so is the population and so are the complexities in our lives – which drive a lot of us to the brink.

TB: There's no question that it's an effective way of, uh, oh, killing a person who society has adjudged responsible for the crimes. And that's about the only things it does. It does *not*, it will never restore any measure of compensation to the victims' families or to the state. None whatsoever. To the contrary, I think, that one of the factors that contributes to the increase in homicide is the fact that there is capital punishment.

If the state can justify the taking of a life, then an individual can, for whatever twisted rationale. And the state, with all its power and majesty – if it can be reduced to the level of killing – then why shouldn't some individuals take that as justification for engaging in what they might believe is justifiable homicide?

HA: You pose some interesting questions there. Let's look at something else that we have explored before but not intimately enough. This model we're talking about, this entity, have you ever thought or imagined this person having any unusual physical manifestations during the time he was "acting out"? Any strange feelings, smells, noises?

TB: That's a pretty far-out thing there.

HA: Any detachment or mood or anything?

TB: Well, there'd be some fairly *eccentric* reactions. You wouldn't be able to say that this was necessarily something that happened, but I... I don't see any indication whatsoever – with the facts we've been dealing with – that the personality we're dealing with suffered from any of those, uh, symptoms.

HA: Any difference in vision, dizziness, or anything like that?

TB: I suppose that if he took peyote or mushrooms, there might be that reaction, but nothing that one might consider as the, uh, spontaneous kind of internal sensation.

HA: Those are some things that psychopaths have related later in describing...

TB (agitated): We're not dealing with a psychopath or an antisocial personality. We're not dealing with a hollow shell or somebody who is a manipulator, uh, per se.

HA: Well, good, that was what I was leading up to. How do you describe this person? He's *not* a psychopath, you claim. He's not... well, he's certainly antisocial at times.

TB: You define him in operational terms and with as much specificity as you can, but you have to tailor his profile *specific* with, a specific reference to the exact nature of his behavior and the exact nature of the facts of the cases he's charged with – and *not* rely on stereotypes. They're grossly inaccurate.

HA: But there *are* some characteristics that we've seen develop in this personality that *do* fit some stereotypes, aren't there?

TB: They do. And they are also incongruous to the same stereotypes in other respects. You don't use the labels, you don't… you can't adopt whole the models we've developed from other studies. You have to approach each individual on a case-to-case basis, maybe gaining some insight from other case studies, but you have to test out those insights to see if they apply.

You just can't apply them blindly and you almost have to experiment with them. "Does this apply? Or doesn't this?" You have to be critical in examining the application of this systemology. It doesn't necessarily apply because this person fits into the general behavioral pattern.

The best definition for these kinds of… of this kind of deviant behavior is an operational definition. In other words, the behavior of the individual in his perceived mental state defines what he is, not some textbook label. We can extract a *lot* of things from that in general lives and hopefully avoid, uh, hopefully gain some insight so it's possible to help others avoid engaging in this type of deviant behavior in the future. Admittedly, it's only a very… a shotgun approach, a generalized application.

HA: You think that if somebody like this picks up this book – and we've been able to explain it properly – it might save somebody from *becoming* like this? Is that what you're saying?

TB: It's possible, but I… I don't think reading the book – I don't care how much insight we could give into the type of person who is capable of committing these kinds of crimes; it doesn't matter how *accurately* we present it – if we were able to present *everything* with a high degree of accuracy and clarity, uh, the mere appreciation for the, uh, mental state of this kind of individual alone is not going to change things. The problems are societal in nature.

They go beyond the individual. They go beyond *any* individual. The things that can be done to prevent persons from engaging in homicidal behavior on a massive scale are things which society has to correct on a massive scale. Not to say that the individual is totally not responsible for that type of behavior, but I doubt you could show a book like this to a – if you could find one – a budding mass murderer, and it would change him. (He is not susceptible to) a rational analysis of his problem.

HA: That's the key right there, isn't it?

TB: However, if society were able to restrict or otherwise eliminate the environmental stimuli that provoke or other-wise create this kind of individual, or the mores that contribute to his behavior, then it would go a long way toward eliminating that kind of behavior.

October 11

Bundy has had several months to reflect on two proposals. One is that he consider confessing everything, in detail, in the first person, to the police. If he is ready to do so, Hugh has offered to act as an intermediary with Florida governor Bob Graham, who could then decide for himself, privately, whether he wanted to make some sort of deal with Bundy or not.

The second idea, Ted's, is that he write an account of the Chi Omega killings as an opening chapter for the book. We, of course, are delighted.

HA: Well, let's see... where are my notes? Oh yes, you were going to think about a couple things. About how to get into that first chapter – maybe an outline or something.

TB: Yeah, well, I told you that I'd thought it out and, uh, when we'd been working on this stuff, and I was... uh, uh... I *know* the type of style that I'm interested in – that it has to be done in... and I found my old outline last night and sketched out, you know, tried to elaborate on it some more last night. Uh, it will take me a couple more days to get it done. I'm still uncomfortable with it, and, uh...

HA: Well, couldn't you just briefly tell what it – I mean, an idea what you're doing, what you're working on? How you foresee it?

TB: Well, it's in the... it's not certainly... it's not going to be a first-person account.

HA: I understand that.

TB: Uh, it would be a third-person narrative... uh, just basically dwelling on... *well*, uh, trying to give you a flavor for what I'm talking about... a touching on feelings... uh, feelings and sensations... as well as the down... the nitty-gritty aspects of the place involved. You know... you can come to say, the, uh, feelings this person had *before*, and what he was doing befo... in the hours, let's say, preceding this.

HA: That's great.

TB: And how these… how it unfolded. The feelings during the commission of the crime, per se. Uh, how he escaped, and, you know, how he eluded the police. And besides that, obviously the chronology of events… the more, uh – the *interior* feelings of this person, whether it be panic or drunkenness… or confusion.

HA: Well, that would be tremendous. And it might help understand this unusual hybrid. But you're having some trouble?

TB: Well, I'm not… it's not… sure, I'm having trouble. I have trouble writing letters to Carole. I mean, I'm not, uh… I don't do that much writing. Writing is like anything; the more you do, the easier it gets. And I have a strong idea how I would like this to look, and no one else can write it but me. Uh, you know, uh, it's very…

HA: Well, we won't attempt to do anything on the Chi Omega situation then until you finish this for us because, like you said, you're the one who has to do it – the only one who *can* do it. But maybe you'd like to talk it out for a while.

TB: Yeah, the problem is… it's one of just phrasing, of sort of getting the feelings… of getting these ideas down into words. I suppose that exchange is not a problem of fleshing out the material. It's a problem of properly… of having all the facts or finding an approach. I mean, I know the type of writing style I'd like to use (long pause). The kind of writing style that I've…

that I've been using is sort of a surrealistic... because it gives a feeling sort of like a dream, a strange, surrealistic dream... uh, based on fact, of course.

The only thing I hate about this damn... damn Chi Omega case, and I hate... I don't want to see the book, uh, the book *should* begin with it, but I don't want to see the book take too much time with it because I still have appeals going, and probably will long after the book is out of print. I can't jeopardize, uh, my... I'll tell you what, Hugh: My mind is having a hard time communicating with my mouth these past few weeks. I want to describe this tumult, this surrealistic experience, but I also have my future to think about.

HA: The Chi Omega situation, while your suggestions and experiences would make it the highlight of the book, there's a lot more to this story than Chi Omega. There must be twenty-five cases in the west that have no bearing on Chi Omega – except that you ended up there.

TB: Yeah. (He shuffles a sheaf of notes he brought in.) You want some hash? There's a little bit left here.

HA: I never have...

TB (laughs): I brought my stash down here with me.

HA: You'd better blow that out.

TB: No, no... there's not enough to get me. Well, well... that's what I'm working on now. Oh yeah, you asked me to sign a note or something for you. What was that all about?

HA: Yeah, to your uncle Jack and grandfather Cowell. I'd like to visit with them.

TB: Well, that's involved, uh… I can't tell you what to do, but I can… I can tell you what I *don't* want you to do – and you can follow that. I *don't* want you to talk to my grandfather. He's in his late seventies and they've shielded him from all this. I don't know if…

HA: It's not that important perhaps. It's just that I want to do the best damn job possible. Why do you feel he couldn't handle it?

TB: He's an old man and they've done their best to keep all this away from him. And I hate to see something like this push him over the edge. And my uncle. I'm sure he… he'd be more than willing to talk to you.
In the case of my uncle, he has a career… and I hate to see him – I hate to see his name used.

HA: I don't see any reason why his name should have to be used. That's not the purpose. I just thought that you considered him a positive influence on you, you really admired him and felt a closeness for him.

TB: I admired him, yeah. I think you'd benefit from speaking with him – although he only knew me as, you know, as a child. I doubt if he could add much to – about my high-school days or my young-adult years.

HA: Well, on another point: We were talking about the situation with the governor. I'd like to make that approach the next time I'm in Florida, three or four weeks or so. They're telling me I can't get in here to see you for several days because the backlog has built up, so I really can't afford to sit around here doing nothing for several days. I think it's an honest backlog; the warden showed me a whole stack of applications.

I haven't decided how to make the original approach. I don't know how much to tell them. I'll have to tell them that I don't speak for you – that you have lawyers – but that if he would be willing to explore it, you might be able to clear up a bundle of cases. Of course, he could make it difficult for me to get with you after that... uh, just handle it himself. I don't know. It's chancy, but I think maybe it's worth it.

TB: Yeah, but see, you're going way out front there. I'm not saying... Think about what you're doing. See, you're an investigator, you're not a lawyer. You don't have any... you don't represent me. He's definitely going to ask his aides to check you out.

HA: I can pass the scrutiny, but I'd hate like hell to lose access to you – so maybe we had better wait a month or two, at least until we get into some more areas I must explore with you.

TB: I can hardly wait.

HA: Now, if you don't want me to do it, hell, I won't. But I just think there's a chance there. I think we can build a case for the uniqueness of this situation; giving society a chance to study somebody who has a problem. You think about it. If you don't want me to do it, I won't do it.

TB: Well, I'm thinking. You have to think beyond that – and the mechanics of it.

HA: What does he (the governor) have to lose? The state is going to fight all your appeals, and it will cost hundreds of thousands of dollars or more; perhaps new trials. You might successfully fight 'em for six or eight more years.

For *what?* To kill somebody? When you put it in that light, why, you know... and he might be able to do something for society. I don't know. Maybe it's completely off the wall.

I'm trying to figure out. Maybe they'll let me in again next week. I've got work to do in Washington and Utah, though. Damn, I need to be there, but what I'm really concerned about is getting that Chi Omega stuff moving, because it is so important.

TB: Well, I think you're going to... whenever I'm finished with that, I think we're going to have to go over it.

HA: Yeah.

TB: So whenever you can get back out here... and I'm not... I'll send word through Carole.

HA: Okay. Will you just say something like your "project" is finished, or something of that sort? So nobody will understand what it is we're talking about here. And I'll try to come back the next week.

TB: I've been thinking about the book. I think it's a dangerous trap for it to fall into the "True Detective" format of... you know... which is nicely exemplified by all three books that have come out – a dry sort of reportorial you know, quasireportorial… you know, "this is what happened." I see this as more of a *story*. I mean, like we're used to reading in fiction – only this is fiction with fact – which is much stranger than fiction… to use that cliché.

HA: Right.

TB: The scope of it certainly has… I mean, probably one of its most salient characteristics is the scope, which can be introduced in ways other than just locking it into a report. Think about how the story unfolded. The discoveries were made by *people*. The investigations were done by police officers. These things just didn't happen. They happened as a result of people discovering and people *doing* things. And show how judges act and how attorneys and clients really relate or don't relate to each other. There's so much *in* the story other than just the facts – to give it dimension.

HA: Well, we're going to have to get a hell of a lot more from you – about the feelings, the sensitivities… whatever reasoning goes on, no matter how convoluted, irrational, or bizarre.

TB: Yeah, I understand… but try to use a quasifictional kind of style, because your characters will have something to say. This is why you almost have to visualize what's going on, what you're writing about. The other books about me lack any depth at all. They are so stagnant.

So stilted, I mean. It's abnormal. People don't talk that way. Things don't happen that way. And this story you have – on the one hand is no more or less interesting than the others, but you have a hell of a lot more information, you have a better writer, and you have the ultimate edge – and as a result, you should do well with it.

HA: What we hope to achieve, also, is the psychological view, you know, the overall picture of *why* and what happened. We don't have... how it *fit*... what you're going to describe in that first chapter. The sensations, the feelings. We're dancing all around that. I hope we can get it down, legitimately.

TB: Yeah, and I think you can *visualize* the story, get a feeling for the characters and for the intricacies... of what *happened* – believable actions between people. I can help you make this something nobody will ever forget. Even though we know it's fact, I visualize, for instance, the characters, places, and events in a work of fiction. Like *Shogun*, a recent television movie. I was startled at just how my visualization of the book, as I read it, corresponded with the television movie. I said, "This is just as I saw it!"

(The guard signals that there are only five minutes remaining.)

TB: Here's this (handing over a magazine piece). This should give you some insight into how *I* relate to this place. It's a very important article for me. And I suggest that you think about it, and there may be some quotable quotes in there about... to help you construct any portions of this book that might – that would deal with my prison life.

In my mind, this is probably the most important article I've read in years. It's called "Mind over Matter." There's so much super stuff in here. I want this back. Please send it back to me.

HA: I'll get it back to you.

TB: It talks about alpha and beta personalities and stuff like that. I'm trying to find the most (leafs through for a minute or two)... Listen to this! I'm trying to find a statement or two that characterizes this article and here is one. It says: "Just as there is a cancer-prone personality, there's apparently a personality that seems to be able to throw off cancer. Someone with high ego strength and high esteem, flexibility of thought, the ability to tolerate stress and what Simon calls social economy, that is, a healthy enjoyment of people, coupled with a capacity to be comfortably alone. I believe these things can be learned," he says, "because I see people who initially have relatively few resources for dealing with the disease improving physically as their psychological profile changes. People can transform themselves or be transformed by disease. The threat of death can shock them into making changes they otherwise might never have risked."

And I think that's the... really the essence of this article – but there's so much more to it.

HA: I'll copy it and send it right back to you.

TB: It says here, if you get sick, it's because you've been thinking screwy... and I can only say "amen" to that. Now, we're not talking... we're talking about disease, and I apply it in a much broader sense.

HA: You're thinking of a sociopath or, at least, a person with deviant behavior.

TB: Yeah. If, in fact, a disease model is applicable to aberrant behavior, or abnormal mental processes – and I think it is, to a degree, especially as disease is presented in this article. Wait a minute. Here's something else! They're talking about a woman who had breast cancer and, it says, "She did not make herself sick, but her sickness was an expression of something more than the activity of a virus. And the problem she faces is to find a less physically compromising way," – now listen to this – "a less physically compromising way to express her blocked needs." Think about that. "To express her blocked needs," or *better yet*, to change the situation for which those needs became blocked in the first place.

HA: (hurriedly, as the guard returns): Now, you never did figure out a way to write down a number, so I'll know what I'm talking about in this case. You remember we talked about a number? Something you could simply write down and then grab and throw away. But I'd know.

TB: Oh, that. Oh, well…

HA: Did you figure out how to get it done for me?

TB: As a matter of fact, I, I, I… haven't figured out how to do it, Hugh.

HA: I know you don't think that's very important.

TB: Well, no… it's not that I don't think… I'm sure it's important to you. I'm just trying to… I'll have that ready for you.

HA: Okay, have Carole contact me and I'll be back in three or four days – when you're ready, okay?

October 20

HA: I know this is hard for you to get back into because you've got things here that are your prime interests right now. But damnit, we've got to get this sonuvabitch moving.

You've suggested giving us something startling at the beginning. Something, you said, that'll make 'em pay attention – about the Chi Omega thing. We agreed that's the best way to start it. You were gonna try to write that. Did you ever do anything on that?

TB: I sketched out, uh, an outline… but I haven't written it down, because, uh, the last time you were here… I haven't done anything on it, uh, since that time. I, uh, oftentimes work on it, uh. I have been absent… my mind has just fallen out of that mood that we were in.

HA: I understand… but I'd like to get back on it. If you can. I sure need to, because I've been sittin' around here playing semantics. We need to move this forward. Well, will you try to do that?

TB: Yeah.

HA: You know there's a lawsuit by the Leach family against the school district?

TB: Uh huh, I've heard, yeah.

HA: I've always felt that Andy Anderson was wrong (about seeing Bundy kidnap Kim Leach from the school) and you said he was wrong. How do you feel about the testimony?

TB: Well, I don't know. I knew he was wrong about me. That's what I'm saying. You're asking about how I feel about him testifying?

HA: Yeah.

TB: Well, I've... I've been privy to how publicity generates, uh, false eyewitness identification since Utah, and any number of people, from the Aspen case to any number of false sightings in Utah and Washington since my name has been in the paper, and, uh, simply... a person would see my face, uh, you know, on television or in a newspaper and with the attendant publicity, would begin to... Some people just begin to hallucinate or visualize all sorts of encounters – some of them to be helpful, some perhaps just because they wanted the attention. I don't know... but I think that is Andy Anderson's case, from the best I can tell. Over the course of being exposed to my picture and the publicity for eight months, or whatever it was before he came forward, he just, uh, he just convinced himself he had seen something.

HA: Okay now, there are certain things... we've spent so much time going into your background, your politics, your college days, growing up, and everything of that sort. It's time – really past time, to get to the nut-cutting here.

Incidentally, I talked to Liz. She wouldn't see me personally but talked to me on the phone. I sent her the tape you made for her.

Her daughter's fourteen now and she said she's doing fine, with "all the problems all fourteen year olds have." She's still married. We chatted a little bit but not a great deal.

She asked me, very frankly, "Does Ted want to live?" and I said, "Hell yes, he wants to live. You bet he wants to live. Why shouldn't he?" I don't know why she asked the question. She *did* say something that was interesting, though. She said that when you told her about being illegitimate, you cried. Do you recall that situation?

TB: I don't recall it. I could have been emotional about it. I can't say for sure. I wouldn't say... I wouldn't...

HA: She said she thought it really bothered you, more than, you know... Naturally you're going to say it doesn't bother you, but she claimed it bothered you – and *deeply*.

TB: Well (long pause), that's just her... that's just her opinion. I just, uh, I can imagine it being something that, uh, you know, was and *is* of a certain amount of concern to me – although not as much now as it was ten years ago even.

HA: She told me, also, that you had mentioned that you'd been disciplined... or that you were, as a small child, disciplined rather harshly. Do you recall that?

TB: I *wasn't* disciplined harshly as a child. I can't imagine that I told her that!

HA: You've never had any harsh discipline?

TB: Oh, I mean spanking, or like that. But that's, I didn't consider... I would not now, and did not then, consider it to be extreme.

HA: Maybe she's reading too much into a lot of things.

TB: She's probably looking for some way of saying, "Well, why?" you know. And who knows?

HA: Okay now. When people read this book, they're going to want certain questions answered. They're going to say, "Why in hell did Aynesworth go to prison and talk to him all those hours? And why didn't he ask Bundy the tough questions?" So I'm going to ask you some tough damn questions.

TB: Sure.

HA: I've got to have some kind of response. To this point, some of our conversations have been ridiculous in that you have weaseled out of everything. I don't know what all you're good for, but we both know – and get that shocked look off your face; it doesn't go well with this mood of sincerity you muster up – you've been around the horn and back again.

I've asked you to be as honest with us as you said you would be when this project began. It has become quite apparent you can not, or will not. You claim innocence in every case you've been charged with. You say you're innocent of *all* the murders. Yet, from my investigation and from Stephen's interviews and mine, we know damn well it's just a matter of how many.

So can you give me an explanation, in your own words? Whatever you want to say about it. I'm not trying to put words into your mouth, but...

You claim you didn't do any of the murders you've been charged with. What about all the ones you've been suspected of back in the west?

TB: Well, I mean... I suppose there are things I'm guilty of that I haven't been charged with, uh... We're talking about *serious* crimes.

HA: Right.

TB: You know... and I say, whether or not I've been charged, I mean, I can't be innocent of something I *haven't* been charged with.. The thing... I'm just saying that, uh... to be broader in that statement, that I'm not guilty or innocent of those cases – both (those) that I've been charged with and those I've allegedly been suspected of being involved in. Obviously I'm not innocent of everything!

HA: Okay now... if, in fact, you had nothing to do with any of the murders, how do you explain (that) you were in the vicinity of several of them? Picked out of a lineup by several witnesses. Identified by photos by others. Generally fit the description of the alleged murderer in others. Drove a Volkswagen which was described by some.

If you're not involved in any of this, why are you in here? Why are you convicted of three murders and suspected of others? You must be the unluckiest person in the world. Why? Why you?

TB: Well, I think you have to look at it as a, uh, the, the, whole, uh, situation as a, uh, uh, continuum… that is, to go back to Utah and work forward to understand the kind of momentum that built up behind the investigation. I mean, well initially the interest was generated, and I think, the calling my stock and trade, or whatever it was…in Utah back in August of '75… that the initial investigation was sparked because of a somewhat similarity between some of my things found in my car and, and, uh, the DaRonch kidnapping. And, and that was the beginning.

And initially the police weren't even interested and they showed a lack of – not in, a lack of, not a lack of interest, but a lack of conviction that they had a hot suspect, and, uh, once the police…

The police were skeptical from the beginning in Salt Lake City and I think it was the, uh, credit card matches from Colorado that convinced them that they had to, uh, get some case at any cost. And at one point, I think they made a commitment to creating, or taking an extremely vague and undec… indecisive witness in Carol DaRonch and making her feel that I was the person she should identify. And once that whole ball got rolling and the suspicions and innuendoes about my involvement in a variety of cases, uh, from Washington to Utah and Colorado…

It was so *sensational* at that point that eyewitness identifications were fairly routine.

Uh, to give you an idea – I mean, eyewitness identification of Theodore Bundy. When I escaped in Aspen, the first time… and stayed within five miles of the city of Aspen the entire time I was gone – they had people who called in and identified or reported seeing me in Seattle and Wyoming, California and all over the country. So eyewitness identification for a highly publicized defendant is not an unusual thing.

And especially in *my* cases where, without exception, all the alleged eyewitnesses came forward... how do I say it? Including Carol DaRonch – all had exposure to me and my face at one point or another on numerous occasions before they made eyewitness identification. They were aware of the publicity surrounding me – and that's from Carol DaRonch all the way down the line. You know, with the inclusion in the last case of Andy Anderson.

All of them were publicity-inspired identifications, with the possible exception of DaRonch and uh, and uh, the other one – Nita Neary (a Chi Omega sister who identified Ted), who, while she saw a number of pictures of me in the paper, I think something else happened there, too.

HA: What do you think happened there?

TB: Well, you just have to – you just have to look at it. We had a case of... in the Chi Omega case... where they had one eyewitness who witnessed everything. We know that she had a, a limited opportunity to observe and a limited amount of... of person to see because (of) the way the individual was dressed. She saw him for a flash as he was going out the door. And she was the only witness they had. And shortly after my arrest on February 15, I became the key suspect in the Chi Omega case.

Within three days after my arrest, several people in the Tallahassee and Jacksonville areas were shown a Polaroid photograph that had been taken of me in Pensacola and flown by special plane to Tallahassee. So they were taking extra pains to have my picture shown to *anybody* who might remotely place me in the vicinity of Chi Omega. However, they neglected... if you want to believe this, to say anything to Nita Neary, the *key* witness.

HA: What do you mean, "neglected" to say anything?

TB: They neglected to show her my photograph until, uh… almost two months later. In the interim, of course, Nita Neary knows I've been arrested. She admits to seeing a number of photographs of me and I simply have a situation here where – given the vagueness of her description of the individual and the limited time of opportunity to observe – that she went from being a vague witness, based on what she'd heard and what she'd seen, to being a positive witness.

I mean, when she identified me in a courtroom, they kept saying, well… Her testimony was she saw a flash of him from the side. She saw his profile. She saw his nose, essentially. And she couldn't remember eyebrows or eyes or anything else. However, in the courtroom – to show you how ludicrous this little game was – they had her from forty feet away, uh… with looking at me full face, point the finger, and say, "That's the man I saw!"

Well, *if* we believe her, she couldn't have made that kind of identification. She didn't ask for a profile. She looked right at me and said, "That's the man!" She knew who she was looking for – based on photographs in the papers and on TV.

HA: You're claiming that because the momentum built up, eyewitnesses came forth under pressure to testify a certain way. But remember now, there is hair evidence and there's some fiber evidence in some of these cases.

TB: Yeah. Well, it's just that fiber and hair evidence is, uh, uh, again such a…
The conclusions you can form based on those kinds of examinations are *so* general and *so* vague that we don't

know what the probability is. The police don't know what the probability is of finding any given fiber or set of fibers or any hair or given set of hairs if they're in a location where there is a lot of opportunity for hairs to be dropped and left there for an indefinite length of time.

Hair blows. Fibers blow, and they're tracked in on shoes – and on clothing. So you just can't say with any certainty how, I mean, how long a fiber has been in a given location. And the same goes for hair.

And it's unlike blood, I suppose, or fingerprints. Supposedly, the only way a fingerprint can get on a surface is if the person with that print puts it there. A fingerprint doesn't blow around. It doesn't last for an indefinite length of time, like a hair will, and it can't be tracked in on someone's shoes. So it's better evidence in that respect – and more individualistic, more characteristic of a given individual. Whereas you can't say with a questioned piece of hair and a *known* hair – just how many people have, other people, besides the known individual – have that kind of hair.

HA: You can only exclude a certain part.

TB: The best thing you can do is exclude.

HA: What would you say if I told you that the fiber situation was even stronger than the testimony indicated – that certain jerseys were made from faulty fiber, and it had thirty-one threads or strands instead of the usual thirty-three… and that the manufacturers said that that could *only* happen in two or three different jerseys made from that one spool. And that it matched *exactly* the fiber with thirty-one strands found in the (Leach case) van. Now, that would seem to make it a bit stronger, wouldn't it now?

TB: Uh, it's all hypothetical... and I don't, uh, uh, uh... I don't think the state of the science of fiber identification is such that, uh, uh... they can say with any certainty.

HA: I could have written that response. I knew you'd say that. Let's move on for a while. You've said you're innocent of all this – and you explained how you got caught up in it. The biggest problem you've had *all* the way is that you claim to have *absolutely* no memory of where you were.
Where were you when the Lake Sammamish girls were killed? When Healy was killed? Parks? Rancourt? Any of these people? Can you give me just *one* alibi – just one damn date that you know where you were?

TB: Oh, I *know* where I was. That's not to say I don't... I mean, I... at *some* times, in some instances, of course, I *don't* remember where I was because it's been so long ago. I can't say on that. I have no recollection. If you would ask me any date back then, whether it was a date on which a murder occurred or a disappearance occurred or if...

HA: Well, you remember Lake Sammamish. You remember that at six p.m. or so, you were over having hamburgers with Liz. Where were you earlier in the day?

TB: I remember I went over to Liz's house in the morning, uh (long pause)... I don't know what time it was. It was before she went to church. It was eight or nine o'clock in the morning.

She was going to go to church. We'd been having, you know, an argument here and there. I just... I had been sick. I'd been home from work for a couple days that week. I, uh, I was just going to spend the day piddling around the room I had on the other side of the university.

HA: Freda Rogers's?

TB: Yeah... and the best I can recall, I stayed home most of that day. And later on in the day, (I) went over and picked up Liz and went for a hamburger.

HA: Where in that house did you live? Where was your room? If there were people there all day, would they have seen you come and go?

TB: It would be the southwest corner. Second floor, southwest corner.

HA: The back? Left? Is there a back way in and out of there?

TB: No.

HA: Just the front door?

TB: Right. Well, I can't, uh, I can't provide any documentary evidence to say that I...

HA: Do you think I *really* expected any? Okay, let's try another way... What about Chi Omega? Where were you when Chi Omega happened?

TB: You mean… you're talking about the evening, Saturday evening, Sunday morning?

HA: Yeah… say midnight on.

TB: Well, those, uh… I tried piecing that day together and I remember the Super Bowl… and going back from that point I can only say that the, the, uh, the best I can recall is that, uh (long pause), my usual routine at that time was to go out. I went out and got a couple quarts of beer and came back and watched TV in my room at night because I wasn't spending much time on the streets at that time.

I tried to stay on… I tried to stay *off* the streets as much as I could, and, uh, the first time I heard about the Chi Omega case was the next morning when I heard some people in the hallway talking about it. And that Sunday I watched the Super Bowl. I mean, I'm just not in a position, you see, uh, how many people have an alibi, uh, for Sunday morning, February… oh, January… whatever it was? At two in the morning?

HA: Well, maybe you don't have for one specific date – but you don't have for *any* date, and damn it, that's – isn't that a bit unusual?

TB (agitated): Well, let's try and pick *any* day. I don't care. Pick any day.

HA: How about last night? I'll give you a chance.

TB: Yeah… I mean, it's a pretty, we've fairly dwelled on this, but, uh, pick any day or two several years ago and say, "Can you prove what you were doing on that day?"

HA: Well, you remember when you stayed at the Holiday Inn in Lake City? What'd you do that night? You visited with someone at the bar for a while.

TB: Oh, yeah, I, I, I, uh, had a few drinks at the bar and I went back to the, uh, my room – and slept in my room.

HA: What happened the next morning?

TB: I got up the next morning. I was going to have breakfast, and I – before I left – I saw a state patrol, a couple state patrol cars, parked in front of this… in front of this main entrance, and I decided to keep on goin'.

HA: West?

TB: Goin' back to Tallahassee.

HA: Did you go out 90 or did you take 10?

TB: Well, I don't know that… I don't know that… that I-75 goes on out. You get on the ramp there and you go north and there's a cloverleaf and you get on the freeway going west.

HA: Yeah, I-75 is right next to the hotel there. Okay, let me ask you: We talked about this in June and we didn't get much out of it. But I wonder. if indeed you're innocent of all these murders and kidnappings, why in hell are we doing this book about you? We've spent weeks and months tracing your early life, your school, your personal and political life – your dreams and frustrations. The last time I asked you about this, you know, you said, "Yeah, it is sort of unusual. We need some kind of a bridge." Have you thought what kind of a bridge? Have we got a bridge?

TB: Well, let's see. I don't know if I'm really keeping up with you, Hugh, on that. Uh, uh, a bridge for what? For *what?*

HA: Why are we doing this book? If you're innocent, why are we interested in the fact you failed Chinese, that you broke up with Marjorie and why?

TB: Because she… I've, I've… I can't explain it, I'm not…

HA: I know guys who've stolen more cars than you have. I'm tired of that kind of crap. Why can't you start telling me what we both know you've got rolling around in that head?

TB: I'm not the one who's saying I'm newsworthy! Why is the news media so interested in me? I guess because I'm an enigma and they're assuming contradictions… because there are so many unresolved questions. Uh, uh, I'm not saying people should be interested in what I did as a young man… that I took Chinese or who I slept with or who I didn't. I don't, quite frankly, I wish nobody had ever heard of Ted Bundy. And, uh, uh, but, uh, we're doing this book because (pause)… we're doing this book. That's about it.

HA: You said one time, "I don't think I'm unique, but maybe I am."

TB: Well, I, uh, I'm unique and I'm not unique. I mean, you're unique. Each of us is as unique as a snowflake might be. But that's not to say that I'm so special that no one can understand me or that nobody has the capacity to understand me. I mean, I'm an existentialist to the degree that I don't believe anybody can know fully what another person feels and why another person does something – because we act as such a complexity of things. Uh, but I'm not... I'm not unique – although obviously special.

HA: Your jailer in Tallahassee was telling me about the deal you cut – for a contact visit. Was that in an office or a cell?

TB: Well, actually it was the interview room they use for, uh, attorneys' visits, on the first floor of the jail, behind the booking area. And it's no holding cell. It has a regular door on it and a plexiglas shield – and no bars and a blank ceiling.

HA: Well, let's get back to your expertise – on this so-called individual we've talked about. I've listened to tapes – we must have a hundred hours of 'em by now – until I'm blue in the face and I still can't... You've said that the abductor, the killer, got *no* sexual satisfaction out of killing. And very little out of the actual possession itself. Where *did* the satisfaction come from?

TB (long pause, long sigh): We'll have to go back through all the things I've... that we've said... and was postulated about this kind of an individual (sighs). I'm trying to think – to try to refresh my *own* memory as to what, uh, we've covered.

HA: Well, you said at one point the actual planning and the build-up process was the high point.

TB: Well, uh, er, certainly, I think that is the, in all part... it would seem that all parts of the planning and this "acting out" would serve some function. You know, I think that if I, in trying to be precise in describing this kind of individual to you, used the word "satisfaction" in that respect, I might have done so, you know, with precision because I think I also pointed out, you know, that we'd expect this kind of person to be a recidivist or to repeat these kinds of crimes.

Because he *wasn't* satisfied – because he was, it was an *illusion* of some kind of ultimate, uh, satisfaction or resolution... whatever.

The complexities of whether it impelled him or compelled him to act in that way... The satisfaction was probably, uh, was distinguished by its absence, you might say.

HA: But where *did* the satisfaction come from? Why would you do it again, again, and again, if you got nothing out of it?

TB: Well, he, uh (long sigh), it's quite possible that there was... you might call it... I don't know that we're talking about an individual who – at least in terms of the conventional idea of satisfaction – uh, was satisfied.

He, uh... what I'm saying, we may have a situation here where the individual is *seeking* to satisfy certain urges – unconsciously or whatever – but it's the absence of this *fulfillment*, to use a different word, that, uh, we would expect to drive him to, in fact, out again and again in that kind of futile exercise.

HA: What about enjoyment from inflicting pain? You said you thought this person did not get any enjoyment – or anything – out of inflicting pain.

TB: Yeah.

HA: Why would he mutilate a young girl? Like sticking an instrument up her vagina or biting her breast or choking her after she was dead. That is mutilation. How would you explain that? We know that happened here.

TB (clears throat): Well, if something like that happened...

HA: You know damn well it did. And worse!

TB: It seems to me that that kind of behavior would be an exception as opposed to the rule here. If we have a person – given the type of hypothetical person we're talking about – uh, I don't, uh...

HA: Well, even if it's an exception, what would cause it? Let's say that happened three or four times. What would cause it?

TB: Well, you can only imagine that some kind of intense rage... of the kind that would perhaps be uncharacteristic... uh, built up – and that kind of individual might, uh (long pause), act out in an uncontrollable fashion, with the results you mentioned.

HA: Like the Chi Omega night? Right?

TB (softly): Possibly.

HA: Well, let's go back a bit further. You told us you thought this person is refining his M.O., he had found... he had learned to live with it. He had gotten very adept at what he was doing and he got *more* in control in the planning of the situation, and yet – maybe later on – something like this completely blew up on him. It was an exception, but it showed he wasn't *really* in control.

TB: Well, it's, it's, uh… if I didn't make it clear before, I should make it clear now, that we're talking about… If I made reference to this individual being under control, it would be only in the most superficial, uh, way. Uh, he is clearly ill.

The person obviously doesn't have control over *all* of his life or else he would, in all likelihood, would not be acting out in that way. I mean, it's clear. He is not in control of himself to the point where he knew, or would know that he was doing something that was, uh, not just illegal, but immoral.

There's control. Yeah, you're right. We can say there's more control because the M.O., the modus operandi, became more familiar – but on the other hand, we see that with the greater incidence of… the greater success this person had – the more likely that part of him that required that sort of stimulation would be to want *more* of that kind of stimulation. And with the security of having, quote, successfully carried it off, there would be a greater, uh, uh, the urge to do it, we'd expect, would become more frequent. Perhaps even more, the feeling would be to become more bold, if that's the word.

HA: Well, where this person might have dealt with only one or two persons at a time – usually one person at a time – then all of a sudden he decides to kill four, five, or six… whatever. How would that happen? Is this total rage or a controlled situation? I don't understand how the change comes. That's a radical change, it seems to me.

TB: I don't understand, uh...

HA: Well, as he becomes more familiar with an M.O. that works – and this means greater success, partially because of his increased confidence – he still becomes more bold. Why would he change his M.O. from, say, a single victim to several? Why would he need this radical a departure?

TB: Well, uh, assuming that it was that kind of departure, then we'd just say that... the only thing to be said was that the, the *need* that he was hoping to fulfill for one reason or another became, uh, would not be filled by one. And perhaps he found himself in a situation where he could – in a situation where he *could* victimize more than one individual... or perhaps as a result of his contemplating or fantasizing about that kind of conduct, he just... It occurred to him at some point in time that he *could* involve more than one individual. There are any number of alternative explanations.

HA: In other words, several victims might have always been his ultimate fantasy, but he considered the risks too severe.

TB: Possibly.

HA: Well, it seems that if it happened all of a sudden, it might seem that he wouldn't have time to really think it out. Right?

TB: Well, I don't think anybody's ruled out the emer... he wouldn't evaluate the conduct at each step, saying, "Am I fulfilled?" I mean, it's so... we can only imagine that, uh, that someone who is committing what is cold, calculating murder of someone is really *not* fully in control of his faculties, fully aware of himself.

He's driven by whatever it is that's driving him to commit that, so I don't imagine that he has the normal ability to access, you know, the feedback he's getting.

HA: What could cause the *intensity* of this person? Would it be a fear of being caught? Would it be the risk factor? What would make a person be this intense?

TB: Well, we talked again, about... we have to go back to the root causes of the person, the causes we can identify in trying to determine why any individual would undertake to kill persons in this way. And we said that this person was reacting inappropriately to stress from his own environment. We're talking about stress as an umbrella label for any number of things.

Uh, stress in his personal life. Let's say, a financial situation... uh, his own sense of self-esteem and fulfillment. The failures in his life... other forms of anxieties. You might be talking about conditions even after environmental stresses we've talked about. Sexual stimuli in the environment that he may be paying attention to on TV, or even a highly violent, stimulating kind of movie.

But you see, if you hang up on an accentuation of this stressful... these stressful influences, we'd expect as a consequence the intensity, uh, of that condition – you'd expect that that condition would be exacerbated even further by intensification of those... those very stressful factors.

HA: You said that ordinarily this person would not inflict pain or mutilate; yet we know it happened in several cases. This is, as you explain it, a radical departure from the norm – if you can call any of this normal. Do you suppose you really understand this individual, or is it too hard for you to tell me?

TB: Well, I don't know. I mean, I don't know for sure if I can give you an explanation for each and every facet of... for each and every... uh, hypothetical crime that you've asked about here.

HA: Well, when you stick an instrument up a person's vagina or you cut a person or bite a person, that seems to indicate a certain amount of rage. That's getting even or something. What would it be? I mean, that's not normal sexual gratification. Can you dig a bit deeper?

TB (angrily): Well, we've said, when we... We're not talking about normal sexual gratification. We're not talking about *normal* anything! Okay? Certainly it's abnormal. You aren't suggesting and I'm not suggesting... certainly, that it's normal. Uh, uh...

HA: Would he ever understand exactly what it was he was fighting and reaching out to attain?

TB: That's a possibility. No one, I think... Can you really understand fully why you do everything you do?

HA: No, of course not.

TB: You know, a normal, everyday thing... so when there's something done in rage, it's an extraordinary kind of rage that, uh, is involved in the murder of innocent, unsuspecting persons. It's a kind of curious puzzle that maybe you – maybe even normal people – have trouble understanding their actions.

And persons who are obsessed or *possessed* by that kind of destructive urge, uh, probably have less of a chance of fully comprehending why they act the way they do.

But, getting back to the question you asked earlier about mutilations, et cetera... and its relationship to pain, I think you're also concerned about. I don't know of any case, any *real* case, quite frankly, in the eases we're concerned about here, that involved mutilation... in a, uh, *premortem* condition.

I think that even if we're assuming that somehow Chi Omega can be explained by this hypothetical person, I think the documents were inconclusive as to whether, uh, whatever the girl's name was, uh, was alive or dead when the Levy girl... when the injury was sustained. Or conscious or whatever.

HA: But the perpetrator of the act maybe wouldn't know that either. So it really wouldn't matter whether she was or not. He didn't know, for sure, whether she was alive, I assume. Wouldn't you assume that?

TB: I don't, uh... I don't know.

HA: Well, I mean, doesn't that sort of knock out your argument? Obviously he did not know for certain. He didn't wait around there, I'm sure – stand around and wait.

TB: I'm not sure, but there was evidence that... in the form of bark and certain bruises on Levy to suggest that she had been hit. And we know the other girls had been struck, uh, while they were sleeping. The two who lived were struck while they were sleeping. We can assume then that the two survivors were struck. And their testimony said they were not sexually molested before they were struck, so it would seem that this individual's first act was to strike the victim while the victim was sleeping.

This seems to be true in the case of, uh, both the girls who died at Chi Omega – and so it's quite possible that Levy would be unconscious. It's hard to say... hard for me to...

One would assume that if, if the pain had been... if those injuries had been inflicted while she was awake, that other members of the sorority house would have heard her screaming or making some outcry. And there's no testimony of that.

HA: Do you remember, getting back to Utah, the hairs that were found in your car? Are you saying that the police had to have put those hairs there – if they, indeed, were Melissa Smith's? Is that essentially what you're still claiming?

TB: Yeah. In the Utah situation, there's no question in my mind that the hair of the respective victims had been placed there. And I say that for this reason. I mean that, you might say, "We'd expect Bundy to say that," right? But, uh, we're talking about...

Let's talk about Carol DaRonch, for example. We had testimony from her as to what happened to her, and I believe what happened to her did happen to her – but she just got it mixed up as to who the attacker was she saw, or who she thought she saw. But she was in her abductor's car for anywhere from five to fifteen minutes – depending on whose story you believe – in November of 1974. Now, in ten months, uh, eleven months later, my car is seized. Nearly a year later.

After a year's worth of use – with people in and out of that car – the car itself was six years old, it was prepared to be sold by... I had taken everything completely out of the inside and I put in *new* carpets, put in, uh, new plastic carpets, uh, cleaned it from stem to stern... and, uh... I probably couldn't prove this, so I never made a point of it, but allegedly the runner, or the item covering the floor... they said they found a hair from Carol DaRonch on... was something I had purchased from a junkyard.

HA: The floor mat?

TB: Floor mat... there you go. Purchased it from a junkyard, you know, in September of 1975. I mean, I knew that I was... I seriously doubted if any of Liz's hairs could be found in that car. So many people had ridden in it. There was no telling how many people *like* Carol DaRonch had been in that car. Or Melissa Smith or any of the others.

But nevertheless, I knew there was not a grain of sand in that interior of that car, uh, uh, *after* I sold it, that had been there before September 1975. That's how clean it was. New floor mats, new carpets, new side carpets, new seat.

HA: So you're saying that that was a situation where the police made a case against you by planting hairs there?

TB: Well, it was also an explanation. Given the nature of hair, how do you think it could have remained there throughout such a thorough cleaning?

HA: In all our lengthy conversations, I have noticed that in *every* case you tend to blame others. They planted this evidence. They lied about this or that. She couldn't have *really* seen me – and so on. Nowhere do I hear you saying, "I shouldn't have been at the Fashion Place Mall when DaRonch was kidnapped. I shouldn't have been seen in the Viewmont High School auditorium just before Debbie Kent disappeared. I shouldn't have been at Lake Sammamish the day two girls disappeared and were killed." What is Ted Bundy to blame for?

TB: Well now, Hugh, no matter how you approach it, you're not going to get what you're hoping for. And you know the reasons why. But, of course, I'm at fault for many things. It's just that we're far apart on what we're both driving at here.

HA: It's frustrating, Ted, to bounce up against this stone wall. What does it matter if you tell us the truth now? None of the crimes in Washington, Oregon, and Utah can ever be tried. And it's obvious Colorado couldn't keep you in jail long enough to try you for the Snowmass killing. I know what you've done; Stephen knows. I feel sure Carole knows. C'mon, let's get moving in the right direction. Hell, it won't cost you a thing to clear them all up, once and for all. Frankly, I don't know how we're going to finish this book unless you become a hell of a lot more receptive to telling us the truth.

TB: That's your problem, not mine.

HA: Okay, but at least, will you try to work on the opening chapter – the Chi Omega thing? You suggested it. We all got excited about it, and now – nothing. When I come back, will you have some notes at least for me?

TB: I'll try. Actually, as I said, I've been working, thinking... Will you take this (handing over a letter) and mail it to Carole for me?

November 12

The conversation begins with Ted's views on the insanity defense.

TB: If I took... if I ever decided to take that route, I'd just kinda sit back and smile. I've taken the opposite approach – absolutely opposite approach. I said I wouldn't have *anything* to do with an insanity defense. I mean, I did everything I could to stay away. I was strongly opposed to even, you know, even considering the idea because I *knew* I wasn't crazy. I *know* I'm not crazy! Insane, incompetent, or anything else. And I was insulted by even the suggestion by my attorneys that we should consider the defense. They knew damn well I wasn't crazy.

HA: They also knew that it might be your best defense.

TB: They also knew it might be a viable defense. Well, that's their job, but still I felt it would be – it should be clear, it should be clear to a jury that I wasn't crazy. Then the best way to go was to go for, uh, a defense on the merits – the lack of reasonable doubt (sic) rather than going for insanity.

HA: Have you ever had second thoughts about it?

TB: Absolutely none, no. I can't *afford* to. I couldn't have gotten away with allowing myself to be a part of an insanity defense, *just* as I couldn't allow myself to plead guilty.

HA: What do you mean, you couldn't have gotten away with it?

TB: I wouldn't have, personally. It didn't *fit!*

HA: But you know there are those who say that anybody who gets into a whole lot of trouble – kills people – is somewhat crazy.

TB: That's true, but *everybody's* somewhat crazy.

HA: People have a view of you – very bright, articulate, handsome, and so on. They also think you killed a lot of people, and you must be a split personality, a madman, an animal or whatever. Some of these things you might be some not. How would you like people to recall Ted Bundy?

TB: I guess my initial response is, I don't care. I mean, really. I'm not really concerned about my image; it's so bad anyway. I mean, the media image. I know who I am, what I am, and know where I've been, and hopefully, I have some idea about where I'm going. I have absolutely no desire to relate to people or impress people or project myself to people at all... that's not it. The Ted Bundy that people are going to be thinking about and reading about... really bears very little resemblance to *me*. I'm not in a popularity contest as far as that goes. I don't care about a reputation, and if I had my druthers, I'd never, *ever* have walked into a courtroom. I'd never have seen a police officer. I'd have never been in prison or on TV or in the newspapers.

I hate the publicity! I hate the image. I hate the notoriety with a passion. I'd love to be the most obscure person in the world right now. And so I really don't care what people think of me... because it's none of their business.

HA: Some would find it unusual that you say you hate publicity. You seemed to bask in it – especially in Colorado and Utah and in the early days here in Florida. But so much for that. Let's talk about one of your favorite topics – how psychiatrists envision you.

TB: Because of my association with all these crimes, the experts refuse to perceive me as being, uh, even remotely – you know, anything that approaches being normal. I mean, I'm not an *animal*, and I'm not crazy and I'm not a split personality. That's all there is to it. People refuse to believe that. That's their problem.

There's nothing in my background – I swear to God, and I know it – I've analyzed my own background and I know... there's no doubt in my mind that there's nothing in my background, no one factor or collection of factors that would explain (long pause) or would otherwise (long pause) lead one to believe that I was capable of committing murder.

HA: Many experts, those who deal with this kind of homicide on a regular basis, say that such a person as we're looking at here would keep little mementos – maybe a diary, jewelry, hair, even pictures. Or he might want to confide in somebody.

TB: Well, you know, we're positive we're dealing with an individual whose primary concern is not to be detected. I think we've seen this over and over again. Obviously, if we attribute the murders, for instance, in the Seattle area to a person with this kind of mentality, it's clear he didn't want to be captured. Because he *hasn't* been captured. He hasn't been charged and he hasn't been convicted. All right?

So he doesn't want to get caught, and he's rational enough not to talk to anybody about it – rational enough not to write anything down. I mean, that's just common sense. So we wouldn't expect him to have a diary. We wouldn't expect him to share any information, because no one could be trusted. I doubt that anyone would seriously believe that they could tell other civilized human beings that they'd committed any number of murders and not expect that person to come forward at some time, you know.

HA: Would he recall *every* one of the murders? Would some of them stand out more clearly and be recalled easier?

TB: Well, since we... you know... we've said that this individual did not have a split personality and did not have temporary amnesia, uh, assuming that he is a fairly rational – at times at least – a semirational person, we would expect that he had normal brain functions. We'd expect him to remember every one of the crimes he committed – and everything else that he'd done, with the qualification that we all tend to forget the small details, or even large details.

HA: Would some be more memorable than others?

TB: Oh, yes. I, I couldn't say for sure. We have discussed the fact that this individual might have used alcohol to facilitate the minimization of inhibitions under these circumstances, uh, prior to and during the commission of the crime. And knowing what those of us who had alcohol – especially under heavy amounts of alcohol – should all know, we tend to remember less than if we weren't under the influence. So we'd expect this person to remember more about those crimes he committed when he wasn't intoxicated

HA: When I suggested he might talk to somebody, I meant somebody qualified to help him with his problem – a psychiatrist, perhaps.

TB: I'm not trying to avoid the question. You asked twice before if there was ever a point where this person sought help. Or had considered it or checked out the idea. I addressed myself to that question somehow and it brought something else to mind.

Perhaps the only *firm* trend I ever ran across in the study of abnormal behavior was that the younger that a person… that he or she was when they manifested abnormal behavior or thought pattern… the more likely it was that there was going to be a condition that would be lasting. And, uh, permanent. A chronic disorder.

Persons who suffer such disorders in later years, or a quick onset of the particular abnormal behavior pattern, suffer *acute* conditions. And it seemed to make sense to me – and the literature is fairly consistent – that the younger it was that a person would develop these problems that more likely, the higher the likelihood that they would continue on with those problems, unless treated, without hope of some kind of remission.

Now, in developing and creating this psychological model that we've applied to various situations and cases, uh, we've been unable to spot a *particular* cause – something that would say, "This is why it would happen"… uh, uh, "This is what," you know. Then perhaps a withdrawal of this condition would make it go away – would rehabilitate the individual.

It's hard; it's not like pushing a button and flipping switches, certainly, but we're looking for a remedy. If there is one, it's gonna be a long answer.

HA: Take your time.

TB: But (pause)… so you must first ask yourself, not knowing the specific cause, you have to speculate as to the cause and then consider various therapeutic avenues in treatment.

Let's consider the possibility that this person suffered from some sort of an acute onset of a desire that resulted in the pattern of, of, of, *killing* young girls. And that there was no other explanation for that, other than it was some sort of genetic or even congenital condition whose time had come… that, uh, I mean, that unless you could get it under an electron microscope somewhere and you could understand the complex circuitry of the brain, you'd never know just why, because there'd never be a satisfactory explanation. Everything in the person's background might be known, but how do you account for it?

There's just no established model of behavior that would account for it. So you'd have to... somewhere in the chemical, uh, finery of the brain, something went wrong, temporarily. Whether it's temporary or permanent, under those conditions we might not ever know. And the only way to find out would be just to watch the person and see how long the conduct lasted. If it lasted indefinitely, then we'd know that something was permanently wrong.

Now, let's see... let me, uh... it's not a, some chemical imbalance or some genetic switch gone wrong – that somehow maybe there was a predisposition, you might call it a condition which, uh, I've alluded to before. I referred to it as a weakness or predisposition, which, absent certain stresses and certain environmental conditions, would never have resulted in this behavior but *did*.

So what we're saying is the personality... the weakness in the personality which becomes malevolent because of a certain set of complex environmental factors and opportunity factors as well here... we don't know *exactly* what combination resulted in his wanting to murder young women – exactly why or even remotely why – but we do know that its environmental, it's specific to an environment, a certain set of stresses, and we can go from there.

It's unlikely this person would change – ever change – unless he recognized at some point and time, was forced to recognize what was causing him to act the way he was and tried to find, or even confronted the irrationality of the whole, the real destructiveness of his behavior. And, in combination with that, was able to learn how to deal with that stress – the kinds of stress which had aroused this urge. He'd have to be able to pinpoint these urges, uh, the stimuli, and deal with or otherwise eliminate them from his daily life.

And he would have to change environments entirely. He could go to a kind of society or community that did not exert upon him the kinds of stresses and pressures which aroused his feelings of anger or hostility and doubt... uh, low self-esteem. I mean, if you could find that kind of environment or society, then we could expect that this person – this kind of person – would cease committing these kinds of crime.

HA: Like prison?

TB: It would be highly unlikely for the normal individual, especially one who is subject to these irrational and horribly destructive acts, to be *able* to confront himself in the way that I've described, because he'd be so caught up in this cycle – this vicious cycle that we've referred to so often, uh, of mur-... you know, of abduction, of possession, and murder. Self-recrimination... and back through it again and again.

He would not be able to step back from it and analyze it. And certainly – getting back to the question you asked before – he wouldn't be able to seek help, because, as we said, this kind of person would not want to get caught.

And I doubt that; I know myself... I mean, I know that if someone came to me and told me that they'd done a large number of uh, committed a large number of serious crimes, that as a responsible member of society – even though I'm a psychiatrist – I would be *obligated* to turn this person in.

You would never know, but I think that'd be the response and that would be the professional and ethical response for that kind of thing. So if that individual understood that society does not really treat – would not treat him in his attempt to rehabilitate himself or make him whole to normal again – but, instead, would punish him or attempt to kill him, it's highly unlikely that he would or *could* seek out help.

In fact, he might hold out the possible belief that he could deal with the problem himself. But, as I said, it's unlikely he'd be able to confront it because he would be enmeshed in that continuing cycle of the building of an urge, the commission of a crime, and so on and so forth.

HA: Getting to another subject briefly, I read an interesting evaluation of you by a former friend of yours, a woman writer, and she…

TB (interrupts): Yeah, I know what you mean. I don't know where in hell she got her facts about me, about anything – but she approached me and wanted me to contribute to the book she was writing. I'm just glad I didn't waste my time. The sheep dip she calls fact! I don't care *who* you are, if you can't see that the great bulk of my personality is alert and vital and reality-oriented and *normal*, then there's really something wrong with your analysis or whatever psychiatric model you're trying to use. I *do* have a conscience. It may have gaps in it, but I have a very *strong* conscience!

HA: What do you mean, "gaps in it"?

TB: Well, we all have gaps in our conscience. Some people feel guilty if they don't come home right after work. Others don't care if they stop off for a few beers. Some don't care if they pick up a little something at the supermarket without paying for it. Some people wouldn't be able to handle it. I, uh, stole textbooks when I was going to college. Some people couldn't handle that.

HA: But to the more serious aspects of what you've done...

TB: I mean, I feel no guilt or remorse, but they don't understand. She wants to adopt this theory that I'm just ashes inside – no conscience, just a shell. Anybody who believes that... that's fine; they're just doing me a favor.

HA: Why? How does that help you?

TB: What she's doing – she's saying this guy can't function, right? He's really... his function is going to go deeper and deeper into this compulsive state. This *madness* – and he's devouring himself. He's just falling apart. And that's just perfect!

As long as the contemporary impression is that I'm just a, uh, incapacitated, uh, uh, incoherent – unable to handle myself or am no longer an energetic, healthy young man – then they're always going to underestimate me. *Always*. They'll never *truly* understand what makes me tick.

HA: What does it matter if anybody underestimates you? You're in prison.

TB: If, if.

HA: I'm serious. What does it matter?

TB: Because it, just – it just matters a great deal (laughs). I want to be forgotten. I want people to forget me. I don't want people to remember what I look like or what I sound like. I want them to think I'm just laying there on my bunk quivering. I hate the limelight, the news media.

Yeah, I knew how to battle in public and to use the media, but that doesn't mean I liked it. I was fighting back. I always fight back.

HA: Speaking of fighting back, you've fought a damn good battle every time I've asked you this question… or even tried to weasel around about it. But we've got to get serious here.

How many are there, Ted? We've been back and forth over this for months. You say you want to tell us the truth for this book. The "third-person" ploy is understandable in that it protects you from further responsibility legally and your loved ones from further complications, but how can we manage to even understand the situation without having an idea of how many?

TB: I'm not going to commit myself. It's an impossibility. I can't.

HA: One of these days, all this is going to be moot. The only way you're going to get out of this place is… well, I won't say that because you might make a run for it some time… but you must – with your intelligence – realize that no appeal is going to work. And that they are going to eventually put you in that chair. How do you feel about dying?

TB: Well, nobody wants to die… but *everybody* will. I may live longer than you. If I don't, I don't. But I *do* have strong feelings, *humane* feelings, about society's alleged right to take another human being's life. The death penalty is motivated solely and exclusively by the perceived need of the state, the prosecution, and the victim, or uh, the family, to obtain revenge.

It's an eye for an eye. There's nothing more. It's no deterrent. There's no doubt it is an effective way of killing a person whom society has adjudged responsible for the crime. It does *not* and never will, restore any measure of compensation to the victim's family or the state. None whatsoever.

HA: Well, if a person kills and kills and kills, and is finally caught, what should be done with him?

TB: I don't know. I don't know if anything *should* happen to... uh, uh.

HA: Well, you can't – well, maybe you can, I don't know – I started to say you can't really claim that it's proper to go around killing people all the time.

TB: No. It's, it's, it's ultimately improper (laughs). You know, there's probably no other behavior that society condemns more vigorously than killing of the kind, that, uh – well, society condones a lot of killing, in a massive scale in war, in abortion, and things like that. Even the slaughter of animals for its own food, but I guess I'm saying that if a given society or community has a reverence for life, it cannot be *selective* in how it applies that reverence.

It cannot have reverence for the two-year-old, but kill the fetus. It cannot have reverence for the victim's life and kill the murderer. It's inconsistent.

So if the life of the victim is worthwhile, then the life – the life of the killer is sacred as well. If society chooses not to observe that kind of consistency; it chooses to kill the fetus and preserve the infant and kill the murderer in retribution for the victim, then it must accept the consequences for the violence that it self-generates.

HA: You mentioned abortion. You were once involved in an abortion.

TB: Well, I think that society accepts... the majority of Americans seem to approve of abortion. We, uh, accept that as a necessary means of controlling population and we just say the fetus isn't really alive. It's really dehumanization, as it were. Society thus says it's justified.

1981

February 5

Bundy's refusal to be more explicit is causing us problems with our editors. He has also complained to Carole that Hugh has been unrealistic and a bully.

Translation: He's been ragging Ted for the truth. Since Bundy has begun repeating himself to Aynesworth, indirectly trying to discourage any further interviews, there have been no visits to the prison since November. Then a letter arrives, promising that he has prepared "those items you're so interested in." This turns out to be untrue.

HA: You don't look so hot today. Have you been staying out

late again? Here's your CARE package for today. You can have my cigarettes. I'm going to quit.

TB: Just give me the opened one. I can always buy those here. I've got a little money in the account. There's a few people who still love "The Bun."

HA: I've heard.

TB (straining to see if the guard is outside the door, close enough to hear the conversation): I've got a problem. I've got this red-headed bull back there who enjoys pushing me in shit. He agitates some of the blacks... tries to turn them against me, but, of course, that won't work because they know I'm down with them, but he's pulling my chain every chance he gets.

A few days ago he came in and ripped down some extra-large pictures I had on the wall. Bobby Lewis (then Ted's best friend on The Row) used to have twice as many, twice as big. But while he was doing it, he rattled around through my books and papers, loud-mouthing about "Wonder what we'll find under here?" and "Don't suppose Teddy is getting ready to run for it, is he?"

HA: I would imagine they would always roust you around. There can't be any love lost. And I'm sure they resent the fact you play lawyer back there for other inmates. That might help your relationships with the inmates, but it won't necessarily make you a hero to the management. And, let's face it, some of those guards might even live over around Lake City.

But, more importantly, what's this crap about Stephen or me telling people that you are planning an escape?

TB: Where else could it have come from?

HA: That's the most ridiculous thing I ever heard of. In the first place, though we've discussed escape, you've never done anything but try to avoid the whole subject. And I understand why.

TB: Last time, I said…

HA: Let me finish. Secondly, if you *had* told me you had such plans, why would I talk about it? The book won't be out for more than a year and we need more time with you to square up some facts we've discussed before. I don't want to lose access to you because the prison thinks you're heading south some morning.

Thirdly, I don't think you can do it. It's a hell of a lot different escaping from the Aspen courthouse or the Glenwood Springs jail than it is out of this fortress. Hell, sometimes after we finish talking, I am not sure *I'm* going to get out of here.

TB: Well, I didn't think you would do anything, but, uh, Carole…

HA: I think you have to face it, Ted: Carole thinks you're innocent and we *know* otherwise, so she can't imagine why we're not coming up with all sorts of evidence that proves you innocent. In fact, since I last saw you, she has written to Stephen and asked that he come back to talk to you – that you two have more rapport and so on. You're not going to hear anything gracious or good about Michaud and Aynesworth from your wife. You, of all people, should realize that.

TB: Yeah, but you know you kept trying to get me off on talking about escape the last time... uh, the last *two* times you were here. And right after that, I started getting bugged about it. And I am not even comfortable talking with Carole about such things.

All you've done that I can see is upset some of the family and write a couple chapters about my escapes. If I had wanted somebody harassed and...

HA: I cannot imagine what family members we have upset or offended. I telephoned your uncle in Arkansas and asked to discuss your youth with him. He explained that he might lose his position if he were to become associated publicly with you, and so we left him alone and made no further effort to talk to him.

On the escape chapters, yes, we got those done pretty well because they are about the only relatively current facts you're willing to help us with. Outside of your step-by-step tales of how you outsmarted the people in Aspen and the jailers at Glenwood Springs and your successful career of boosting everything from a benjamina tree to cars, you haven't been all that helpful. I know that...

TB: You knew going in that I wasn't going to confess to anything. If I *was* guilty (pause) – and I'm *not*, of all these things you think I did, do you think I would just come out and lay it on the line? What would be my motivation?

HA: Well, when I first started on this project, I thought you *must* have had some exculpatory information – something that could shed doubt on *something*, but long ago I determined you did not. That was, I figured, the only good thing that could come out of your participation. Now I honestly don't know why.

(Bundy raises a hand, rolls his eyes, and takes a moment to closely scrutinize all wires present in the room. They all seem to be firmly connected with the interviewer's recorder.)

TB: All right, but you know I don't feel right about our deal. Nothing has happened, and as I sit here month after month I have to wonder if you two have taken everything and forgotten about me. You promised that you would...

HA: We promised, as we are both abundantly aware, that we would investigate any and all possibilities that might lead to exculpatory information for your defense. Free. For nothing! Gladly – and professionally. In return, you agreed you would make yourself available to us, as often as needed, and tell us the *truth* about all your activities.

For several months, I traveled all over the west and southwest trying to run down rumors and possibilities – things that you and Carole thought might be productive. Want to know the scorecard on that? About twenty to nothing, pure ass crap! We haven't been able to find enough to get one of those credit card thefts of yours turned around!

And you know why? Because you've been absolutely no help. That's Number 1. And Number 2, because you don't *have* anything to help with. You can't even tell me where you were on a given holiday... sometimes, even, on your birthday.

TB: Well, maybe I just won't participate anymore. I don't see anything good coming out of it.

HA: Would you have wanted Stephen and I to just sit and talk and act like we believed everything you told us about your innocence? Would that have pleased you? I guess you expected us to come up with a real mystery here: "Is Ted Bundy, that wonderfully clever fellow, being railroaded by circumstantial evidence?"

We made it damn clear – and to the family and to Carole also – that we would investigate for you and give you and your attorneys anything that might help you. Almost in the same breath, we said we would be compelled to write the truth as we saw it – no matter which way it fell.

Now you just don't like the way it fell. And we're well aware that Carole thinks we're a couple of shits. I don't know how it works, but you've got her fooled. She *really*, I think, believes you didn't do anything. And so she thinks we are out to cause you even more grief.

You *have* been cooperative in some ways, I'll admit. You've given us access to your school records, letters, court documents, and the like. But you got pissed off when we tried to interview Liz, you made us promise not to interview your grandfather, and you've stonewalled on what you promised to write about Chi Omega – which you offered to contribute months ago.

TB: Now wait a minute, Hugh, it's true that I've been somewhat less than helpful in some areas, but it hasn't been intentional. It's a combination of being in here, of not trusting several people I used to trust on the outside, and just going through an emotional period where I have forgotten a lot of details.

Can you tell me where *you* were on December 8, 1975, or even February 5, 1980? Why are you grinning and shaking your head? This may be funny to you, but...

HA: No, it's not funny to me. I have spent a lot of time dealing with you and Carole and at least a dozen weirdos these past months, and Stephen and I have spent every bit of the advance money the publisher gave us just trying to catch it. That, and running down the bogus investigative leads you two have provided us.

I only think it funny – and a little sad that you're not realistic about all this. *Every* fake lead I ran down cost us. We spent the time and money. We realized, and it didn't take very long, that you weren't leveling with us on *anything*... and now you complain to us that you feel left out, that you think, somehow, *we* have reneged on our agreements.

I'll be the first to agree that we haven't moved the project along as fast as we would've liked, but that's not our fault.

TB: Well, it seems that both you and I are dissatisfied with this relationship. You want something I cannot give you... and yet, you act like I promised it.

I've done my best, and at some personal cost, to describe to you the person that did these crimes – from my knowledge from reading of the crimes and my study of the psychological bent of such people in our society. I've tried to explain the moods, feelings, and subtleties.

I thought that by now – it's been almost two years of this – you and Steve would have the book done. It seems as though you have done little toward it. You're still trying to get me to step quite a ways further than I ever agreed to.

I don't need any more of this. Just last month I had an offer – you saw the letter, I think – to do a big, big interview with a major network. I didn't even answer it.

HA: It is up to you; do what you want. But to get back to the main reason I came down here – well, actually, there were about three, but we've discussed most of them. We don't want you to believe that we've said anything publicly about you planning to escape… or *not* planning to. In the first place, as we both know, you have refused to talk about it – even though I *was* curious a couple times.

It would be ridiculous for us to comment on such a thing. In fact, if it were in the works, I don't *want* to know about it. I think it would be suicide for you – with the feeling Florida has about you. And, frankly, right up until today, I hoped you still had something to share with us. And while I didn't think you'd ever be *pleased* with the book, I thought you would understand that we went about our task honestly – and came to our conclusions honestly.

TB: I guess you are justified in your arguments, but let's just say that one becomes paranoid in here. No way to get out your frustrations. Oh, you can get 'em out, okay, but the results might be worse than the frustration. And I keep hearing about the questions you've been asking people. I don't know. And you never seem to want to meet with Carole. And she is definitely a part of this.

HA: I understand your concern, but it's hard to deal with a well-intentioned person who lives in the dark about the subject. That's a problem *you* have fostered and nurtured… and someday you're going to have to deal with it in a much sounder manner. But that's *your* business, not mine. But it *does* become a problem for Stephen and me.

(The guard stops by the door and says, "Five minutes.")

TB: See? They know everything that's going on. Next time we ought to try to get that other room. It's louder. The heating and air conditioning in there sort of vibrates or something.

HA: Hell, if they wanted to know anything, they could just take my tapes when I leave. I'd raise hell, but by the time they had to give them back, they could have them copied. Well, anyway, where *were* we?

TB: You were leaving, a very dissatisfied man... and I was telling you that you shouldn't be; that you have more information in these months of interviews than anybody will ever have about Ted Bundy. Are you planning to come back tomorrow?

HA: No, they've told me there are a dozen lawyers or so that need a lot of time with their clients and that I probably couldn't get back in for a few days. I'll have to go back home and do some transcribing. But I'll check with Carole and see how things are.

March 31

Another letter from Bundy: "I need to talk to you. What's going on?" This will be the final meeting with Ted.

TB: I didn't know if you were coming back or not. Carole

said she had not heard from you or Steve. I got to thinking, after that last get-together, that I had been somewhat testy with you and that your remarks about your relationship with Carole – while not particularly pleasing – may have had some merit. Like you said, she is in a peculiar situation and there's no reason why *any* of us should like each other, uh, necessarily.

But I'd certainly like to feel that I can trust you two. I haven't the slightest idea what's going on with the book, and I *have* to feel like my further help is just lost time. You have not kept me informed. You have told me, in effect, that my suggestions are meaningless to you. And who does this New York person think she is, writing to me and telling me she wants me to confess!

HA: Well, nobody has used the word "confession." But we have told our editors, constantly, that you insisted on writing what you suggested for the opening chapter, the Chi Omega thing. God, we've talked about it so much, I'm almost blue in the face.

You told me last summer, then last fall, and again this year that you were "working on it." Last time I was here you told me you'd try once again. You said we might have to work on it a bit, redo it or whatever... but that it would be unique, something unusual, something damn hard.

TB: Uh, I don't know how hard it would be.

HA: Well, not hard, but I mean something new, something, you know – because you said you'd go into this person, what his feelings were that night, you know, the day before, what he was doing, that sort of thing.

TB: As I recall, I formu –... uh, advanced the idea of me writing something, *simply* to help you and Steve get an idea of what I continue to believe would be the only way to approach this thing.

HA: We talked about it three or four times.

TB: We talked about it.

HA: I asked you point blank, "What do you envision in this thing?" and you told me "his feelings, how it would have operated, how it would have happened" We agreed it would be something that nobody would know about but it would be striking enough to grab the reader.

TB: Yeah, actually, I suppose it would be.

HA: And I have done nothing on the idea with the governor because, once again, the ball's in your court. You seemed completely disillusioned about the project – and your role in it – last month. You said nothing about it in your letter and, as you know, without your *complete* cooperation, I'm not about to raise the issue.

TB: What do you think I could do – in *here*?

HA: The same thing we discussed in the past. One, make a list of all the cases you were involved in. A no-shit list – times, places, dates, names if you knew 'em. Two, give the list to me or give it to Carole when she comes in.
No, that won't work, will it? Okay, just write me a letter with the dates listed in it. Then a few days later, send another letter with just the names of the towns. Listed in the same

order if you can. Then I'll come back and we'll sit down and get specific... but first, after checking with some of the police jurisdictions – and we know pretty much what we're talking about here, don't we? I'll then contact the governor and see if they want to work out some sort of a deal.

TB: That sounds all well and good, for *you*, but it means nothing to me and, as I recall, I long ago rejected it as an idea or an approach.

HA: No you didn't.

TB: Now...

HA: Okay, after talking to Carole, I figured you might have changed your mind, but listen to this... damnit, listen to *exactly* what you said, uh, last October.

(A tape of the lengthy session in which Hugh offers to contact Governor Bob Graham is played. Bundy smokes three cigarettes and chews his nails, acting nonchalant, disinterested.)

TB: Then I reject it now. The word "confession" is used... or "will confess" or something to that... on that order. You're filled with ample material on tapes where I say again and again that I'm not going to... there's no point, there's... there's nothing to confess.

HA: You say you'll help with the crimes. How are you going to help somebody with crimes if you don't confess?

TB: I'll tell them I didn't do it. Wouldn't that help (laughs)?

HA: I don't think so. You've already told 'em that.

TB: That's their problem. But I... what I'm saying is that, uh... if you color (it) by making that kind of approach, uh, come-on... you're coloring the kind of response you get... the bias and, uh, that... that's going to lead you *not* to accurate information but to (unintelligible) information.

HA: All right, you want to talk about accurate information. Let's talk about accurate information. You've lied to us on several occasions, Ted.

TB: I don't know what about.

HA: Well, on several occasions you've lied to us. Well, let's see... let's just... Christ, I'll turn it off if you like! You know, this is ridiculous! You're sitting there and telling me you've never lied to me. In the first place, you told us you had nothing to do with *any* of these crimes. That's not reasonable!

TB: Sure it is.

HA: Look, you like for people to have respect for your brain, your mind and yourself. Well, maybe I'd like that same respect. I don't understand. You know if you had visited with me and you had investigated many crimes that I was concerned with and you came to the conclusion that I was guilty and I kept saying, "No, I'm not... I wasn't there. I can't tell you where I

290 Stephen G. Michaud and Hugh Aynesworth

was, but I wasn't there." This one and that one. You know, how would you feel? You'd feel like your intelligence was being insulted, wouldn't you?

TB: I, uh, well, I might feel that way. It depends on just my mood. It may not simply be a case of insulting intelligences because, I mean, I have no best interest in insulting your intelligence. I certainly get no gratification from it. I know you have to make a living... and you have to produce something that's... that's, uh, uh, acceptable to persons who have different priorities than I do. And I have different priorities than they do. What we're trying to do is reach a compromise. I don't think it's a matter of insulting intelligences, uh, necessarily.

HA: All right. You remember when I asked you *five* times... maybe six times, if you would tell me a number; how many victims... how many people. And you said, "Well, I'll try to think of a way to do that." You said to me one time, "Well, perhaps I can." You said, "Bring me a list of the names and dates of those"... and then you stopped and said, "No, that won't work because they're all attributed to me and I'm not going to be involved in *that!*"

Well, what the hell were you? You know, what were you going to help me with? You were just going to make up a number?

TB: Hmmm.

HA: You're... you're not... Ted, you're not innocent, goddamnit. I don't *care* if you're innocent or not, but you're *not*... and you lied to us all the way.

TB: I never made any promises I didn't keep.

HA: Bullshit! When Stephen and I agreed to investigate every possible nook and cranny to try to find exculpatory evidence for you – because you swore it was all *out* there, just waiting for somebody to pull it together – you swore that you would tell us the truth, the absolute truth.

Of course, we skirted that, didn't make an issue of it, for months, until Stephen left and I was your conduit. Months ago I stopped acting like I thought you innocent and you stopped thinking up places for me to go and investigate ridiculous allegations and "evidence." And we, of course, realized that to confront you any stronger than we did was to risk losing your input, the cooperation you have given. After all, you had virtually nothing to gain – and potentially, plenty to lose.

And, I'll have to admit, that despite what your original intentions (were), you've given us considerable insights into a killer's mind. You can always say you are innocent, but there are those who will know you are talking about yourself.

TB: That would be foolish for them to do so, to think that.

HA: When I suggested the possibility that law-enforcement people might flock to talk with you, bringing psychiatrists and psychologists by the dozens, I was seriously trying to do something worthwhile, for you – and for the cops and the victims' families.

I don't know how long you've got, but it can't be more than seven or eight more years. You say you're not going to try to escape. Your appeals, though I'm no lawyer, seem spurious at best... so you're *going* to die. It's just when... and how.

Something like this might buy you another year or two –
and give you a decent feeling that you'd done all you could to
make up for…

TB: To make up for *what?* I think you succumbed to the
same things that the police succumbed to, hoping, you know,
that he'll come through. For whatever reason, I don't know.

HA: I can see we're not even close to being on the same
wave length here. It's too bad, because we both appreciate the
time and effort you have given. And, let's face it, when you
suggested coming up with that Chi Omega stuff, I damn near
fell off my chair. There's no way we could expect anything like
that in reality.

I have to tell you, the first part of our arrangement, I always
thought, was beneficial to you at the time. You enjoyed talking
out some of your thoughts, and you didn't have much outlet for
that kind of self-examination inside these walls. And I think
you always considered yourself so smart, so wily, that – at least
in *your* mind – you always thought there was a chance the book
could make you look good.

So, to that point, you got your money's worth. But we
couldn't provide even a doubt in any of the murders – probably
because there *is* no doubt. You lost on that. We've turned over
the rocks – and there's nothing there to make you look or feel
any better.

But if you had come through with your description of what
went on in the killer's mind in Tallahassee that night, it would've
far surpassed all the ruminating and postulating you've done –
and though it wouldn't have helped the girls at Chi Omega, it
might have added something to the world's knowledge about a

very disturbing sociological phenomena.

TB: I *wanted* to do it... but it was just too hard. And I couldn't do it part way, edit it, work with it back there. Somebody would've... could've found it and used it against me. And it was too important, uh, to...

HA: I thought you came close two or three times. And I thought that talking about it would be a great burden off your mind.

TB: A burden? No, I carry no burden, except being in prison.

HA: You can compartmentalize better than anyone I've ever known!

TB: It's not a matter of... well, it *may* have been a matter of compartmentalization, which is *not* the process by any means. I've learned to live absolutely and completely and totally in the *here and now*. I don't worry, think or concern myself with the past, or, for that matter, with the future, except only to the extent necessary.

That in itself is not pathological. If you study, which I have been studying to some degree, oriental philosophy – Buddhism and Taoism and spiritual-physical traditions of the East are much in tune with the way I have become.

As a result, I find that the pressures on me have actually permitted me to enter into a period of growth – for whatever value that has for me. It's not going to be relevant to *you* or somebody at large... I don't know. But I tried to give you a measure of my optimism when I gave you that book on... uh, pardon me, that article on holistic medicine.

HA: And that means you have no further desire to cleanse anything from the past? I don't understand.

TB: Well, whatever I've done in the past, you know – the emotions of omissions or commissions – *doesn't* bother me.

Try to touch the past! Try to deal with the past. It's not real. It's just a dream! In fact, it's as real as the future.

HA: I wish I could treat the past two years with the same philosophy.

TB: It had to come to this! I was sitting around – those first few months – and just being affected by everything that went on, with Carole, with my family, with you and Steve and this book thing. God only knows why I got involved, though I actually enjoyed parts of it. Only parts, now.

Now, it is a lot easier for me to write a nasty letter than to sit here and get really uptight. You know… my letter to you guys… it was a lot easier to write that than to confront you with the same vehemence today.

I've never gotten close to you, Hugh, but I've never done you any wrong, either. I didn't bring you into this project and then dump on you. I may have not given you what you wanted, but God's sakes! I haven't given a lot of people what they wanted. I do regret that it's come to this point.

But what did I *ever* have to gain? I don't give a damn about what is written about me, and I…

HA: You sure did when you thought it might go your

way.

TB: Not so. Not so. I knew you both were professionals and you would write what you believed. I dreaded it anyway, because every time I hear about some book or magazine article written about me, I'm always deeply distressed. I haven't won too many so far.

I mean, certainly there was a time when I used the press, but, you know, only as a technique to cause confusion and to bolster my defense. That was not for publicity's sake. At any rate, I regret that this state of events will, in some way, hurt you and Steve and your attempt to write a good book. That was not my intention.

Actually, I can't see why you don't have enough right now to finish it. What else do you need?

HA: Are you shoving this situation back into a comfortable compartment, Ted? We have spent days, weeks, and months, getting your feelings, remembrances, your instincts, and the like. But what we need – or at least what is needed for the best book – is the truth from you.

I need to know what *really* happened in the Leach and Chi Omega cases. I need to know whether we're writing about half a dozen murders or fifty. I need to have some idea how the murderer felt, how he was transformed from an acceptable member of society into a madman. And I'd like to know where most of the bodies are.

I can understand your unwillingness to talk about the Florida cases in detail, but there's nothing but good (that) can come from understanding and, in effect, solving, the cases in the West.

TB: But I don't see the problem. You know enough about all of this that you and Steve can just fill in the holes. I told you a long time ago that you could make up as many as you like. It'll sell better. And who cares?

HA: Well, it's like our editor said recently, "He's already confessed... that plea-bargain deal. He's guilty and everybody knows it. Why won't he just tell you?"

TB: Well, we live in different worlds, obviously. We look at the world differently, that is, she and I. We *all* look at the world differently.

HA: Yeah. Well, I can understand where you are and how you feel. But there's something that I *don't* understand. You say the past is not real and doesn't even matter. And yet you remember the past. So why in hell don't you talk about it... and get it all out and get it done?

TB: Well... I remember, as you might remember... a Humphrey Bogart movie. When it's over, you don't talk about it all the time.

HA: Going to a movie isn't exactly like killing people, Ted! Now, goddamnit, you're straining reality here again!

TB: Are we? We're *always* straining reality... every day. I don't know what to say to you except to tell you that, uh, I just view things a lot differently.

Prison has helped me, because it forces me and everyone else to live in the here and now. Only I do so differently. Some people in prison try to escape from being right here, right now. They do it with drugs or they do it with any number of cute devices. But I've been able to use that tremendous gift of living *right now* – to see everything where it is – as much as I can right now.

It's to my advantage. It took me four or five years until I could reach that point, because I didn't know what it was. I used to live each day at a time, just to protect myself. Now I live each day, and each moment, to try to expand myself. It may not make sense to you, but...

HA: Actually, it doesn't make sense to me.

TB: Well, a lot of people, uh, *most* people – at least those I'm most familiar with – are encumbered with a kind of mechanism that is called guilt. And as I understand it, guilt *is* a mechanism. To a degree, I have certainly experienced it, but much less so now than ever while I was on the streets. Or even two years ago!

HA: What do you mean, less?

TB: I mean I don't feel guilty for *anything!* I feel less guilty now than I've felt in any time in my life. About anything. And it's not that I've forgotten anything, or else closed down part of my mind, or compartmentalized. I compartmentalize less now than I ever have.

It's just done! It's back *there* in the mists! I say "mists" because I don't think anyone actually touches the past the way they can touch the present or the future.

Guilt? It's this mechanism we use to control people. It's an illusion. It's a kind of social control mechanism – and it's very unhealthy. It does terrible things to our bodies. And there are much better ways to control our behavior than that rather extraordinary use of guilt.

It doesn't solve anything, necessarily. It's just a very gross technique we impose upon ourselves to control the people, groups of people. I guess I am in the enviable position of not having to deal with guilt. There's just no reason for it.

I don't think I need to feel guilty anymore, because I try to do what's right, right *now!* And I either do or I don't. And that's it. Now, some people could listen to what I just said and say, "See, he's a sociopath," or whatever term they use. "He doesn't feel any guilt. Oh, how terrible! He doesn't feel any guilt!" Hah!

I feel sorry for people who feel guilt. I'm not talking about the *act*. I'm talking about the emotional consequences of the act. I feel sorry for people who are drug addicts or who are *criminals*. I feel sorry for business executives who have to lust after money and power. I feel sorry for a lot of people who have to do things that hurt them.

But I don't feel sorry for anyone who doesn't feel guilty because the guilt doesn't solve anything, really. It hurts you. You don't need guilt to do the right thing. You don't have to feel bad about the past to be able to do well right here and now. And it's the here and now that carries us to the future. You don't need to feel badly. You don't need to regret.

HA: Well, that seems easy enough for someone who simply doesn't want to face the facts about a life that went astray. I'm not sure it bodes well for the future, however. Don't you care, for instance, about how others feel about you – and, more particularly, how they would feel if they knew you had absolutely no remorse, guilt, or sorrow?

TB: Sure, that's, uh... that's just part of the social reinforcement scheme. We do well because of what our peers and our families think about it. We try not to do things that hurt them, or make them feel badly about us. It's a positive-negative reinforcement and all that. That's part of the illusion of our contemporary existence.

We do a *lot* of things that are just really bizarre, if you stop and think about it. That are just terribly destructive. I don't want to get into preaching again, but I mean, I've done a lot of, uh... I've done a lot of self-inspection – I guess that's the word – and I try to understand what I do in each and every minute.

But for all our progress, Hugh, for all the great things this society is accomplishing, look how sick we've gotten. What kind of testimony is that for the rational mind? Or to our civilized social structure? There is something terribly wrong with the way things are going.

It manifested itself in me, okay? I saw what it did! I can readily see now what it did to me. We've tried to discuss that. I've tried to explain it to you. Okay? I can *understand* what it did to me and I'm not trying to externalize the blame or place it on anybody else.

I *do* understand it! I acted in concert with my environment, or allowed myself to be absorbed in my environment. I understand that now, better than before – especially when I see a lot of the young people and the way they're headed today.

You know, they know better, but at the rate they're going... I see the way we live. I see the way a lot of people destroy themselves, Hugh. Now, Steve is a real nice, bright guy. I don't know a *lot* about him – except during our contacts – but here's a young fellow, a young man, who doesn't eat right, abuses his body with alcohol and cigarettes, and lives just a hectic existence. And he thinks it's peachy! He thinks it's just the greatest thing in the world.

HA: Yeah.

TB: And I'm not trying to be self-righteous about it. I'm not saying I'm better or anybody's better or worse, but there's got to be something wrong with an existence that makes us feel good about destroying ourselves a little bit at a time. That's where I'm coming from. It's kind of an individual experiment right now. I don't know how it would translate into being back in society – and being subjected to the old stresses and pressures which were a part of my mental, uh, program.

HA: Many people go through such stresses – and though they are obviously *affected*, they don't act such things out.

TB: True, well, there are those, too… it's not a problem that lends itself to a very satisfactory analysis. If you choose one set of circumstances over another, who knows what errors you're making? I would guess that, a hundred or two hundred years ago, a lot of the men who are in prison *now* would not have been in prison – simply because of the environment they lived in.

They would not have had the opportunity or the need to engage in criminal behavior or socially deviant behavior. It wouldn't be there – the temptation or the perversion, the corruption or what have you. So, yeah, it's environmental.

What's happening, I think, is that modern society is testing our genetic materials to capacity… and those who have certain weaknesses or predispositions – which would probably have not manifested themselves in a less indulgent society – are being identified and thrust into deviant action.

Steve, as a matter of fact, in a letter he wrote to me, quoted a passage from a book on psychopathology that, in effect, said just that. I guess I was pretty impressed because I thought he was doing some research in that area.

I forget the title, but it more or less said that society is driving some of its individuals past the point where they can conform. The kind of environment we're producing the social and physical and what have you.

I doubt that my chromosomes are radically different from those of people who lived quite lawfully in centuries past. But modern forces will test these. It's a rather cold way of looking at it, but I *do* believe it's possible to retreat. But you have to be able to totally shut yourself off from the, uh, forces.

HA: Well, you seem to know yourself much better today than before. If you had it to do over again, would you be able to avoid getting trapped by this?

TB: There are lots of things. If I knew myself as well as I do now, yes. I would've never gone to college, for instance.

HA: Never gone to college?

TB: I would never want to be an attorney.

HA: Why wouldn't you have wanted to go to college?

TB: That may have been a rather extreme statement. But all

college does is refine the rather shortsighted ways of thinking that we accept in society. It gives us the ability to seek the goals of society, uh, more efficiently – and that's good whether it's for power, greed, or to have physical possessions, or just to live in harmony with other people.

HA: But there have to be some parameters set somewhere.

TB: I think if I had it to do over, I'd, maybe, be a lumberjack.

HA: A lumberjack?

TB: I'd have as little contact with modern society as possible. If I could have recognized fifteen years ago the poisonous consequences of modern life – not only the physical things that are being done to us but the intellectual, spiritual, and poisoning we get – I would have certainly withdrawn.

Or I might have interacted in society in a way that I would have tried to debunk the contemporary notions that we accept as success. You know, the house, the good job, and all that. There's nothing wrong with feeding and clothing and sheltering oneself, in a family, but there's certainly something amiss when we have to deal with the multi-expectations of today's society.

HA: It isn't the easiest thing to disengage from society, though.

TB: It isn't. It's like we're on this runaway train. We know it's running away with us, but it would be a hell of a thing getting off! You might make it; you might not. You're sure to get a bundle of bruises any way you look at it. But, you know, jumping off that train – even when it's at its fastest – might save you the pain and grief of going off the cliff later.

HA: Don't you wish you'd been more mature eight or ten years ago?

TB: Sure, I wish I had been exposed to a lot more.

HA: You really were somewhat sheltered, you know. Except academically. Socially, you were pretty immature.

TB: I think that was my most glaring limitation, the cause of a lot of grief over those years. Once I was able to see the world... see people and things around me, in a less dispassionate, uh, more compassionate way... I felt much more comfortable with myself. And with everything around me.

HA: You know, when you delve inside yourself like this – without all the bravado and arrogance – I find myself really hating to see your life end up like this. A man of your intellect, your ability. I've sometimes been harsh with you because I thought you were always playing games with me, but when I see you truly suffer, it's a hell of a thing to see.
And I'll remember it for a long time.

TB: Well, I... I'm glad you are able to feel that way about me – not that it makes me feel better, necessarily, but that it makes me feel better about *you*. You know, you've been able to see some things that maybe other people can't see. There are a lot of people out there that for one reason or another are going haywire!

And when they do, they don't go haywire like, uh (pause)... some of the guys in here. They may require a psychiatrist. They may get a divorce, they may take up drinking. But no matter what, they are less effective people. God help 'em if they go all the way!

HA: I can't even imagine.

TB: Some malfunctions, you know, are more spectacular than others. And we're seeing more and more of the spectacular. And, as time goes on, with increasing ferocity, you're going to see more of it.

HA: What about you? Are you going to be all right?

TB (pause): Oh, yeah. Yeah. I'm all right.

HA: You say that rather flippantly.

TB: Well, I try not to struggle with it. I don't mean to be flippant. Actually, where I am right now... I'm in the best possible shape I could be. Well, I mean, uh, for someone here in prison and living on Death Row.

I'm *always* making improvements – and you can put that in quotations. I feel *good* about me. I feel that I'm doing the right things and moving in the right direction. I'm doing as well as I could've ever imagined myself doing. I look back, a few years back, when I was in prison in Utah or jail in Colorado, and I shake my head and I just felt like I was sort of engulfed by my plight. And the jail life was threatening my well-being.

But I no longer have this angst. I'm not, of course, at the

mercy of outside influences – at least not like I once was. I'm still jeopardized, but I don't let that have a negative effect on what's going on inside me. I recognize it and know it's not good, but you know, I realize what my situation is and I'm minimizing the effect on me. It just doesn't mean as much as it once did.

HA: But you *must* feel it. Outside influences decide whether you live or die… when, where, how…

TB: Yeah, but for me, right *now*, I can't even describe… I don't know if I ever could have reached the point to have seen things as clearly as I can now, Hugh.

If all this hadn't happened – let's say something else happened and I went on to become an attorney. If I were to have a dream tonight and it would come true – that I graduated and became a lawyer, married Liz, and had a perfectly *miserable* life for the remainder of my days… got totally caught up in the law and all the politics and controversy, the mortgages and marital discord, the alcohol and all that stuff…

I'll be serious with you right now. I would not trade where I *am*, in this year, right now… for a new shot at my old existence. It would be too painful.

HA: Not even if you had today's ability to sort things out?

TB: Well, that'd be a different matter. Carole and I were discussing this the other day. And I said that if somebody came to me and promised that if I went back and I was assured that everything would be peachy, if I became a lawyer, I'd go on out there and the day after tomorrow I'd resign from the firm. And I'd go live a different life, completely.

HA: Unfortunately, we don't ever have those chances. In your new-found serenity, how do you react to others who don't understand this convenient rebirth, as it were? For instance, I'm sure the prison officials don't think of you as some Gandhi-like philosopher who just dropped by the Florida prison to help inmates find inner peace. And how do you feel about people like me? I sit here and say, "I think you're a murderer. I think you're guilty." I mean, how does that make you feel? Do you care?

TB: It's not a matter of caring. It doesn't have any meaning for me.

HA: You don't have any animosity, do you?

TB: No, absolutely none. I mean, I may have in the past. I may have acted defensively in the past or manifested that kind of need to defend myself. That's, you know, the nature of the ego. One of the things wrong with this society is that everyone is trying to protect or nurture egos; our little false beliefs of having an identity that is separate from everything and everyone else.

That which separates you from me is our egos. And so I would have felt the need to preserve that – that false sense of separateness, by becoming hostile. But there's no such need now. What you say just doesn't even register with me; I care nothing about it.

And what I try to feel toward you is, you know, the best possible feelings. Certainly we're locked in – in one of those arrangements which, unfortunately, are part of these artificial obstructions in our society. The book. The guilt or innocence

– all those things that are really meaningless.

But they brought about unpleasant, you know, clashes between you and I (sic). But I now have positive protection against that. It really doesn't matter to me *what* you think.

HA: Well, I've enjoyed visiting with you. *Sometimes* I have! Sometimes I haven't. To be very frank about it, it's often been quite a strain.

TB: It's unpleasant (pause). I reached a point, in May or June of 1979... or was it 1980? I'm trying to figure all this out. Yeah, it was '80, after the Lake City trial in Orlando. Steve had been coming around for a few weeks, then there was a delay of several weeks, and then here he came again.

And I noticed, I started running down, unconsciously making my way down through the path which I see more clearly now. That is, trying to disengage myself from that way of thinking which so severely influenced me before and trying to see things as they *really* are.

When I was in jail in Lake City, or Leon County, and then off to trial in Miami, and then I was here and then on trial in Orlando, I was locked into that struggle, struggle, struggle, fight, fight, fight... think like a lawyer, talk like a lawyer, play the game. And the whole thing reached a point where just thinking about this business became totally disdainful to me. *Not* just because it involved me; that was obviously a major part, I'll admit, but it was just so senseless. So meaningless. Such an absurd exercise.

And then, every time I was forced to talk with you and Steve, it moved me along. I cannot say I didn't enjoy some of the sessions, for they brought back good and decent memories, but you never gave me a full day, even, of that. It was always back to the slime, back to the allegations, back to what I'd been fighting in the system for years.

HA: But, in fairness, it was *your* actions that set the tone of our relationship. And I'll have to admit that while I *did* react with furor on a few occasions at your lack of remorse or inability to relate to others' pain, I handled many questions with as much gentleness as I could muster, because I full well realize you are a human being, also.

I often felt touched by your situation. But before long, reality always had to return... and my pity – yes, I guess it was pity – for you, became tempered with the knowledge that there were many parents whose lives will never be the same because of you.

TB: I guess I was arrogant, at least in your eyes. But I always knew – you see, I *am* able to understand the outside world, too – I always knew there was this tremendous interest. Not in me, particularly, but in that monumental question, "What *is* a Ted Bundy?"

HA: I think the compelling factor was that you are not an ordinary fellow. You're not the kind of person society envisions as doing these things. That's the main thing, don't you think?

TB: I think so. It's not because *I'm* different from most of the men back there on Death Row. It's in large part because I got so much publicity and so I have a very high profile. And people tend to think about me a lot more than the others back there... those who are virtually nameless, without publicity.

And people are fascinated by anyone who kills, especially anyone who is attributed to have killed frequently.

HA: Right.

TB: I have guards who ask me questions – like they expect me to answer. One of them'll say, "Why, you're such a nice, intelligent guy!" Blah, blah, blah. "And what I can't figure out..." I can understand the interest, why that interest is there. And I can understand how important it would be for some people if I said I'd done it all.

If I could, you know, get out in front... and answer the questions you and everybody else have asked me, it would titillate everyone's imagination and, maybe, temporarily satisfy the need to do it. But it wouldn't broaden their consciousness of really what is the matter!

I know there is that great interest out there to see Ted Bundy. Partially because the crimes are unusual. Well, they *are* and they aren't. As your editor put it, there are a lot of men back there on Death Row whose stories aren't that much different than mine.

I understand that. I mean, the story has been told before, again and again. The really scary thing is that there are a *lot* of people who are not in prison, a lot of people who are not in prison, who are *far* more successful than I.

HA: How do you know that? It's just a gut feeling. You don't know that.

TB: Every day I know it. The Atlanta (Wayne Williams case) situation is just an aberration.

HA: I don't believe that's just one person over there.

TB: That's *not* just one person – but you see, someone is being *so* obvious or some group of people is being so obvious about it, and they are still getting away with it.

There's a case now down in southern Florida, where a man – they're digging up bodies on this man's farm! One girl disappeared in 1975. The man's in his fifties, okay? So he's now in prison on sex offenses. They're trying to put all sorts of other cases on him. They say his property is just full of bodies. Not the ultimate skeleton in the closet situation.

And this guy's in his fifties! And in all probability, they don't have anything to link him up to these crimes – and probably won't, because all they have is skeletons. So what! But (in) all probability, from what little I know about things like this, he's been at it for twenty or thirty years, and has never been caught – until now.

HA: How do you know that? How do you know when a man starts? That's a hard thing to determine, isn't it?

TB: I think a man starts early. The problems… are with him early on. The problems may not manifest themselves until the twenties. But I think more often than not such a person – now, I'm not talking about the kind of thing where a man secretly goes around abducting girls and disposing of them secretly. A guy who abducts girls like that, that comes from some incident that manifests itself very early in his life. In every case that I've read about, without exception, Hugh, that behavior started somewhere in the twenties.

HA: That would mean this guy operated for thirty years. Damn!

TB: There's no exception I've ever seen where a man has been known to have started in his forties and fifties.

HA: Well, what about John Gacy? He didn't start in his twenties.

TB: I don't know. I haven't read much about him but my impressions are that he was in trouble for a long, long time. I mean, on the fringes of trouble, anyway. I understand he had been arrested and confined for this type thing before.

What may have changed him into a more dangerous individual is that he saw the act of murder and concealment as a way of avoiding detection for the, uh, sex crime.

We have a man in back – that's what happened to him. He was in and out of mental hospitals in Maryland ever since he was a teenager. He first started beating up little kids. Then he started molesting young boys. They kept putting him in these institutions and he kept escaping. And they kept releasing him.

Finally, it got to the point where they got real serious with him. They told him that – he was in his early twenties – they said if he got in trouble again, he would be treated as an adult. And this kid just walked away from an institution and picked up a young boy and molested him. When it clicked in his mind that they were going to throw the book at him, he killed the kid. Killed him to conceal the crime. And kept on doing that until, several years later, they caught him.

HA: Well, in effect, that's one of the biggest points

you made: Killing wasn't the big thing. It was often just a necessity.

TB: It would seem so. That would seem to be the case. Uh, let me finish a little bit here and I'll let you get on your way.

HA: Yeah, I guess I'd better get over to Jacksonville and see if I can get a flight out tonight (long pause). I just saw Watson (the assistant superintendent) go by with some people. I guess they have a lot of people who just want to look.

TB: There are. They all want to see Bundy. A lot of 'em do. "Where's Bundy?" I'll hear. "Let's go see Bundy." They'll drift by. There've been a lot of 'em.

HA: Well, if you get tired of that, you could just expose yourself to them and maybe they wouldn't come back.

TB: Well, what I generally do is confound them. "Hi, how are you doin' there? Isn't this a nice cell?" You know, my cell is always clean and neat – and I'm not afraid of them. And I know their little secret: They're afraid of Ted Bundy!

HA: What makes you think people are afraid of you? *I'm* not afraid of you. I don't understand.

TB: I know you're not afraid of me. You've been *around* me a lot. You're not responding exclusively to that old belief that says that anybody who has been accused of doing what I've done is some kind of crazed, malicious, tyrant monster.

I had this one guy who put his arm around this woman

and walked her toward my cell. She was just scared to *death!* Other people show their fascination other ways. Some just stand to one side and look at me. I can see them mirrored in my television. They all cluster around in groups of four or five... and I'll whip around... and they'll scatter (laughs)!

HA: Oh, (laughs) that's good.

TB: Some of them have this *morbid* curiosity. I mean, it's like looking at the great white shark. I'm not creating this because I get a big thrill out of it, but this is really the way people act around me. I don't want people to be afraid of me. To the contrary... but I even try to pacify them to an extent. That's why I say, "C'mon in. How are you? What are you up to today?" I give them a little spiel about something, you know, and they'll sometimes say, "Well, I read a lot about you."

Then I do my "You haven't read a lot about *me*. You've been reading about somebody... somebody named Ted Bundy." Then they'll whisper, "Boy, he must *really* be crazy!"

I'm not... I'm just not... the Ted Bundy they're reading about. They don't know me. They don't understand what I'm getting at. They think I'm crazy. They have no idea what I'm like. I don't care. I really don't care.

HA: They haven't had any more trouble down there lately, have they?

TB: What's that?

HA: Any more guard trouble.

TB: Not since we had that stabbing in October. Since then, they've had us locked down so tight, there hasn't been any trouble, but conditions have deteriorated considerably.

HA: You're still handcuffed everywhere you go – every time you're out of your cell.

TB: Every time the cell door is *open*.

HA: Did they cut back on your exercising?

TB: They cut back from three times a week to once a week. In fact, for a while they cut back to once a month. Then it was once every couple of weeks and, finally, to once a week.

We're in a phase right now – and I think the Reagan assassination attempt (the previous day) might galvanize it to a large degree. I can see the prisons becoming what they were in the 30s and 40s.

Whether in fact the wave of… the anti-crime wave is real or not… the FBI statistics came out yesterday and they said there was a 13 percent rise in crime. In Florida it went up 18 percent – all in violent crime.

There's going to be a incredible public reaction to that, in general… and to Reagan in particular. It's not going to (be) healthy, either; it's going to get oppressive.

HA: And they're going to start executing people.

TB: Oh, yes, there's no question about that! And not just executing one now and then. The theory is that if they kill criminals, the criminals can't commit crimes anymore.

The anti-death penalty people are prone to say, "See, the death penalty doesn't work." Those in favor of it say, "It's because we haven't exercised it enough."

And, of course, that kind of mentality – it's logical conclusion is that we execute anybody who commits a crime. I think it's a deterrent – to the person who commits the crime. So if you execute everybody who commits a crime, from, let's say, armed robbery up to murder, you're not only going to get rid of the criminals but reduce the populations of the prisons. And, thereby, the budget.

It's going to happen. Rather dramatically in the next decade.

HA: Does that worry you a lot?

TB: Me? I don't sit around and worry about it, no. If it's going to happen it's going to happen. I've always had the death penalty. It's just a matter of knowing *when* you're going to die.

HA: Well, here's a good sign: Two men were scheduled to be executed in Louisiana last week and both got stays.

TB: Well, that may last for a while, but they're eventually going to get Congress to pass legislation whereby state prisoners have limited access to federal habeas corpus. It's coming, but it doesn't worry me that much. Not like being on a plane. Does the thought of, you know, crashing on an airliner worry you? It's in the back of your mind, but...

HA: Yeah, but when you board a plane you haven't already been told that you are going to die – maybe not this year or this month, but soon.

TB: Yeah.

HA: But I guess if you knew, it would make you not enjoy your remaining days.

TB: Sure. Or to take advantage of them. That's precisely what I'd like to do. Well, thanks for coming by, Hugh, and…

HA: Yeah, I've enjoyed visiting with you more today than ever before. I hope to see you again, but I don't know if I ever will or not.

TB: Yeah, uh, the pressure, that element of pressure always separated us because *you* always felt you had to get something from me and I felt that your interests were not *my* interests, so we floundered a bit all the way.

HA: Well, we both learned some things, I believe. I was glad to hear you say that in the rediscussing and reliving… going back over some of these years… you made an important breakthrough for yourself.

TB: Yes, and I'm glad, too. I think it was important. That's why I feel that all this was not a waste. It started to put me on the path to where I am now. Just thinking about this business was so *terrible*, so *horrible*. You really jarred me a couple of times, knocked me back from where I thought I was to where you thought I ought to be. I don't recall exactly when it happened, but while I was facing all this from you – which wasn't easy for any given session – I slowly began to understand what I had to do next, how I had to restructure my life. I'm in a lot better shape now.

· Oh well, who'll remember either one of us in a hundred years?